Simpler Living
Compassionate Life

a christian perspective

foreword by Bill McKibben
with Cecile Andrews
Wendell Berry
Shantilal Bhagat
Frederick Buechner
John Cobb
Calvin DeWitt
Alan Durning
Duane Elgin
Richard Foster
William Gibson
Gerald May
Evy McDonald
James Mulligan
Henri Nouwen
Juliet Schor
Michael Schut
Jerome Segal
Philip Sherrard
David Shi
William Stringfellow
Timothy Weiskel
Terry Tempest Williams

edited and compiled by Michael Schut
published in cooperation with Earth Ministry

Morehouse Publishing
NEW YORK · HARRISBURG · DENVER

Morehouse Publishing, 4775 Linglestown Road, Harrisburg, PA 17122
Morehouse Publishing, 445 Fifth Avenue, New York, NY 10016
Morehouse Publishing is an imprint of Church Publishing Incorporated.

Cover Design and Photography : Val Price
Photography : (p. 9) Maryknoll Fathers & Brothers, Fr. Joseph Towle, MM
                          (p. 160) Regan MacStravic
Illustrations : Victoria Hummel
Contributing Graphic Designer : Jim Lemons

Printed in the United States of America

The scripture quotations used within are from The Holy Bible, New International Version,
© 1973, 1978, 1984 by International Bible Society. Used by permission of Zondervan
Bible Publishers.

ISBN : 978-0-8192-2369-2

Table of Contents

Study Guide by Michael Schut

Acknowledgements

Any book is the result of the combined efforts and wisdom of many people. I think this is true even for books written by only one person, for individuals are expressions of all those who have influenced their lives. Their writing embodies the wisdom and inherited worldviews garnered from their community. This is even more the case, then, for an anthology such as this, combining the work of not only all the included authors and the communities which have influenced them, but the input and wisdom from many members of my community. This book is all the richer and fuller for it, and I am grateful. For many of us it is not all that common to be able to work on a project which so closely expresses what we value. This book has been such a project for me. I remember when I first began to write: all I could do for some time was sit silently in deep thanksgiving.

For making the work of Earth Ministry possible, thank you to all our donors whose gifts keep our work alive. Thank you to St. Mark's Episcopal Cathedral (Seattle, WA) for your grant. Special thanks to two foundations—The Greenville Foundation (Sonoma, CA) and The Dudley Foundation (Bellingham, WA)—for their generous support of this project. Both foundations were able to see beyond the perceived boundary typically drawn between environmental and religious concerns.

In 1996, Earth Ministry published *Simplicity As Compassion (SAC): Voluntary Simplicity from a Christian Perspective*. SAC was an eight-week curriculum that included an anthology of 15 essays. It formed the core from which this book has been expanded.

I am especially grateful to James Creasey and Liz Riggleman of Living the Good News. Your enthusiasm for the project was very encouraging. Thank you, Liz, for your editorial advice, good humor, kindness and guidance. Thanks for your patience in answering all my many questions. James, I have appreciated your ability to help varied audiences understand the breadth of this book's message. And your suggestions and advice were always insightful and to the point. Thank you to the rest of the staff at Living the Good News for your support.

My deepest thanks to Rev. Jim Mulligan, Earth Ministry's Executive Director, for the camaraderie we shared on this project and in all of our work together. Jim provided constant support, editing, and constructive feedback; he read everything here a number of times! We spent many hours discussing ideas back and forth. He also helped me to see my own blind spots, which have a way of creeping into my writing! Jim wrote Meeting Six. His wisdom, keen perception, and gentleness are felt throughout this book.

The rest of Earth Ministry's staff and volunteers also played important roles. Pete Dorman, Phebe Gustafson, and Sheryl Wiser were always available for various administrative and marketing support. They also provided comments on various drafts of the introductory essays. Rev. Carla Berkedal was supportive of this project throughout. Rene Dubay, Intern, researched articles and provided input on the topics covered in *SAC*. Jeanette Carlson, Earth Ministry volunteer extraordinaire, deserves many thanks: she typed, re-typed, and proofed the curriculum as it matured through various stages. In addition, Rene and Jeanette, as well as Intern Greg Peters and Earth Ministry staff, contributed ideas in various brainstorming sessions. Alison Galambos helped write author bio-sketches. Anne Quigg assisted in the process of electronically scanning articles.

A special acknowledgement goes to Dr. Bill Gibson, a leader in the field of Christian eco-justice for over 30 years. Though there are many demands on his time and his eyesight makes it difficult for him to read, Bill thoroughly read the original *SAC*. He provided many thoughtful suggestions that have been incorporated here.

Scott Warner and John Hoerster provided professional, friendly and pro-bono legal advice as we developed *Simpler Living, Compassionate Life*. Their expertise and thorough attention to detail was invaluable to us lay-folk!

The majority of the content of this book comes from the hard work, perceptive thinking, and deep care that all the included authors bring to their lives and work. They are leaders in their fields of expertise with many demands on their time. Each one with whom I had the opportunity and privilege to interact was very kind, helpful and supportive of the book. I have personally benefitted from their writings a great deal. I hope including them here helps many others. My thanks and indebtedness to: Cecile Andrews, Wendell Berry, Shantilal Bhagat, Frederick Buechner, John Cobb, Calvin DeWitt, Alan Durning, Duane Elgin, Richard Foster, William Gibson, Gerald May, Evy McDonald, Henri Nouwen, Juliet Schor, Jerome Segal, Philip Sherrard, David Shi, William Stringfellow, Timothy Weiskel and Terry Tempest Williams.

Two of these authors, both also from Seattle, offered not only their writings but friendship and support as well. First, Cecile Andrews, thank you for meeting with me way back when *SAC* was only an idea! Your good-natured, talented leadership in the voluntary simplicity movement brings a smile to my face! Second, while all other essays were first published elsewhere, Evy McDonald wrote her powerful, personal essay specifically for this book. Thank you, Evy, for sharing your wisdom. Thanks to Evy's community members at the New Road Map Foundation for their kindness and support of our work at Earth Ministry.

Thanks to the many publishers for permission to reprint the works contained herein. To all those who used the original *SAC* curriculum and either sent in written evaluations or spoke with me in person, your comments and encouragement were always appreciated and helped in forming this second edition.

Monique Miller, David Perry, Paul Schafer and Wayne Schut read drafts of the introductory essay. Van Bobbitt, John Current, Joyce Kelly, Ruth Mulligan, Joyce Schut and Sharon Wilson read draft versions of the curriculum. Katrina Schut helped proof the essays. Thank you kindly.

MICHAEL SCHUT
September, 1998

Foreword

As a young man, I came across the gospel account of the rich young man who was told by Christ to give away all his goods. The story hit me like a ton of bricks—it was my first intimation that the Bible was really for *me*, that simply abstaining from murder and adultery and high-grade lying was not all that a good life required. And the story hit me like a ton of bricks because it seemed so damn hard. I am a good child of suburbia, acquainted with most upper-middle-class forms of material comfort. I was supposed to renounce all this? And what? Live on a cot like the men in the small homeless shelter I'd helped start in the basement of my church? Jesus never seemed sterner—the young man went away "sorrowfully" and so, in a sense, did I.

But the story has never stopped haunting me, and as I've grown older I've seen that it involves much more than a moral *diktat*. For one thing, in my work as an environmentalist I've come to understand the kind of burden our accumulation places on the planet. But much more fundamentally, I've come to understand the kind of burden it places on our lives. I once wrote an odd book on television, which involved watching everything that came across the world's largest cable system on a single day. If you boiled it all down into one idea, the archetypal idea of the consumer society that we are born into, it would be: "You are the most important thing on earth, the heaviest object in the known universe." There's no message possible that runs more nearly counter to the message of Jesus (and indeed to the message of most of the gurus who dot human history), the idea that in losing ourselves we find ourselves, the idea that in caring for the least around us we make ourselves whole and real.

So seen in that way, Christ's admonition to the rich young man is less a stern commandment than a piece of loving advice. The young man went away sorrowfully, and we do not hear from him again. But perhaps as *he* aged he began to understand more fully the wisdom he had heard from the Source in that short encounter, and perhaps he began to rearrange his life, to cut down the dense shrubbery of wealth and privilege that kept him from contact with the world, with God, with his own soul. This book and study guide offers you a chance to walk—slowly, with plenty of switchbacks and rest stops—that same road. It is filled with old wisdom applied to new situations. Sometimes it will be painful, as painful as that encounter between Christ and the rich man.

But it will be tender, too. Here, perhaps, is one of the first times in your life when someone outside your family and friends will take you seriously as a person, not as a consumer. Be open to the spirit of it, and know that it is offered in love and hope, the same love and hope that led Jesus to ask more of people than they thought they could ever give. In Mark's version of the story, the young man's repeated questions bring out a kind of gentleness in Christ. "And Jesus, looking upon him, loved him." Loved him enough that he didn't trim his message. That love for us, that desire that we find something deeper, and happier and more real than the ersatz lives we often live, undergirds every word of this good book.

BILL McKIBBEN

Introduction

Lasting change happens when people
see for themselves that a different
way of life is more fulfilling than
their present one.

—*Eknath Easwaran*

Introduction

I have come that they may have life, and life abundantly.

—John 10:10

∞

There is in Western culture a shared restlessness, a vague sense that we are "off-center." We have achieved more, created more, conquered more, and realized more than anyone in the history of the world could have ever imagined. And yet, for many of us, there remains a longing within. How can this be? How can we have so much and still be wanting?

I suspect a kernel of the answer lies in the very human tendency to try to fill our longings with things, material and otherwise, that never fully satisfy.

As Christians, we recognize the abundance of which Jesus spoke as essential to our wholeness. Yet more often than not, we don't experience or feel that abundance. Could it be that in seeking and attaining more things, we have actually lost something of inestimable value? Perhaps we're beginning to perceive the depth of our personal and collective loss: a loss that comes from the misunderstanding that this abundance is essentially and primarily material; a loss that may in no small measure result from confusing our society's ideal of the "good life" with the "abundant life."

If the good life is materialism and the pursuit of the American Dream, the abundant life is authentic wealth. If the good life is individualistic and me-centered, the abundant life is characterized by the extension of compassion to all of creation. For our purposes, the ethos of the abundant life is modeled after the person of Jesus, the things he taught, and the way he lived.

This book brings together a rich collection of voices represented by each author's essay. Whether reading through it alone or going through the study guide with a group, it invites your own voice into the dialogue. The anthology begins with a beautiful piece by Frederick Buechner encouraging you to listen to your own story—to hear those longings that call us all to the abundant life.

Voluntary simplicity is an important component of, and pathway to, that abundant life. So, the anthology continues with concerns that first draw many of us to simplicity: time and money. But it proceeds to discuss issues of overconsumption and justice, food choices, theology, spirituality, history, and community.

I suspect if we could truly see the abundant life in all its fullness, we would gladly drop our confused, dogged pursuit of the good life and embrace true abundance as if returning at last to a place we've always known. But we cannot completely escape the ways the pursuit of the good life pervades our culture and our own lives. The rest of this book seeks to provide further images of the abundant life and to suggest ways of moving toward it personally and culturally. We're glad you joined us for this exploration!

verview

by Michael Schut

This book is a tapestry woven with the voices of many different authors. The following overview should help you hold its many threads together. The piece begins with the question, "Is simplicity only a fad or can it lead to lasting change?" The answer partly lies in simplicity's ability to incorporate the many issues discussed in the rest of the book. The overview piece, therefore, continues by briefly introducing each section with comments and short summaries of each author's essay. You may find it helpful to look back periodically at this essay to re-orient yourself.

Lasting change happens when people see for themselves that a different way of life is more fulfilling than their present one.

—Eknath Easwaran

In 1994, the Trends Research Institute identified "voluntary simplicity" as one of the year's top ten trends. Trends, of course, are usually not equated with lasting change, often becoming the latest passing fad. David Shi's *Epilogue* points out that it is only during periods of "martial, economic or cultural crisis" that statesmen and reformers have "successfully invoked" a wider participation in some form of simplicity. "The genuine sacrifices on the part of citizens during the two world wars and the oil embargo demonstrated the way in which simplicity has provided an emergency reservoir of moral purpose during times of crisis." Once the perception of crisis passed, however, simplicity reverted to a minority concern.

If the voluntary simplicity movement is to become more than a minority concern and a foundation for systemic change within individuals and society, it must recognize as valid the varied reasons people are drawn to it as well as the varied ways such a movement might express itself. *But, it must go beyond that to call people to a broader vision*—a vision that sees the connections between ecological and social decline; between environmental and social justice, between personal choices and global issues; a vision of the abundant life that emerges as a prophetic, compassionate response to today's world. Whether or not voluntary simplicity can provide such a foundation and lead to lasting change will depend partially upon its ability to incorporate the following:

- Celebrating those things for which we are grateful: friendships, community, family, the arts, good health, the beauty and mystery of creation. Enriching our lives with such lasting gifts rather than with the increased consumption of consumer goods.
- Recognizing that simplicity must not only be a path to personal growth but a path leading to greater equity and justice; and that without equity, sustainability cannot be achieved.
- Recognizing the importance of developing communities of support—small groups celebrating life and supporting one another's change.
- Recognizing that both individual change and political action are necessary; and advocating for a society characterized by a "politics of simplicity."
- Recognizing that change is needed not only in daily living habits but in our ways of thinking (worldviews).
- Recognizing that simplicity for the Christian community is not just self-actualization but a spiritual pilgrimage, "loving the Lord your God with all your heart, soul and mind and your neighbor as yourself."

This broader understanding of simplicity informs and ties together this anthology and curriculum. Once people begin to explore simplicity as it speaks to their own concerns, they often see how that concern connects to many other issues. Therein lies one of the simplicity movement's great strengths and possibilities. Those wanting to change their relationship with time and/or money begin to see how that change could be expressed in a concern for environmental justice. Those passionate about ecological degradation may for the first time realize that minorities are most often the first affected by such degradation. And those in the process of modifying their own daily choices might discover the need to work for political change as well.

A Map to This Book

This collection of essays has been arranged in a certain order. But it is not necessary that everyone read it in that order. The book begins with some of the practical areas of everyday life that drew many of us to simplicity in the first place: issues of time, money, consumption and economics. Some of you will want to start there. But for those of you who like to begin by first considering the larger framework of ideas supporting simplicity, you might begin with the sections entitled "Simplicity Is Nothing New: A Brief Historical Overview", "Theology in Support of Simplicity and Eco-Justice" and "Worldviews: The Lens through Which We See". These sections focus on the history, theology and worldviews (ways of thinking) behind simplicity. Finally, the study guide at the back of the book guides participants through the readings in an order different from either of those mentioned above.

With these comments about the ordering of the essays, let us now turn to a brief introduction to each of the book's sections.

The Sacred Journey: Seeking the Abundant Life

Frederick Buechner, in the introduction to his autobiography *The Sacred Journey*, proposes to "try listening to my life as a whole...for whatever of meaning, of holiness, of God, there may be in it to hear."

While this may well be an unusual place to begin a book on simplicity, it sets an important tone: recognizing the value and sacredness of each of our life stories. As you read through *Simpler Living, Compassionate Life*, you will be "listening" to the authors' stories and ideas. We encourage you to reflect on your own life; as you consider the various authors' voices we hope you will listen deeply to the voice of your own life experience. What fits? What's new? What do you agree with? What invites you to new directions? The section concludes with the essay "The Good Life and The Abundant Life" which provides a thematic framework for the book's content: that pursuit of the societally-defined good life has all but replaced our vision and pursuit of the abundant life. Cultural idols such as materialism, economic growth, and productivity have led us astray.

Time as Commodity, Time as Sacred

Many people feel drawn to simplicity because they sense it offers a different, more balanced experience of time. Slowing down provides an opportunity for considering how our "use" of time might more fully reflect our core values.

The four essays in this section reflect and contrast the various ways we experience time. Juliet Schor asks why, in such an economically affluent country, do so many of us feel fatigued, overworked, stressed-out, and deeply conflicted over such little time with our families? Cecile Andrews continues this theme, contrasting "time anxiety" with mindfulness. She says that much of our time "is spent in ways that kill our spirit, our capacity to enjoy the moment," whereas practicing mindfulness can lead to a much richer experience of time as a sacred gift. The writings of Henri Nouwen and Gerald May both reflect this latter sense of time. May suggests that in our busyness we become "addicted to fulfillment," and leave little room "for love to make its home in us." Nouwen writes of a contemplative spirituality that can enable us to see the whole world as "sacrament," that which both reveals and embodies the mystery of God's love.

Your Money or Your Life: The Place of Money in Modern Life

Those within the simplicity movement emphasize that the opportunity to re-think money has nothing to do with "deprivation" and everything to do with living a life of "immeasurable wealth," reflective of our core values.

Through telling her own very powerful and provocative story, Evy McDonald writes of how she brought her spending habits and relationship with money into alignment with her Christian values. Like so many of us, McDonald significantly defined her self-worth by the power, prestige and status her good job (think money) provided. During the process of redefining her relationship with money she began to see that "money is something for which you trade your life energy—your time."

In his essay titled "Money," William Stringfellow connects the idolatry of money to justice: "in this world human beings live at each other's expense, and the affluence of the few is proximately related to, and supported by, the poverty of the many." He writes passionately about how freedom from this idol can come through seeing money as a *sacrament*.

How Much is Enough?: Lifestyles, Global Economics, and Justice

In our culture where at every turn we are encouraged, if not induced, to consume more, more, more...the question "how much is enough?" is radical.

Today's global economy has created more wealth and material well-being for more people than at any other time in history. Yet it simultaneously does not provide for the basic human needs of a *majority* of the world's population and increasingly degrades the rest of the natural world. The Christian faith, and its call to compassion and justice, brings into question some of the basic assumptions and consequences of this economy.

Four articles make up this section on economics and justice. My essay explores the connections between poverty, ecological degradation and overconsumption. I suggest that one of the primary flaws in our economic system is that the human economy does not see itself as embedded within nature's economy. The essay provides a framework for considering these two economies in the context of relationships and faith. John Cobb's article examines our economy's view of humans as individuals-in-a-market rather than persons-in-community. He critiques this view from a Christian perspective and suggests ways to create alternative economies that value community. Alan Durning's essay statistically challenges the cultural assumption that the more we have the happier we are. He specifically analyzes daily consumer choices—such as transportation and food choices—and the broader impacts of those choices. Wendell Berry's essay concludes this section as he wisely draws attention to the appropriate *scale* of our response to global economic issues. The scale of our competence, he says, is to work toward preserving each of our "humble households and neighborhoods." Were the health of all such neighborhoods preserved, many of the global problems we face would disappear. His ideas can be seen as a call for economic bioregionalism.

Social and Environmental Impacts of Everyday Food Choices

The previous section focuses on what is often an overwhelming issue: the global economy. Next we turn from this broad overview to a closer examination of one area of this larger system: food. From how it is grown, packaged and transported, food has certainly become one significant element in that economy. What's so exciting about food choices is that we of necessity make them every day, so we are given the opportunity to make a difference every day!

Whether offering hospitality, gathering for an over-flowing potluck with friends, or celebrating significant life-passages, many pleasurable memories are associated with the gift of food. Wendell Berry's essay suggests a significant element in the pleasure of eating is "in one's accurate consciousness of the lives and the world from which food comes." He provides seven practical suggestions for increasing our consciousness of the ways daily food choices impact people and the land.

James T. Mulligan's essay explores in a straightforward and insightful way the continuum of options available to us for purchasing food. His "Hunter-Gatherer Continuum" considers buying exclusively from Farmers' Markets and subscription farms rather than supermarkets. Along the way he discusses how each option does or does not support local agricultural communities and economies, and which options are most healthy for people and the earth.

Social Structures and the Politics of Simplicity

The simplicity movement has by and large emphasized the need for individual change rather than political action. But for simplicity to reach its potential and help create a more compassionate society, not only must we as individuals change but the structures and institutions that shape our everyday lives must also change.

The three essays collected for this section offer an overview for just such a politics. John Cobb considers the ways in which Christians have historically responded to the political realities of their world. He presents five "images of appropriate Christian response." Into Cobb's framework, Cecile Andrews' article interjects a wonderful overview of some of today's best ideas and policies integral to a politics of simplicity. Among other things, she discusses new kinds of taxation, regulating corporations, and developing new standards of economic health. In the final essay in this section, Bill Gibson maintains that a Christian lifestyle begins with "sharing the servanthood of Jesus and standing…with the poor." But he also recognizes that individual identification with those who are poor must be "synchronized with political activities directed toward (economic) redistribution."

Simplicity Is Nothing New: A Brief Historical Overview

At this point the book steps back a bit. So far, we've looked at issues that often first draw people to simplicity—time, money, economics and consumption—and recognized the need for both individual and political action. The three articles in this section reveal that simple living has been part of American culture since before our country's founding…and part of Christianity since its founder walked the earth. So even though voluntary simplicity is recognized as a "trend" of the '90s, its strains can be heard throughout the American and Christian tradition. Tapping into those traditions can provide a rich, supportive backdrop for those desiring a simpler, more fulfilling way of life today.

For a very detailed and rich account of the history of simplicity in American culture, we refer you to David Shi's book *The Simple Life*. The first essay, by Jerome Segal, gives a concise overview of Shi's themes. The second essay, Shi's *Epilogue*, thoughtfully discusses the simplicity ethic's historical strengths and weaknesses. Richard Foster's essay presents his understanding of the practice of simplicity from the early church depicted in Acts, through the desert monastics and St. Francis, to present-day writings and practices.

Theology in Support of Simplicity and Eco-Justice

Just as delving into the Christian tradition uncovers a history of simplicity, so does it uncover a biblical and practical theology of simplicity. The theology presented here is not disembodied or overly-academic; rather, it is immediately applicable to everyday life. And theology (implicitly or explicitly stated) is an essential thread in the fabric of simplicity. As Timothy Weiskel believes, "our theology determines the character of our engagement" with all of life.

Three essays, representing authors from quite diverse perspectives, comprise this section. Harvard Divinity School's Timothy Weiskel, in his provocative essay, minces no words: the only "real chance we have of surviving as a species is through a radical theological revolution," which must address the most pervasive religion of our day: "growthism." And, he continues, that theology must speak to the many left behind by growthism.

Calvin DeWitt, a biologist and evangelical theologian, presents his perception of several scriptural principles using the Bible itself as an "ecological handbook." You might be surprised at how much the Bible has to say about ecological concerns. Richard Foster is one of the better-known Christians writing on simplicity. In his essay he lays a foundation for a biblical perspective on economics and writes that the Christian discipline of simplicity is an "*inward* reality" resulting in an "*outward* lifestyle." He then shares ten principles helpful in practicing that lifestyle.

Worldviews: The Lens through Which We See

The theology we hold to is one important element of our worldview. Worldviews provide a lens through which we interpret reality and see (know) the world. Yet, just as fish swim oblivious to the water surrounding them, many of us move through the world oblivious to our own "way of seeing" that so determines our personal experience of the world. We are largely unaware of where our worldviews come from, as well as the assumptions behind them—unaware of why some things in life *grab* our attention while others *slip by* in the background.

My opening essay in this section briefly discusses a few of the major influences responsible for constructing our worldviews and also specifically deals with how worldviews determine our "sense of self" and our perspectives on simplicity. The next two essays, by Duane Elgin and Shantilal Bhagat, work well in tandem. Elgin uncovers some of the primary assumptions underlying our Western culture's worldview, such as dualism and individualism. While Western Judeo-Christianity has been very susceptible to those tendencies, Bhagat's essay strongly points out how Christianity (and the Bible) are not inherently dualistic or individualistic. His essay specifically highlights four "beliefs that need rethinking."

This section concludes with Philip Sherrard reflecting on one of the essential characteristics of a worldview that strongly supports voluntary simplicity. That is, a worldview that affirms the sacredness of all creation and which therefore values all life. Such a perspective would fundamentally alter the ways in which we relate with and treat the natural world and each other.

Widening Our Circle of Community: Journey to Abundant Life

As you read through *Simpler Living, Compassionate Life*, you will notice many authors speaking to the importance of community. The presence of community is a powerful reminder that authentic wealth does not consist in the size of your bank account and investment portfolio, but in the depth and diversity of relationships: the mechanic who won't overcharge you, the neighbor you can trust with your kids, the landscape and other creatures so familiar to you that you know you are home, and the people and creatures whose unseen labors keep the world working.

Usually it is those within our community to whom we feel connected. And here is where worldviews come in: does the circle of our community extend only to those who share our ethnicity, our race, our humanity? Or does the circle extend also to those who share our earth home? Does it extend to earth?

Two essays comprise this section. Cecile Andrews focuses on human community, offering practical suggestions for reinvigorating community life: from urban villages, town centers and celebrations, to joining service projects. Terry Tempest Williams' provocative essay speaks poignantly of her sense of our connection to the non-human community.

Epilogue

The anthology concludes with two stories. Each in its own way helps evoke two of the book's foundational themes: that we need fundamental changes both in the way we *think*—characterized by an increasing ability to see the sacred in the ordinary—and in the way we *behave*—characterized by acts of compassion.

The Study Guide: Developing a Community to Facilitate Learning and Change

While the study guide will be helpful to individuals, we encourage you to consider the benefits of going through it with a small group. Movement toward simplicity requires swimming upstream against dominant cultural messages; it requires redefining success and the characteristics of "the good life"; and it is certainly made easier with celebration—of friendships, community and all the beauty around us. Developing a community can both support such movement and make the process more enjoyable. The study guide is easy-to-use and flexible; the role of facilitator rotates each session so no one person has to lead the course.

A Note on Inclusive Language

We are committed to using inclusive, non-sexist language, including when referring to God. You will however find non-inclusive language in this book in some essays. We received permission to reprint those essays in their original form, and thus were unable to edit such language.

The Sacred Journey: Seeking the Abundant Life

Simplicity of living, if deliberately chosen, implies a
compassionate approach to life. It means that we are
choosing to live our daily lives with some degree of
conscious appreciation of the condition of the rest
of the world.

—Duane Elgin

The call to simplicity and freedom for Christians
is the call to move from achievement oriented
spirituality to a life centered on a shared vision
of relatedness to people and things,
a relatedness of gentleness, of compassion,
of belonging to one another.

—Richard Bower

Introduction to The Sacred Journey

by Frederick Buechner

Frederick Buechner is the highly celebrated author of many works of fiction and nonfiction, including his autobiographical trilogy *The Sacred Journey, Now and Then,* and *Telling Secrets.* His novel *Godric* was nominated for the Pulitzer Prize (1981) and he has been honored by the American Academy and Institute of Arts and Letters. Buechner was born on July 11, 1926. He attended Princeton University and Union Theological Seminary in New York, after which he was ordained in the United Presbyterian Church. Through his own story, including his father's suicide and, to hear him tell it, his unlikely conversion, he invites us to reflect on our own stories. Buechner and his wife Judith live in rural Vermont. They have three grown children.

Buechner's writing is profoundly honest and revealing. It is through listening for God's voice in his own life that Buechner gently invites you to listen to, and discover the sacredness of, your own story.

∞

About ten years ago I gave a series of lectures at Harvard in which I made the observation that all theology, like all fiction, is at its heart autobiography, and that what a theologian is doing essentially is examining as honestly as he can the rough-and-tumble of his own experience with all its ups and downs, its mysteries and loose ends, and expressing in logical, abstract terms the truths about human life and about God that he believes he has found implicit there. More as a novelist than as a theologian, more concretely than abstractly, I determined to try to describe my own life as evocatively and candidly as I could in the hope that such glimmers of theological truth as I believed I had glimpsed in it would shine through my description more or less on their own. It seemed to me then, and seems to me still, that if God speaks to us at all in this world, if God speaks anywhere, it is into our personal lives that he speaks. Someone we love dies, say. Some unforeseen act of kindness or cruelty touches the heart or makes the blood run cold. We fail a friend, or a friend fails us, and we are appalled at the capacity we all of us have for estranging the very people in our lives we need the most. Or maybe nothing extraordinary happens at all—just one day following another, helter-skelter, in the manner of days. We sleep and dream. We wake. We work. We remember and forget. We have fun and are depressed. And into the thick of it, or out of the thick of it, at moments of even the most humdrum of our days, God speaks. But what do I mean by saying that God speaks?

I wrote these words at home on a hot, hazy summer day. On the wall behind me, an old banjo clock was tick-tocking the time away. Outside I could hear the twitter of swallows as they swooped in and out of the eaves of the barn. Every once in a while, in the distance, a rooster crowed, though it was well past sunup. Several rooms away, in another part of the house, two men were doing some carpentry. I could not make out what they were saying, but I was aware of the low rumble of their voices, the muffled sounds of their hammers, and the uneven lengths of silence in between. It was getting on toward noon, and from time to time my stomach growled as it went about its own obscure business which I neither understand nor want to. They were all of them random sounds without any apparent purpose or meaning, and yet as I paused to listen to them, I found myself hearing them with something more than just my ears to the point where they became in some way enormously meaningful. The swallows, the rooster, the workmen, my stomach, all with their elusive rhythms, their harmonies and disharmonies and counterpoint, became, as I listened, the sound of my own life speaking to me. Never had I heard just such a coming together of sounds before, and it is unlikely that I will ever hear them in just the same combination again. Their music was unique and unrepeatable and beyond describing in its freshness. I have no clear idea what the sounds meant or what my life was telling me. What does the song of a swallow mean? What is the muffled sound of a hammer trying to tell? And yet as I listened to those sounds, and listened with something more than just my hearing, I was moved by their inexpressible eloquence and suggestiveness, by the sense I had that they were a music rising up out of the mystery of not just my life, but of life itself. In much the same way, that is what I mean by saying that God speaks into or out of the thick of our days.

He speaks not just through the sounds we hear, of course, but through events in all their complexity and variety, through the harmonies and disharmonies and counterpoint of all that happens. As to the meaning of what he says, there are times that we are apt to think we know. Adolph Hitler dies a suicide in his bunker with the Third Reich going up in flames all around him, and what God is saying about the wages of sin seems clear enough. Or Albert Schweitzer renounces fame as a theologian and musician for a medical mission in Africa, where he ends up even more famous still as one of the great near saints of Protestantism; and again we are tempted to see God's meaning as clarity itself. But what is God saying through a good man's suicide? What about the danger of the proclaimed saint's becoming a kind of religious prima donna as proud of his own humility as a peacock of its tail? What about sin itself as a means of grace? What about grace, when misappropriated and misunderstood, becoming an occasion for sin? To try to express in even the most insightful and theologically sophisticated terms the meaning of what God speaks through the events of our lives is as precarious a business as to try to express the meaning of the sound of rain on the roof or the spectacle of the setting sun. But I choose to believe that he speaks nonetheless, and the reason that his words are impossible to capture in human language is of course that they are ultimately always incarnate words. They are words fleshed out in the everydayness no less than in the crises of our own experience.

With all this in mind, I entitled those Harvard lectures *The Alphabet of Grace* in order to suggest that life itself can be thought of as an alphabet by which God graciously makes known his presence and purpose and power among us. Like the Hebrew alphabet, the alphabet of grace has no vowels, and in that sense his words to us are always veiled, subtle, cryptic, so that it is left to us to delve their meaning, to fill in the vowels, for ourselves by means of all the faith and imagination we can muster. God speaks to us in such a way, presumably, not because he chooses to be obscure but because, unlike a dictionary word whose meaning is fixed, the meaning of an incarnate word is the meaning it has for the one it is spoken to, the meaning that becomes clear and effective in our lives only when we ferret it out for ourselves. *Heilsgeschichte* is a more theological way of saying the same thing. Deep within history, as it gets itself written down in history books and newspapers, in the letters we write and in the diaries we keep, is sacred history, is God's purpose working itself out in the apparent purposelessness of human history and of our separate histories, is the history, in short, of the saving and losing of souls, including our own. A child is born. A friend is lost or found. Out of nowhere comes a sense of peace or foreboding. We are awakened by a dream. Out of the shadowy street comes a cry for help. We must learn to listen to the cock-crows and hammering and tick-tock of our lives for the holy and elusive word that is spoken to us out of their depths. It is the function of all great preaching, I think, and of all great art, to sharpen our hearing to precisely that end, and it was what I attempted in *The Alphabet of Grace*. I took a single, ordinary day of my life, and in describing the events of it—waking up, dressing, taking the children to school, working, and coming home again—I tried to suggest something of what I thought I had heard God saying.

That was ten years ago. By now my children have mostly grown up and mostly gone. I am not by a long shot entirely grown up myself, but I am ten years' worth of days older than I was then, and lots of things have happened to me, and I have had lots of time to listen to them happening. Also, since I passed the age of fifty, I have taken to looking back on my life as a whole more. I have looked through old letters and dug out old photographs. I have gone through twenty years' worth of old home movies. I have thought about the people I have known and the things that have happened that have, for better or worse, left the deepest mark on me. Like sitting there on the couch listening to the sounds of roosters, swallows, hammers, ticking clock, I have tried to make something out of the hidden alphabet of the years I have lived, to catch, beneath all the random sounds those years have made, a strain at least of their unique music. My interest in the past is not, I think, primarily nostalgic. Like everybody else, I rejoice in much of it and marvel at those moments when, less by effort than by grace, it comes to life again with extraordinary power and immediacy—vanished faces and voices, the feeling of what it was like to fall in love for the first time, of running as a child through the firefly dusk of summer, the fresh linen and cinnamon and servant-swept fragrance of my grandmother's house in Pennsylvania, the taste of snow, the stubbly touch of my father's good-night. But even if it were possible to return to those days, I would never choose to. What quickens my pulse now is the stretch ahead rather than the one behind, and it is mainly for some clue to where I am going that I search through where I have been, for some hint as to who I am becoming or failing to become that I delve into what used to be. I listen back to a time when nothing was much farther from my thoughts than God for an echo of the gutturals and sibilants and vowellessness by which I believe that even then God was addressing me out of my life as he addresses us all. And it is because I believe that, that I think of my life and of the lives of everyone who has ever lived, or will ever live, as not just journeys through time but as sacred journeys.

Ten years ago in those Harvard lectures, I tried to listen to a single day of my life in such a way. What I propose to do now is to try listening to my life as a whole, or at least to certain key moments of the first half of my life thus far, for whatever of meaning, of holiness, of God, there may be in it to hear. My assumption is that the story of any one of us is in some measure the story of us all.

For the reader, I suppose, it is like looking through someone else's photograph album. What holds you, if nothing else, is the possibility that somewhere among all those shots of people you never knew and places you never saw, you may come across something or someone you recognize. In fact—for more curious things have happened—even in a stranger's album, there is always the possibility that as the pages flip by, on one of them you may even catch a glimpse of yourself. Even if both of those fail, there is still a third possibility which is perhaps the happiest of them all, and that is that once I have put away my album for good, you may in the privacy of the heart take out the album of your own life and search it for the people and places you have loved and learned from yourself, and for those moments in the past—many of them half forgotten—through which you glimpsed, however dimly and fleetingly, the sacredness of your own journey.

The Good Life and The Abundant Life

by Michael Schut

In his former position as Associate Director for Earth Ministry, Michael Schut was responsible for program delivery, leading retreats and workshops, speaking, teaching, writing and more. Schut was the primary author of *Simplicity as Compassion: Voluntary Simplicity from a Christian Perspective,* Earth Ministry's eight-week curriculum which served as the core for the study guide for this book. He works closely with churches, small groups and individuals interested in deepening their awareness of the connections between caring for people and caring for the earth, between Christian faith and relationship with and care for creation, and how to express that in everyday life.

Schut holds degrees in Environmental Studies and Biology and has a professional history which includes a wide variety of experiences in the social service and environmental fields. After serving as a resident manager for homeless men, he worked for Environmental Safety and in the Agriculture and Natural Resources Division of the International Science and Technology Institute. He has also enjoyed a wide variety of outdoor education work experiences including teaching environmental education and leading wilderness backpacking and rockclimbing trips. Schut enjoys basketball, backpacking, playing guitar and singing. He is also very fond of ice cream.

Pursuit of "the good life" has become a powerful idol in our day. Movement toward simplicity challenges this pursuit at almost every turn. Simplicity just may be a component of, and a pathway to, what in Christian terms we call the abundant life. This essay introduces these topics—the restlessness many of us feel when pursuing the good life, the idolatries found within that pursuit—and closes by suggesting characteristics of the abundant life to which Jesus referred.

∞

...I have walked at night and gone into your homes and found people dying unloved. Here [in the West] you have a different kind of poverty —a poverty of the spirit, of loneliness, of being unwanted. And that is the worst disease in the world today, not tuberculosis or leprosy.

—Mother Teresa

∞

The Good Life

If asked, most of us could easily compose society's picture of the good life. Its images are constantly paraded before us on TV, billboards, newspapers, and magazines. While perhaps most prevalent in the U.S., the messages and products of that life are now exported throughout the world. Rural villages across the globe boast TV sets. Little wonder, especially for those whose basic needs go largely unmet, that the supposed "good life" as advertised is so attractive. But, unwittingly, our culture's highest ideal of the good life, the American Dream, has become a nightmare—for the earth (through ecological degradation), for those whose poverty is a necessary by-product of Western affluence, and for those who have attained the Dream and found it lacking.

One sign of this nightmare is the restlessness and dissatisfaction many of us feel in the pursuit of the good life:

I'm worn out. I just don't have time for what's important to me anymore, like time with my family, time to exercise, or time alone to think or read a good book.

I spend more time than I'd like, working to get stuff I don't really need. And in some ways my way of life prevents others from simply having enough.

I long for a way of living that reflects my true values, nurtures deeper relationships and builds community.

When we consider the following, it is little wonder that we experience life as out of balance:
- Americans spend 40 minutes a week playing with children—and six hours a week shopping.[1]
- About one in every four vertebrate species is currently on the road to extinction unless we work to change their circumstances.[2]
- The average amount of pocket money for American children—$230 a year—is *more than the total annual income* of the world's half-billion poorest people.[1]
- During the 1990s, 57 million children will be born in the "North," 911 million children will be born in the "South." Those born in the North will consume and pollute more than those born in the South.[3]

- American couples spend an average of 12 minutes a day talking to each other.[1]
- Sixty percent of the total U.S. African-American and Hispanic populations live in communities with one or more uncontrollable toxic waste sites. These communities are disproportionately exposed to air, land, and water pollution.[4]

These are serious signs of cultural and ecological imbalance—reflected in the restlessness so pervasive today. This is not to say that the good life is entirely negative. In some concrete ways it mimics the abundant life (which we will discuss shortly) and most of us have benefitted from its pursuit. But when it becomes our top priority, then the good life has drawn us into a life of idolatry.

The Good Life Gone Bad: The Inevitable Dilemma of Idolatry

The good life functions as a powerful idol of our time. The concept of idolatry often seems archaic, relevant only to biblical times when the Israelites' neighbors bowed down to graven images and Paul preached in Athens, a city full of silver and stone deities. But today's idols are just as real, though perhaps more subtle. An idol is anything we put before God, a partial truth mistaken for the whole "Truth," a lesser good elevated to the ultimate good. I have always found it particularly helpful to think of idols as promising something they cannot finally deliver.

In any discussion of idolatry, it is important to point out that no matter how genuine our desire to discern and offer our ultimate allegiance to "the Truth," idolatry is an inevitability of life. In Christian terms this inevitable fallibility is called sin, part of the human condition. We need to accept such an inevitability with humility but not disgrace. This discussion is included here to help unmask some of the idolatries associated with the good life in order to help move us toward the freedom and fullness of the abundant life to which Jesus referred.

If pursuit of our society's definition of the good life is one of our more subtle, powerful idols, what "lesser good" does it promise? And how does that compare with the abundant life?

First, the good life promises to meet basic human material needs—certainly one aspect of the abundant life—but does so for only a few, at the expense of the many—certainly not a characteristic of the abundant life. Second, the good life promises a level of happiness that bears some resemblance to the abundant life's promise of deep joy. Finally, the good life promises the ability to care for all those in our community—a characteristic of abundance—but either incorrectly assumes everyone in the community has equal opportunity and access or does not seriously concern itself with questions of equality. To the extent that the good life successfully mimics the abundant life it becomes understandably difficult to distinguish between the two.

The good life is itself comprised of a number of other cultural idols. Let's consider four of these: materialism and economic growth; productivity; anthropocentrism and individualism; and simplicity itself. I will attempt to give credit to the good each idol intends while also drawing attention to its limitations. Highlighting them is not meant to lay blame, but to see how their pursuit has contributed to transforming the dream of the good life into a nightmare for many. Along the way we'll also consider what simple living might have to say to these idols.

First, *Materialism and Economic Growth*—One of our culture's most prevalent idolatries is materialism. Economic growth is the politician's Holy Grail, the unquestioned priority. It is Western culture's *implicit religion*—that is, its core value system that significantly shapes its overall orientation. One of the underlying assumptions of economic materialism is the belief that the free market economy will eventually bring the good life to everyone.

But the problem of inequity has not improved. Economic disparity has increased along with economic wealth. Yachts are the only ships raised by this rising tide of economic wealth:

- the richest fifth of the world's population receives 82.7% of total world income, while the poorest fifth receives 1.4% (United Nations Development Program, 1992);
- Americans comprise only 5% of the world's population but consume 30% of its resources.[1]

These vast inequities in human wealth do not convey the very high cost the economic system imposes on the rest of the natural world. These costs, generally unaccounted for in the economic system (and considered externalities), include air and water pollution, habitat loss and species extinction. Unrestrained materialism leaves in its wake those who are poor, and today the earth and her creatures are numbered among them.

On a more personal note, we all struggle with the place of money in our individual lives and often feel a good deal of anxiety about future economic security. Such concerns are understandable and inevitable. Many people still grow up with a sense of scarcity, anxious about whether there will be enough. Our cultural memory reminds us that for most of human history survival itself was precarious and "having more" simply meant having enough to survive the next life-threatening time. The need in our day for some of us to exercise restraint is a relatively new phenomenon. Discerning how much is enough is made particularly difficult in our culture, which teaches that security lies in "having more than I have now." While the Christian message does not give us formulas for enough, it does consistently point us away from a security based on materialism. The moral work of discerning the point of "enoughness" is left for each generation to determine.

To its credit, our economic system has provided more material well-being to more people than any other system at any other time in history. Besides this "good," materialism reflects other positives characteristic of our culture. First, materialism rejects the Gnostic notion that spirit is good while matter (including our earth and the body) is inherently evil. Second, it reflects the desire to have a more healthy, satisfying life. While *voluntary* poverty can be a beautiful offering of one's life, poverty itself can crush not only the body but the spirit as well. Finally, materialism reflects the good of taking care of others within our communities by meeting basic needs and providing for a few luxuries. But the circle we draw in our minds, defining those who do and do not belong to our community, is most often too small. Those living outside the circle effectively have no claim to moral treatment by those within.

Perhaps the prophetic word that simple living has to offer materialism centers around justice and freedom: justice that can be lived through reduced consumption and more equitable distribution of the earth's finite resources, and acting justly toward the rest of creation: freedom that allows each of us to move from life-draining acquisitiveness toward a joyful, generous spirit that recognizes the worth of all God's creatures.

Second, *Productivity*—Our culture has made an idol of productivity itself; we desperately need to "be productive." We pack as much activity as possible into most all our days. We applaud efficiency. We are much better at doing than simply being.

Of course there is nothing inherently wrong with efficiency. And the sense of accomplishment from a job well done is worth celebrating. The good within this idolatry is the desire to fully utilize our gifts and to make a genuine contribution to our community. Such contributions are a gift back to the communities that sustain us. But in our driven busyness we do not take time to *listen*. We no longer know who we are and the "still, small voice" is lost in the cacophony of voices urging us on to the next task. Lacking the ability to listen and follow God's voice and our own inner direction, we become increasingly susceptible to the marketing of the good life. We lose touch with the understanding that who we are is larger than simply what we do.

Into this hyper-productive life walks simplicity. Simplicity requires us to slow down, to consider how our lives reflect who we are and what we value. We are allowed to find time for regeneration and to nurture and be nurtured. Gerald May (see page 41) refers to this slowing down as creating space: "space is freedom: freedom from confinement, from preoccupation, from oppression, from drivenness... We need space to allow the compulsions to ease and the bonds to loosen." If the abundant life is more than just consuming, it is also more than just producing.

Third, *Anthropocentrism and Individualism*—Anthropocentrism is human-centeredness, valuing humanity above absolutely everything else. It is perceiving ourselves as separate from, and superior to, earth and other creatures. If other creatures and their habitats have no (or little) value to us, their subjugation or even destruction poses no moral dilemmas. An outgrowth of this idolatry is unlimited confidence in our collective intelligence and ingenuity, faith in our ability to solve any problem through science and its technological applications.

Like materialism, anthropocentrism includes good within it. One could make the case that anthropocentrism reflects a strong sense of responsibility. If humankind is the only creature capable of moral discernment and if we are the conscience of creation, then we are indeed in a centrally significant role. Within this idolatry, then, lives the healthy and natural desire to be an important and responsible member of a community.

As far as we are aware, humanity has shaped the world far more than any other creature. With this power, however, comes an equal responsibility. The Bible repeatedly makes it clear that humanity should join with God in caring for the whole of creation. The community of all life is integral to the design of God's earth, and our role in respecting that integrity is significant.

There is another level to the idolatry of anthropocentrism: our culture's extreme individualism. Writer Bill McKibben believes that rather than being human-centered, we are "me-centered," highly individualistic. Were we fully human-centered, we would take care of our own—no hunger, homelessness, or poverty. But we would also take care of the rest of the natural world—no pollution, loss of topsoil, or nuclear waste—for its health is intrinsically bound up with our own.

Individualism has also made significant positive contributions to our society. It is partly responsible for recognizing the intrinsic worth of every human being. This recognition has given rise to the notion of human rights and thus supported numerous people in their struggle against oppressive communities—whether those communities be small racist towns, or powerful totalitarian nations. Individualism also values the unique gifts within each person. What individualism does not fully recognize is that all of us are profoundly relational beings. A person not in relationship with others—human and non-human—can hardly be said to exist. We are defined by our relationships and created for community.

Perhaps what is fundamentally wrong with individualism, as with anthropocentrism, is not an exaggerated sense of humanity's importance but rather a profound loss of the knowledge that all life is sacred. As Philip Sherrard says, "We are treating our planet in an inhuman and god-forsaken manner because we see things in an inhuman, god-forsaken way. And we see things in this way because that is basically how we see ourselves" (see page 200). Movement toward simplicity can not only make us reflect on how our lifestyles affect the natural world, it can also help us reposition ourselves within that world.

Finally, *Simplicity*—Simplicity itself can become an idol resulting in judgmentalism and self-righteousness. That which was initiated out of inner simplicity becomes an external effort to "keep down with the Joneses." That which was meant to be liberating becomes a rigorous list of "simplicity do's and don'ts." That which sprang from a desire to express compassion for those with so little becomes a tool of judgment wielded against those with so much.

On the other hand, simplicity, when combined with genuine Christian spirituality, offers a prophetic, culturally-challenging alternative to the good life. Simplicity stands in quiet contrast to our culture's dominant messages. It reveals and challenges the idols of our day and calls us, individually and societally, to live lives of compassionate integrity. Like the Old Testament prophets who called the Israelites to right relationship with God, the simplicity movement calls us to cast aside our idolatries that we might move toward the abundant life.

The Abundant Life: Freedom and Compassion

A man is rich in proportion to the things he can afford to let alone.

—Henry David Thoreau

Compassion seems to be the greatest power.

—The Dalai Lama

Earlier I mentioned the relative ease with which most of us could create a mental image of the "good life." But I suspect many of us would have much more difficulty creating an image of the abundant life, for its images are not nearly as prevalent. Yet all of us experience hints of abundance—moments that ring true in our hearts and call us to be more fully alive. In contrast to the poverty of love Mother Teresa experienced, the abundant life is a life of love, where the heart is full and relationships are rich. The statement below, adopted by the Methodist church in 1996, provides a beautiful, suggestive vision of the abundant life. Read through it slowly:

> We are people called to live toward God's vision of reconciliation through Christ Jesus. This reconciled world, or "new heaven and earth," includes...a creation where diversity is celebrated as a gift, rather than resisted and destroyed; where loving relationships are supremely valued and the resources of the world are shared equitably and justly; where all persons know their worth and value as children of God and who seek the well-being of God's creation above their own greed.

> It is a world where we live out of a theology of "enough"...a theology that allows us to move away from worshiping the gods of consumption and material need. In living out a theology of enough we will no longer expend our physical resources in consumption and our emotional resources in worrying over status. Our security and sense of well-being will be defined in relationship to God, not by our possessions...

> While Christ does not seek for any of us to be without basic necessities,

a simplified life will move us away from the expectations and injustices
of affluent living. Abundant living is a life of greater simplicity, of more
responsible use of resources and of a deeper faith.

—from "God's Vision of Abundant Living"

The statement concludes by recognizing that the abundant life is a life of greater
simplicity. The simple life is both a *component of*, and a *pathway to*, the abundance
of which Jesus spoke. And the abundant life as described here addresses each of the
good life's idols discussed above. The abundant life "moves us away from the expectations and injustices of affluent living" associated with materialism. In an abundant
life "we no longer expend our physical resources in consumption and our emotional
resources in worrying over status" as is so often the case when caught up in the idol
of productivity. The abundant life "includes a creation where diversity is celebrated
as a gift...where all persons know their worth and value as children of God and
seek the well-being of God's creation above their own greed" rather than the
human- and me-centeredness associated with anthropocentrism and individualism.

The abundant life is a life characterized by freedom: freedom to define our security and well-being in terms of relationship with God rather than the amount of
stuff we've accumulated—freedom to live a theology of enough. It is not the freedom associated with the Western notion of individualism: free to do anything and
go anywhere while paying no attention to the consequences. Rather, the abundant
life recognizes that the flip side of freedom is responsibility to community. The definition of community, those deemed worthy of our care, includes the rest of the
natural world. This abundant life invites us to be fully participatory in, not isolated
from, the community of all creation, "where loving relationships are supremely
valued and the resources of the world are shared equitably and justly."

Finally, the abundant life is a life characterized by compassion, not understood
primarily as a nice, sentimental feeling but in its fullness as "the greatest power."
My favorite definition of compassion comes from Frederick Buechner: "Compassion
is that sometimes fatal capacity for feeling what it is like to live inside another's
skin, knowing that there can never really be peace and joy for any until there is
peace and joy finally for all" (Buechner, *A Room Called Remember*). This definition
includes empathy and justice: empathy as "feeling what it is like to live inside
another's skin" and justice as "knowing there can never really be peace and joy for
any until there is peace and joy finally for all." Compassion, not only *felt* as empathy but *embodied* as justice, is surely a hallmark of the abundant life.

Compassion—literally, suffering with—is particularly powerful in a Christian
context. A willingness to suffer with is not highlighted here to suggest another
path to self-inflicted martyrdom, rather as an invitation to experience life fully—
the pain and the joy. When we look at Jesus' life we see a vibrant, passionate person engaged in life. In his willingness to identify with suffering, to the point of

death, he overcame it. As Larry Rasmussen says, "Compassion is the passion of life itself, even as joy is... The quest of cross theology is precisely for a power that overcomes suffering by entering into it and leading through it to abundant life for all."[5]

May your pursuit of the abundant life, in all its fullness, truly feel like coming home—home to a place you have always longed for. May this book serve as a roadmap to you as you make the journey.

Time as Commodity,
Time as Sacred

We measure our...time in terms of money, and find
that we can't enjoy time at all.

—*Cecile Andrews*

Silence of the heart is necessary so you can hear
God everywhere—in the closing of the door, in
the person who needs you, in the birds that
sing, in the flowers, in the animals.

—*Mother Teresa*

Excerpt from The Overworked American

by Juliet Schor

Author of the best-selling book *The Overworked American: The Unexpected Decline of Leisure,* Dr. Juliet Schor is currently Senior Lecturer at Harvard and Director of its Women's Studies program. She is also Professor of Economics of Leisure at Tilburg University, Netherlands. Her most recent book is *The Overspent American: Upscaling, Downshifting, and the New Consumer.*

A founding member of the Center for Popular Economics and the Center for a New American Dream, Juliet lives in Newton, Massachusetts with her husband and two children. Barbara Ehrenreich describes her as one of those few economists who "can speak plain English and force us to confront some hard questions about who we are, what we are doing, and why we are doing it."

The hard questions Schor raises here revolve around time. Why do 30 percent of American adults report experiencing high stress almost every day? Why do a majority of us get between 60 and 90 minutes less sleep per night than optimum? Why do more and more couples feel the need for two incomes, significantly decreasing time with their family? Why all this in such a supposedly affluent culture? Schor intimates that we are actually impoverished in how we experience one of life's fundamental gifts—the gift of time itself.

∞

Most economists regard the spending spree that Americans indulged in throughout the postwar decades as an unambiguous blessing, on the assumption that more is always better. And there is a certain sense in this approach. It's hard to imagine how having more of a desired good could make one worse off, especially since it is always possible to ignore the additional quantity. Relying on this little bit of common sense, economists have championed the closely related ideas that more goods yield more satisfaction, that desires are infinite, and that people act to satisfy those desires as fully as they can.

Now anyone with just a little bit of psychological sophistication (to go with this little bit of common sense) can spot the flaw in the economist's argument. Once our basic human needs are taken care of, the effect of consumption on well-being gets tricky. What if our desires keep pace with our incomes, so that getting richer doesn't make us more satisfied? Or what if satisfaction depends, not on absolute levels of consumption, but on one's level *relative* to others (such as the Joneses).

Then no matter how much you possess, you won't feel well off if Jones next door possesses more.

How many of us thought the first car stereo a great luxury, and then, when it came time to buy a new car, considered it an absolute necessity? Or life before and after the microwave? And the fact that many of these commodities are bought on credit makes the cycle of income-consumption, more income more consumption, even more ominous. There is no doubt that some purchases permanently enhance our lives. But how much of what we consume merely keeps us moving on a stationary treadmill? The problem with the treadmill is not only that it is stationary, but also that we have to work long hours to stay on it... the consumerist treadmill and long hour jobs have combined to form an insidious cycle of "work-and-spend." Employers ask for long hours. The pay creates a high level of consumption. People buy houses and go into debt; luxuries become necessities; Smiths keep up with Joneses. Each year, "progress," in the form of annual productivity increases, is doled out by employers as extra income rather than as time off. Work-and-spend has become a powerful dynamic keeping us from a more relaxed and leisured way of life.

Faith in progress is deep within our culture.[6] We have been taught to believe that our lives are better than those who came before us. The ideology of modern economics suggests that material progress has yielded enhanced satisfaction and well-being. But much of our confidence about our own well-being comes from the assumption that our lives are easier than those of earlier generations or other cultures. I have already disputed the notion that we work less than medieval European peasants, however poor they may have been. The field research of anthropologists gives another view of the conventional wisdom.

The lives of so-called primitive peoples are commonly thought to be harsh—their existence dominated by the "incessant quest for food." In fact, primitives do little work. By contemporary standards, we'd have to judge them extremely lazy. If the Kapauku of Papua work one day, they do no labor on the next. Kung Bushmen put in only two and a half days per week and six hours per day. In the Sandwich Islands of Hawaii, men work only four hours per day. And Australian aborigines have similar schedules. The key to understanding why these "stone age peoples" fail to act like us—increasing their work effort to get more things—is that they have limited desires. In the race between wanting and having, they have kept their wanting low—and, in this way, ensure their own kind of satisfaction. They are materially poor by contemporary standards, but in at least one dimension—time—we have to count them richer.[7]

I do not raise these issues to imply that we would be better off as Polynesian natives or medieval peasants. Nor am I arguing that "progress" has made us worse off. I am, instead, making a much simpler point. We have paid a price for prosperity. Capitalism has brought a dramatically increased standard of living, but at the cost of a much more demanding worklife. We are eating more, but we are burning up those calories at work. We have color televisions and compact disc players, but we need them to unwind after a stressful day at the office. We take vacations, but we work so hard throughout the year that they become indispensable to our sanity. The conventional wisdom that economic progress has given us more things *as well as* more leisure is difficult to sustain.

However scarce academic research on the rising workload may be, what we do know suggests it has contributed to a variety of social problems. For example, work is implicated in the dramatic rise of "stress." Thirty percent of adults say that they experience high stress nearly every day; even higher numbers report high stress once or twice a week. A third of the population says that they are rushed to do the things they have to do—up from a quarter in 1965. Stress-related diseases have exploded, especially among women, and jobs are a major factor. Workers' compensation claims related to stress tripled during just the first half of the 1980s. Other evidence also suggests a rise in the demands placed on employees on the job. According to a recent review of existing findings, Americans are literally working themselves to death—as jobs contribute to heart disease, hypertension, gastric problems, depression, exhaustion, and a variety of other ailments. Surprisingly, the high-powered jobs are not the most dangerous. The most stressful workplaces are the "electronic sweatshops" and assembly lines where a demanding pace is coupled with virtually no individual discretion.[8]

Sleep has become another casualty of modern life. According to sleep researchers, studies point to a "sleep deficit" among Americans, a majority of whom are currently getting between 60 and 90 minutes less a night than they should for optimum health and performance. The number of people showing up at sleep disorder clinics with serious problems has skyrocketed in the last decade. Shiftwork, long working hours, the growth of a global economy (with its attendant continent-hopping and twenty-four-hour business culture), and the accelerating pace of life have all contributed to sleep deprivation. If you need an alarm clock, the experts warn, you're probably sleeping too little.[9]

The juggling act between job and family is another problem area. Half the population now says they have too little time for their families. The problem is particularly acute for women: in one study, half of all employed mothers reported it caused either "a lot" or an "extreme" level of stress. The same proportion feel that "when I'm at home I try to make up to my family for being away at work, and as a result I rarely have any time for myself." This stress has placed tremendous burdens on marriages. Two-earner couples have less time together, which researchers have found reduces the happiness and satisfaction of a marriage. These couples often just don't have enough time to talk to each other. And growing numbers of husbands and wives are like ships passing in the night, working sequential schedules to manage their child care. Among young parents, the prevalence of at least one partner working outside regular daytime hours is now close to one half. But this "solution" is hardly a happy one. According to one parent: "I work 11-7 to accommodate my family—to eliminate the need for babysitters. However, the stress on myself is tremendous." [10]

A decade of research by Berkeley sociologist Arlie Hochschild suggests that many marriages where women are doing the "second shift" are close to the breaking point. When job, children, and marriage have to be attended to, it's often the marriage that is neglected. The failure of many men to do their share at home creates further problems. A twenty-six-year-old legal secretary in California reports that her husband "does no cooking, no washing, no anything else. How do I feel? Furious. If our marriage ends, it will be on this issue. And it just might." [11]

Serious as these problems are, the most alarming development may be the effect of the work explosion on the care of children. According to economist Sylvia Hewlett, "child neglect has become endemic to our society." A major problem is that children are increasingly left alone, to fend for themselves while their parents are at work. Nationwide, estimates of children in "self"—or, more accurately, "no"—care range up to seven million. Local studies have found figures of up to one-third of children caring for themselves. At least half a million preschoolers are thought to be left at home part of each day. One 911 operator reports large numbers of frightened callers: "It's not uncommon to hear from a child of six or seven who has been left in charge of even younger siblings." [12]

Even when parents are at home, overwork may leave them with limited time, attention, or energy for their children. One working parent noted, "My child has severe emotional problems because I am too tired to listen to him. It is not quality time; it's bad quantity time that's destroying my family." Economist Victor Fuchs has found that between 1960 and 1986, the time parents actually had available to be with children fell ten hours a week for whites and twelve for blacks. Hewlett links the "parenting deficit" to a variety of problems plaguing the country's youth: poor performance in school, mental problems, drug and alcohol use, and teen suicide. According to another expert, kids are being "cheated out of childhood... There is a sense that adults don't care about them." [13]

Of course, there's more going on here than lack of time. Child neglect, marital distress, sleep deprivation, and stress-related illnesses all have other causes. But the growth of work has exacerbated each of these social ailments. Only by understanding why we work as much as we do, and how the demands of work affect family life, can we hope to solve these problems.

The Spirituality of Everyday Life

by Cecile Andrews

At sixteen, Cecile Andrews read a passage in Thoreau's *Walden* expressing the desire to live deliberately and "not, when I came to die, discover that I had not lived." Those words particularly stood out to her: when she was eight years old her father died, so she knew that life could be over in a second. Her concern for "alive-ness" led her to the idea and practice of simple living. She is the author of *The Circle of Simplicity: Return to the Good Life* and is a community educator giving workshops on Voluntary Simplicity, Simplicity Circles and Finding Your Passion.

Though she doesn't mention this much, Andrews has a Doctorate in Education from Stanford University. She worked in the South on civil rights and poverty with the American Friends Service Committee, and directed women's programs and continuing educa-tion at North Seattle Community College. She was born in the Puget Sound area and presently lives with her husband, Paul, in Seattle, Washington. Her two children are now grown. The volun-tary simplicity movement, which now has adherents nationwide, first caught fire in Seattle; Andrews was (and is) a very significant spark igniting that fire. Cecile loves to read mysteries, play her flute and hang out in cafes talking with friends.

Andrews begins this chapter of her book with "Some cultures embody spirituality in everything they do. In our culture...there is simply no room nor time for the spiritual life when you are preoc-cupied with getting ahead, making a profit...managing your invest-ment portfolio, answering the phone, shopping or watching television." This excerpt begins with her thoughts on "mindfulness" (being fully alive and living in the present). Practicing mindfulness, being open to God's voice, is made difficult by the "time anxiety" we so often feel. But slowing down gives us time to notice things: from impulse buying to a friend's smile or the smell of spring. Noticing such gifts of everyday life engenders gratitude, whereas so much of our lifestyle engenders "discontent and resentment."

∞

Mindfulness

...What all this is about, remember, is trying to feel fully alive, to keep ourselves and the earth alive. And, as Thoreau was to say in so many ways, that means living fully in the present. For most of us, our attention is constantly diverted. We're rarely aware of what we are doing.

Take food. Food is probably one of the best symbols of our American way of life. Food is meant to nourish us, but it is also meant to be enjoyed. And the only way you can enjoy it is to pay attention to your eating. But we never do that. Our contribution to world cuisine is fast food. What does it mean to have drive-through windows to get our food? We have invented food that can be eaten with one hand while we're doing something else. It's pathological. We're not tasting the food; we're not getting any real pleasure or even nourishment out of it. And with all the chemicals and petroleum involved in our food production, our way of eating is destroying the planet as well. In other words, we're trashing the planet for something we are not even enjoying.

So one way of being mindful is paying attention to and savoring what you eat. When you eat, focus on enjoying eating.

In living mindfully, we pay attention to whatever we're doing and "suck out all the marrow," as Thoreau said. We become deeply absorbed in what we are doing, appreciating the people we are with, being conscious of the wind on our face. It means paying attention to what you are doing, and not doing ten things at once. Taking the time to notice, slowing down, sitting peacefully, and just being.

Time Anxiety

Being mindful is hard for us because we are always anxious about time. Just as we never feel we have enough money, we never have enough time. In fact, maybe it's because we feel we don't have enough money that we feel that we don't have enough time. Since we measure everything in terms of money, that sense of scarcity pervades our whole life. Learning that we have enough—money, time, love—may be our most important lesson.

Even when we eliminate the apparent obstacles of working and consuming too much, we still have trouble relaxing and enjoying the present moment. So the problem is not just the scarcity of time, it's our attitude toward time. That little voice always creeps in, You'd better hurry, you've got a lot to do, you're not getting enough done, time is running out. What does this mean in terms of feeling alive? Surely, if things keep on this way, when we come to die, we will discover that we have not lived.

We live in constant anticipation of the future, regret and guilt over the past: we can hardly wait for the weekend, for summer vacation, for the kids to be grown up, until retirement. We might as well say, "I can hardly wait until I die."

In the past I read books that told how to get more done during the day, how to find that extra hour so you could study French or learn photography. I would try to do as many things as I could at one time. Now I focus on doing less and slowing down. I try to stop rushing, to practice mindfulness, to practice meditation. I keep working at it, but still I have that nagging feeling—hurry, hurry.

We get upset at everything that gets in our way. We yell at other drivers, using language that shocks us. We switch checkout lanes in the grocery stores, we click through TV shows, we hurry our kids. Once, in a frantic effort to get ready for a birthday party for my kids, I tried to blow up balloons while I was driving.

Is it the universe's revenge? We, who have ruined the earth's resources, have had our only true resource, time, ruined for us. We are a caricature of a whirling dervish. We have made a mockery of so many of the world's spiritual traditions— all of which warn against excessive greed—that we've been set spinning, unable to stop and enjoy life.

I try not to rush and to move slowly as I clean the kitchen. But my husband, who doesn't think about these issues as much as I do, who is still in a traditional job, undergoes a personality change every Monday morning—starting to frown, starting to be impatient, intent on beating the clock. As Thoreau said, "As if we could kill time without injuring eternity." And we are killing time. That used to mean just sitting around; but now, in our frenzied activity, we really are killing time. So much of our time is spent in ways that kill our spirit, our capacity to enjoy the moment, to experience the depth of the moment. Americans, who are so ego-centric, think we have built the best possible civilization, but we have no time to enjoy it.

And why? Because time has become money. What a joke. We value money above all. We measure our most precious commodity, time, in terms of money, and find that we can't enjoy time at all. A Faustian bargain. You want to have all the money in the world? Okay, you can have money, but no time to enjoy life.

Sometimes I will go into my husband's study as he sits there writing on his computer and say to him, "Well, this is it! This is your life! It's probably not going to get any better!" How else can I remind him, and myself, to take time seriously, to not let it slip away.

Moving Slowly

…Why should we live with such hurry and waste of life?

—Henry David Thoreau

To live mindfully, to appreciate your time, you have to move slowly. There's nothing more difficult for Americans, and we have gotten worse in the last twenty years. Court reporters find that we talk faster. We walk faster, our movies are faster. MTV is the perfect example. Just as you start to focus on an image, the camera moves on.

What is this addiction to stimulation? Sometimes I feel addicted to my own adrenaline. If I'm not rushing, feeling pressured, I feel like I'm missing something. Is this the only way we can feel alive now—by rushing? Are we mistaking the rush of caffeine for a feeling of vitality? Does rushing make us feel like we are doing something important, that we are important people? Are we all engaged in such meaningless work that we can only feel important if we feel pressured? Do we have to convince ourselves and others of the importance of our work to justify our existence?

Here is where mindfulness comes in. You must pay attention to your speed and consciously slow down. Maybe make that your mantra—slow down—saying it very slowly....of course, in our rushing, we have no time to talk with people, so we get lonelier and lonelier.

In rushing, we have no time for reflection, no time to notice what is going on around us. We can't reflect on warning signals that come to us—warning signals such as early signs that something is wrong with our health. Signs that you are starting to drive too fast. For instance, whenever I have a near miss in my car, I always say to myself, Ahh, a message from the universe, and I slow down and become more careful in my driving.

Once I walked in on a man in the process of robbing my house. On my walk up to the door I had noticed several little things I later realized should have told me what was happening. But I ignored them. I escaped unharmed, but once again I thought to myself, You ignored the signs. You didn't pay attention.

When we rush, we are much more likely to consume because we are ignoring the little voice asking us if we really need this new thing. Impulse buying is what corporations depend on.

I think that little voice is always there speaking to us, telling us the right thing to do, but we ignore it because we are rushing and have no time to listen.

Gratitude

This is what I would like to feel more than anything. Gratitude. How else can you really enjoy your life? To feel gratitude is to look at everything in your life and appreciate it, be aware of it, pay attention to it. Our lifestyle, of course, engenders discontent and resentment. Because more is always better, you can never be satisfied with what you have. Because commercials are constantly showing us ecstatically happy people with lots of stuff, we always feel that we're just not quite making it. Then, when we see how much money rich people have, we feel envious. All of these feelings make you discontent with your life, causing you to fail to be grateful for what you do have.

So each morning, I consciously think about what I am grateful for and repeat e. e. cummings's *words to myself*:

> i thank You God for most this amazing
> day: for the leaping greenly spirits of trees
> and a blue true dream of sky; and for everything
> which is natural which is infinite which is yes

Entering the Emptiness

by Gerald May

Now a grandfather, Gerald May cannot remember a time when relationship with the natural world was not an essential part of his life. During the five years following the completion of his book *The Awakened Heart,* he spent many hours alone in the mountains and forests. The internal changes brought about by those times in solitude helped him face cancer treatment in 1995. Since 1973 he has worked at the Shalem Institute of Spiritual Formation in Washington, D.C., as an Associate Faculty member, Director of Spiritual Guidance and Director for Research and Program Development. He also established and supervised their wilderness retreats. In addition to his work at Shalem, Dr. May has taught and practiced psychiatry, and held numerous adjunct faculty appointments (including Wesley Theological Seminary and Union Graduate School). May currently lives in Columbia, Maryland with his wife. He has four children and four grandchildren.

In this beautifully reflective piece, May writes of the holiness of "spaciousness": spaciousness of form, time, and soul. He gives practical advice on creating spaces of quiet in our lives. He also recognizes the difficulties associated with opening ourselves to such spaciousness: doing so challenges the idols of efficiency and productivity that we discussed in the introduction; doing so sometimes requires us to face those unpleasant things we keep from our awareness. May reveals that in our tendency to fill up any open space in our days we are "addicted to fulfillment." It is his belief, however, that the emptiness we experience when we embrace spaciousness or quiet is actually our never-completely-satisfied "yearning for love." This yearning draws us to God.

∞

You have made us to be toward Yourself, O Lord, and our hearts are restless until they rest in You.

—Augustine of Hippo

Every risk we take for love, each step we take toward greater consecration, leads us deeper into the spaciousness of love. I have described many kinds of spaces and emphasized the necessity of space for consecration; now we must seek a glimpse of the nature of spaciousness itself. In biblical Hebrew, the letters yodh and shin combine to form a root that connotes "space and the freedom and security which is gained by the removal of constriction." From this YS root come words like yesha and yeshuah, referring to salvation. When you think about it, it makes sense that space would be intimately associated with salvation. Space is freedom: freedom from confinement, from preoccupation, from oppression, from drivenness, and from all the other interior and exterior forces that bind and restrict our spirits. We need space in the first place simply to recognize how compelled and bound we are. Then we need space to allow the compulsions to ease and the bonds to loosen. In the Hebrew sense, our passion needs elbowroom. To the extent that space is permitted by grace and our own willingness, we discover expanding emptiness in which consecration can happen, room for love to make its home in us.[14]

It seems to me that spaciousness comes to us in three primary ways. First, it appears as spaciousness of *form*: physical, geographic spaces like the wide openness of fields, water, and sky and the welcoming simplicity of uncluttered rooms. Second, it comes as spaciousness of *time*: pauses in activity when we are freed from tasks, agendas, and other demands. Third, we encounter spaciousness of *soul*. This is inner emptiness, the room inside our hearts, the unfulfilled quality of our consciousness. Depending upon how we meet this soul-space, we may experience it as open possibility or void nothingness, as creative potential or dulling boredom, as quiet, peaceful serenity or as restless yearning for fulfillment.[15]

The Trouble with Spaciousness

People in our modern developed world are ambivalent about all three kinds of spaciousness. On the one hand, we long for space; in the midst of overactive lives we yearn for peace, stillness, and freedom. We look forward to vacations, and we yearn for our minds to be free of preoccupation. On the other hand, we are liable to become very uncomfortable when such spaces do open up. We do not seem to know what to do with them. We fill up our vacations with activities and compulsions; we fill up our minds with worries and obsessions.

Perhaps I am being romantic, but I think there was a time when we could sit on the front porch and simply enjoy the breeze or watch the sun go down. I remember soft evenings, sitting on my grandmother's lap on the front porch—not a word, barely even a thought. That was simple appreciation. But today many of us have been so conditioned by efficiency that such times feel unproductive, irresponsible, lazy, even selfish. We know we need rest, but we can no longer see the value of rest as an end in itself; it is only worthwhile if it helps us recharge our batteries so we can be even more efficient in the next period of productivity.

Now, on a soft evening, I may retire to my deck (my modern, efficient house does not even have a front porch), and I can just barely recover the old sense of spaciousness and peace I felt with my grandmother. It does not last for long. A few brief blessed moments, and then my mind wants to go back to the work I have yet to do and the worries I feel I must keep picking at. Then I am likely to pour myself a drink. My grandmother never drank; she thought it was a sin. Also, I think, she did not want to fill up her space.

The ancients knew the value of spaciousness for its own sake. The Hebrews ritualized the Sabbath in keeping with God's rest on the seventh day of creation. God did not take that day of rest simply to recoup energy to begin creating another universe during the next workweek. Resting was valuable in its own right. Spaciousness was holy.

The fourth commandment for Jews and Christians is to remember the Sabbath and keep it holy. Many other religions and denominations continue to provide for such times of space and rest, but the meaning has often been twisted. Sabbath was meant to be a day of spaciousness in form, time, and soul. It was to be an uncluttered day, a day not filled up, a day of rest and appreciation, a day of freedom just to be. Now, religious Sabbath is apt to feel like restriction rather than freedom, confinement rather than space. Instead of freedom from having to work, Sabbath came to mean not being *allowed* to work.[16]

I grew up with this kind of reversal. There was a long list of things we were not permitted to do on Sunday. A similar thing was true of silence: silence meant you were not allowed to speak. I shall never forget the liberation I felt when I first went on a silent retreat and the leader said, "The real meaning of silence is that you are free from *having* to speak." Many years later, I came across the following insight from a Tibetan Buddhist text: "Freedom is not the opposite of determinism, but of compulsion, of *having* to act." [17]

We have clearly lost something when we are no longer free just to be, when we must always be active, doing some things and refraining from doing others. Something is missing when we have to force our pauses, carve out our spaces, and then feel we have to justify them. As a result, recreation often means engaging in more pleasurable work, not freedom from having to work at all. The pastor of our church took a sabbatical. He sent regular reports to the congregation about what he was learning. Apparently he felt he had to assure people that he was making good use of his time. Something is amiss when wasting time is something we feel ashamed of, when we must ask a quiet person, "What's wrong?" It is as if a piece of the heart has been cut out; our capacity to be easeful with inactivity has been thrown away and forgotten without our even realizing it.

Think about yourself. How are you when there is nothing to do? When you have a moment of freedom, what do you do with it? Try to take such a moment now: no agenda, nothing to accomplish, just be. Stay with it as long as you can. What happens? Does it feel freeing or confining, peaceful or anxious? Was it different when you were a child? Did it come more easily and feel more comfortable then? If so, what do you think accounts for the change?

Most of us, most of the time, just fill our spaces up or dull our awareness of them. We grab a book, run to the television, work on a project, socialize, have a drink. I used to think women were more comfortable with space than men; nowa-

days I am not so sure. Women perhaps feel more guilty about taking time in freedom for themselves, while men feel more anxious. But it is a tiny difference. Either
way, real space can be very unpleasant.

We somehow must realign our attitudes toward spaciousness. We must begin to
see it as presence rather than absence, friend instead of enemy. This is the most
important practical challenge we face in being consciously in love. It will not be
easy, because we have come to associate space with fear, emptiness with negativity,
lack of fulfillment with dysfunction. The seventeenth-century philosopher Bene-
dict de Spinoza said that nature abhors a vacuum. Modern science has shown he
was wrong. There is far more space than stuff in the universe. The atoms that make
up all matter, including our own bodies, consist of vast distances of space between
tiny subatomic particles. No matter how solid we may feel, we are much more
space than substance. If any nature abhors a vacuum, it is human nature—and
that only because our nature has been so adulterated by conditioning.

I would ask you again, now, to give yourself a little space. Take a moment and
just sit, just be. Waste some time. See and hear what there is around you, and
notice what happens within you. Do not expect any particular experience, and do
not contrive anything. How does it go?

Space and Repression

It is an addiction of the first order that we feel we must always be filling up
our spaces. It goes along with our addictions to work, to productivity, to efficiency.
Sometimes, though, we do not like spaciousness because of what appears to us
within it. Ever since Sigmund Freud's work, psychology has understood that human
beings try to keep unpleasant things out of awareness. The psychoanalysts called it
repression or suppression; a more modern term is selective inattention.

At any given moment, we all have a number of worries, fears, guilt feelings, bad
memories, and things we are procrastinating about that we are simply putting out
of our minds. The difficulty with space, especially interior spaciousness of soul, is
that it allows such repressed and suppressed annoyances back into awareness.
When I pause for a moment and let my mind settle down, what comes in? The
things I have put off, the worries I have been avoiding, the bad feelings I have sti-
fled. Space is like sunlight and fresh air toward which the buried uglies of our souls
crawl in search of healing. It is a very healthy thing. Space is not only potentially
restful but also therapeutic. But like many therapeutic processes, it can be painful.
And in matters of healing consciousness, as in love, there can be no anesthesia.

I know what it is to try to escape from space. A few springtimes ago, I was feeling very overextended and oppressed by my work. I longed for space. A Saturday
morning came when there was no one at home and my desk was momentarily
clear. Ah, I thought, now I have a chance to just sit, just be for a while. Although
I was alone in the house, I closed the doors to my study. I unplugged the telephone,
put my cushion on the floor, and lit a candle. I sat down, took a breath, looked out

the window, and for the first time in days noticed the beauty of the trees and sky. I closed my eyes and noticed a continuing drivenness deep within me, running on its own momentum. I tried to relax, but couldn't. I prayed. I did some stretching and exercise, and then sat down again. But there was no peacefulness. My mind was yammering—no thoughts, just silly, meaningless noise. I tried to let the tension and the noise be. I prayed some more. This is the way it is, I thought, and I just have to sit through it. My eyes opened, again to seek the sky. I noticed that the door-knob was crooked; I could see from where I sat that the screws had come loose. My toolbox was nearby. When I next thought about seeking space, it was an hour later, and I had the entire door dismantled, off its hinges, screws and knobs all over. That afternoon, when my wife came home and asked me how the day was going, I said, "Great. I fixed the door."

It is also possible to create fake space, in which we force our minds into stillness and keep everything repressed. In fact, it is this fake space that most people associate with meditation and concentration—a forceful, effortful attempt to keep the mind silent, focused, and without "distraction." But this is not space at all. It is instead a kind of trance, a deadening of sensitivity, a stifling and restriction of awareness. It is anesthetized; there is no openness in it, no willingness, no participation. True space is encountered only with the willingness and courage to experience things just as they are.

When people tell me they have trouble taking time for prayer or meditation, I often ask them what unpleasant things they might be wanting to avoid. I often ask myself the same question. My answer right now is ironic; the thing I most want to escape from is my longing for love. It hurts too much, more than anything psychological I have ever experienced. There are many times I would escape it or anesthetize it if I could, but it will not go away. Or perhaps *I* cannot go away.

It is a blessing when love is so relentless, because the more we repress, suppress, procrastinate, or anesthetize, the more resistant we will be toward space. Conversely, the more true space we give ourselves, the less we will repress. And to the extent that we consecrate our spaciousness, intend it for love, point it toward love's source, space will be merciful. The unpleasantness of space will never be more than we can bear. Our increasing availability to the truth happens gradually, gently, with grace. It happens in keeping with our own unique personalities; we are given what we need as we need it. Space becomes brutal only if we try to force it, make it a project, or demand that it meet our expectations.

The Myth of Fulfillment

I have described two basic difficulties we human beings have with space. In the first, we are addicted to filling up every kind of space we encounter. We are addicted to fulfillment, to the eradication of all emptiness. In the second difficulty, we fear what spaciousness will reveal to us. We would rather have the anesthetized serenity of dullness than the liberating dis-ease of truth. Together, our addiction to

fulfillment and our flight from truth weave a harsh, desperate barrier against participation in love.

Back in the days when I was doing a lot of psychotherapy, a Roman Catholic
priest came to me with this concern: "I'm nearly fifty years old, and I still don't
have my sexuality resolved."

My response, perhaps a bit too flippant, was, "Join the crowd."

"No," he said, "I mean it. I'm not satisfied with my relationships, and I can't
make peace with celibacy. I can't find any serenity with my desires for intimacy."

I still felt it sounded quite normal, but he wanted to work on it. So for several
months we explored whether psychological problems were causing his distress. He
had not received perfect love and support from his parents when he was a child,
but I thought, "Who does?" He had been traumatized in a variety of ways by early
sex education and experiences. I wondered, "Aren't we all, to some degree?" I
couldn't escape my conviction that he was a very normal example of the male of
the human species.

A middle-aged mother told a story not unlike that of the priest. "I should be
happy with the way things are. I have a fine marriage, two wonderful kids, a good
career. Yet I keep feeling something is missing. I have these dreams about romance.
Deep down I am restless; I want something more. I think my sex life is at least as
good as the next person's, but there's some kind of intimacy I long for. I think perhaps I am repressing something."

I asked, "Is there any particular reason you feel this is a problem? Could it be
that many other people have similar yearnings for something more?" (This was my
attempt at a gentler version of "Join the crowd.")

She paused for a long time. "No, I do *not* believe other people have these feelings. I know a lot of people who are perfectly happy and fulfilled."

"Do you think they really are? Or is it maybe just the way they act and talk? I
know I hear this kind of thing from many people."

"Well, you talk to a lot of strange people. I have some close friends who never
seem to feel the way I do. If they're kidding themselves, they are doing a good job
of it. They really feel contented with their lives."

"Have you talked to them? Have you told any of them how you feel, to see what
they'd say?"

"No, I haven't. They wouldn't understand. And I'd feel—I do feel—as though
there's something wrong with me. They'd give me advice, and that's the last thing
I need. I already feel too incapable."

So we explored her psychology for a while. As with the priest, there were imper-
fections, but again I kept thinking that all experience is imperfect. And I kept
wanting to say, "What's wrong with feeling unfulfilled and restless? Isn't there
something basically *right* about it?"

With both these people, as with so many others who have confided in me, the
real problem was believing that their sense of inner restlessness and lack of fulfill-

ment indicated psychological disorder. They had swallowed the cultural myth that says, "If you are well adjusted, and if you are living your life properly, you will feel fulfilled, satisfied, content, and serene." Stated conversely, the myth says, "If you are not satisfied and fulfilled, there is something wrong with you."

The myth is so widespread that the majority of adults in our culture accept it without question. There are three ways we act out this belief: We may try to "fix" ourselves, our life situations and our relationships because we feel there is something wrong with them. Or we may repress our restlessness, trying to appear to ourselves and others as if we had achieved perfection. Failing this, we dull our concern altogether, seeking to lose ourselves in work, food, entertainment, drugs, or some other escape. Ironically, all three ways easily become addictions in themselves; addictions to self-improvement, to perfect adjustment, or to various means of escape.

The myth has pervaded virtually every aspect of our society. Popular religion promises peace of mind if only we will believe correctly. If we are not completely happy, it maintains, it is because we are somehow not right with God. Perhaps we are too sinful, or our faith is insufficient, or we have missed the one true doctrine. Countless people believe the religious myth, even when a cursory reading of the lives of saints reveals great agony, doubt, and struggle within themselves and with their world. A slightly deeper probing of spiritual growth shows that as people deepen in their love for God and others, they become ever more open: not only more appreciative of the beauty and joys of life, but also more vulnerable to its pain and brokenness.

Popular psychology promotes the myth as well. It promises peace of mind for only two categories of people: those who grew up in perfectly functioning families and those who use modern psychology to rise above the scars of their dysfunctional families. Countless people believe this psychological version as well, even when the knotted lives of our most successful citizens are continually displayed in the media for all to examine and when no such thing as a truly functional family can be found.

Although it is very right to treat our real disorders and maximize our health, we make several great mistakes if we think life should or even can be resolved to a point of complete serenity and fulfillment. To believe this is to commit ourselves to a fantasy that does not exist and that, if it were true, would kill our love and end in stagnation, boredom, and death. It is also to remove our concern from the real issues of our life and world, to transfer our energy to a vague, self-serving agenda that must be carried out before we can get on with the business of living, loving, and creating a better world. Further, the myth perpetuates the willful delusion that we human beings are objects, like machines, to be built and repaired, meant for efficiency rather than love. Most importantly, the myth of fulfillment makes us miss the most beautiful aspect of our human souls: our emptiness, our incompleteness, our radical yearning for love. We were never meant to be completely fulfilled; we were meant to taste it, to long for it, and to grow toward it. In this way we participate in love becoming life, life becoming love. To miss our emptiness is, finally, to miss our hope.

The Secret Hope of Emptiness

Emptiness, yearning, incompleteness: these unpleasant words hold a hope for incomprehensible beauty. It is precisely in these seemingly abhorrent qualities of ourselves—qualities that we spend most of our time trying to fix or deny—that the very thing we most long for can be found: hope for the human spirit, freedom for love.

This is a secret known by those who have had the courage to face their own emptiness. The secret of being in love, of falling in love with life as it is meant to be, is to befriend our yearning instead of avoiding it, to live into our longing rather than trying to resolve it, to *enter* the spaciousness of our emptiness instead of trying to fill it up.

It has taken me a long time to learn this secret, and I continue to forget it many times each day. Befriending emptiness is mostly a tender thing, requiring such immediacy and vulnerability that my heart is rendered very delicate. I cannot maintain it, and it is only through the empowerment of grace that it comes to me at all. Yet nowhere else am I more truly myself. In no other way does the woven tapestry of love and addiction spring into vibrant, colorful life.

Some recovering addicts have discovered the secret as they realize that the awesome, terrifying space left by their relinquished addiction is like that of an empty vessel, devoid of substance yet full of possibility. The recovering heroine of Erica Jong's *Any Woman's Blues* finds that "I was not a victim of fate. Yes, God, Goddess, the Higher Power, the Holy Ghost, worked *through* me; I was a human vessel for a divine energy force. But to be a vessel was not the same as to be a victim or a pawn. Life flowed through me, and therefore my body and mind had to be respected." [18]

Some artists have discovered the secret as they endure what Etty Hillesum called the battlefield of our inner space: "To turn one's innermost being into a vast empty plain, so that something of 'God' can enter you, and something of 'Love' too." Etty Hillesum's life came to an end in the concentration camp at Auschwitz, but her hope—and, most amazingly, her joy and gratitude for life—lived on for us through her oppression. [19]

Oppression by other human beings, like the oppression of our own addictions, can teach the secret. But we can learn it only if we have the courage to face our emptiness with undefended clarity. In nineteenth-century Maryland, the young Frederick Douglass was confronted with his own emptiness as he learned to read. "It opened my eyes to the horrible pit, but to no ladder upon which to get out." Douglass was a man of great courage, most obviously in risking his life for freedom for his brothers and sisters. But beneath this, before this, there was a deeper bravery. He was willing to experience the pain of his own longing. He chose not to run away from his truth. [20]

We can perform service to others for a variety of reasons. We can do good deeds because of fear, guilt, or the desire to inflate our egos. But if we really want to be loving, if we truly wish to respond to the call of justice and freedom, we must first have the courage to look into our own emptiness. We must somehow even come to love it. The poet Rilke, a late contemporary of Douglass, advised a young friend to "be patient toward all that is unsolved in your heart and try to love the *questions themselves*. *Live* the questions now. Perhaps over all there is a great motherhood, as common longing." [21]

We all have experiences of emptiness. Some of these experiences, like losing love, youth, or health, or feeling compassion for the pains of others, are universal for the human race. They are expressions of what Rilke called the great motherhood of common longing. But some experiences are always uniquely our own, carried in the secret places of our hearts, touched only in solitude. Anyone who faces emptiness becomes contemplative in that very moment, for then the truth is seen—just as it is.

It is the contemplative saints, however, who most know the fear and pain as well as the joy and freedom of entering emptiness; they have chosen to confront that which has to be thrust upon the rest of us. They have stretched and yielded themselves to experience cleanly and clearly the hunger and brokenness of their own hearts and of our world. They have willingly sought to deprive themselves of anesthesia. They have claimed their desire to bear the beams of love, regardless of the cost.

At the turn of the fifteenth century, Julian of Norwich wrote, "I learned to be afraid of my instability. For I do not know in what way I shall fall. I would have liked to have known that—with due fear, of course. But I got no answer." She faced her fear and was able to continue: "Both when we fall and when we get up again we are kept in the same precious love. The love in which God made us never had beginning. In it we have our beginning." [22]

Spaciousness is always a beginning, a possibility, a potential, a capacity for birth. Space exists not in order to be filled but to create. In space, to the extent we can bear the truth of the way things are, we find the ever-beginning presence of love. Take the time, then; make the space. Seek it wherever you can find it, do it however you can. The manner does not matter, and the experience you have there is of secondary importance. Seek the truth, not what is comfortable. Seek the real, not the easy.

Perhaps you already have an intentional rhythm of prayer, meditation, or reflection. If so, the form may not need to change at all. Just review what you do and what seems to happen. Does your practice allow some real space, or has it become completely filled with spiritual activity? Is it a time of immediate presence for you, in which you can just be? Or has it become a routine in which you find more dullness than wakefulness, more focused attention than openness to what is?

In my experience, all routines sooner or later become habits I begin to hide behind. I can take the best of disciplines—those that are most likely to really enable spacious presence—and turn them into doings. Then I go through the motions of the practice and escape the space altogether. For this reason, I find I need to bring a certain freshness to all my spiritual practices. This time of prayer or meditation may be something I am very used to doing, but why am I doing it now? What is my real hope? Can I reclaim my desire, form my intent afresh, so that I enter each time as if it were the first? Can I claim my hope that it will indeed be a beginning?

If you do not already have such a rhythm, I encourage you to try to establish one. If you are at all like me, this will not be easy. But I am convinced the struggle is worth it; success or failure do not matter—the attempt is worthwhile in and of itself.

The first step is to look for spaces that occur naturally in your life. We all have them, and they can tell us something about what is uniquely right for us. Perhaps you find little natural spaces after you have completed some work, times that you stretch and look around and just be for a moment. Could times like that be expanded? Could you savor them a little longer? Or maybe you sometimes indulge in a long, hot bath, or find yourself in stillness just before you go to sleep or wake up. Possibly you find space in nature or gardening, in music or exercise. Take a while to go over a typical day in your mind—where are the most likely moments of spaciousness? Are there some such moments that you usually immediately fill by watching television, reading, drinking, or some other activity that dulls you even though you call it recreation? Might you be able to just be present a while longer in some of those moments before you move to fill or dull yourself? Might some of them be expanded and made more intentional without causing them to feel too contrived or artificial?

In addition, you should probably at least try to set aside some regular time each day, in the morning or evening or both, that is simply and solely dedicated to just being. In the beginning, these times may be only a few minutes long. (Many of my times are still only a few minutes long, after over twenty years of experience.) A friend of mine began each morning with only the time it took her coffee to perco-late. I think there is little value in staying there longer than you can remain fresh and present. When busy-ness and dullness take over, it is probably best to move on and come back again later. On the other hand, don't run away when the first repressed unpleasantness surfaces. Try to let it be; stay a little longer with what is.

A set-aside time in the morning, however brief, can establish a kind of attitudi-nal posture (*disposition* is the classical word) for beginning the day. It is a time when you can consecrate the day and yourself for the day, offering your prayer for greater presence in love. Likewise, evening times can include a little reflection on the day. Where were the moments of space? What times seemed to contain real presence? What glimpses of being in love were you given? What enterprises or situations kidnapped you and held you hostage to functioning or fear? And where is the spaciousness right now, in this moment at the end of the day? What do you seek there? What is the deepest desire with which you might drift into sleep?

Finally, keep an eye open for longer spaces. Consider extended spiritual retreats, quiet days, or contemplative prayer or meditation groups where you can spend some dedicated and less distracted time just simply being. Bear in mind that I am not speaking of the talk- and activity-filled conferences that are sometimes called retreats or spiritual groups but of periods in which people truly seek stillness and deepening alone or together. Experiment with whether you find space more easily alone or with other people. Look to your own Sabbath—is it possible to claim some time like that for yourself, when just being is truly an end in itself? What sort of support might you need from other people to help you pursue this?

I have proposed that you seek three kinds of spaces in your life: little moments in the midst of work and play, regular set-aside times each day, and periodic longer times of authentic retreat. In all these, and in the rest of your time as well, I hope you will seek the spaciousness of the immediate moment: the spaciousness of *presence*. In this one single moment, here and now, all three kinds of spaciousness come together: form because it is here, time because it is now, and soul because aliveness is birthed in immediacy.

You will, as I do, find yourself resisting the spaciousness of presence. Sometimes you will know that you simply do not want to face into it; it may seem too painful, or it may require too much letting-go of other investments. That is all right. Do not try to force it. If you fight for presence simply because you think you *should*, you will only stifle yourself. True presence never comes through coercion.

But there will be other times, increasingly frequent, when you know that in spite of your resistance you really do desire presence; you want it deeply regardless of the pain it holds or the relinquishment you must endure. When it happens to me, I pray for help: "God, you are here now; help me be here now." Or I repeat one of the precious phrases: "present moment, wonderful moment," "pure and total presence," "practice the presence," "continually renewed immediacy," "be here now," "be still and know," "come unto me," "bear the beams."

I also try to remind myself of what I know from experience: the two most important facts about the spaciousness of the present moment. No matter how full of wonder or how empty and barren the moment seems, *it is always sufficient*. And no matter how much exquisite joy or pain I may feel in the moment, *it will never be more than I can bear*.

The emptiness of the spaciousness of the present moment is sufficient. It contains everything that is needed for lovingly beginning the next moment; it seeks only our own willing, responsive presence, just here, just now. And we can bear whatever experience we have in the spaciousness of this present moment. If we project it into the future it may seem impossible, but just here, just now, it is not too much. There are no exceptions—not in physical pain, not in psychiatric disorder or emotional agony, not in relational strife, not in war, not in oppression, not in loss, not in spiritual aching, not in dying. Love is too much with us for there to be any exceptions.

Contemplation and Ministry

by Henri J.M. Nouwen

Henri Nouwen, who died in 1996, was a Catholic priest known for his many books on the Christian faith, spirituality, and Christian action and contemplation. He touched the lives of many students while a professor of Pastoral Theology at Yale Divinity School. He spent his last years sharing his life and living with mentally handicapped people in the L'Arche community of Daybreak in Toronto, Ontario.

Nouwen writes of a contemplative spirituality that enables us to see "what is really there." In contrast to the hurried and out-of-control experiences about which Andrews and Schor wrote, Nouwen suggests that when we are able to remove our blindfolds and "see nature as a gift, time as opportunity, and people as persons, we will also see that our whole world is a sacrament constantly revealing to us the great love of God." He believes that our relationships with nature, time and people can minister to us as we can minister to them.

Making the Clouded Clear

What is the relationship between contemplation and ministry? To contemplate is to see and to minister is to make visible. The contemplative life is a life with a vision and the life of ministry is the life in which this vision is revealed to others.

I came to this definition by reading the writings of Evagrius Ponticus, one of the desert fathers who had great influence on monastic spirituality in the East and the West. Evagrius calls contemplation a *theoria physike* which means a vision (*theoria*) of the nature of things (*physike*). The contemplative is someone who sees things for what they really are, who sees the real connections, who knows, as Thomas Merton used to say, "what the scoop is."

To attain such a vision, a spiritual discipline is necessary. Evagrius calls this discipline the *pratike*, the peeling away of the blindfolds that prevent us from seeing clearly. Merton, who was very familiar with Evagrius's thinking, expressed the same idea when he said in one of his conferences to the monks at the Gethsemani Abbey that the contemplative life is a life in which we move constantly from opaqueness to transparency, from the place where things are dark, thick, impenetrable and closed, to the place where these same things are translucid, open, and offer vision far beyond themselves.

I would like to look first at the different levels at which this movement from opaqueness to transparency takes place, to make it clear that all of life can become a vision of the nature of things. Then I want to explore the concrete discipline of contemplation which must undergird this movement from opaqueness to transparency to keep it alive.

The contemplative life is one in which we start seeing our world as transparent, a world which points beyond itself and thus reveals its true nature to us. Just as a window cannot be a real window for us if we cannot look through it, so our world cannot show to us its real identity if it remains opaque and does not point beyond itself.

Nature

Recent decades have shown us that as long as we relate to the trees, the rivers, the mountains, the fields and the oceans as properties which we can manipulate according to our real or fabricated needs, nature remains opaque, and does not reveal to us its true being. When a tree is nothing else than a potential chair it ceases to tell us much about growth; when a river is only a dumping place for industrial waste, it can no longer speak to us about movement. They become opaque, an opaqueness which in our society manifests itself as pollution. The dirty rivers, the smog-filled skies, the strip-mined hills, and the ravaged woods are sad signs of our false relationship with nature.

Our hard and very urgent task is to realize that nature is not primarily a property to be possessed, but a gift to be received with admiration and gratitude. How differently we would live if we always sensed that the nature around us is full of desire to tell us the great story of God's love, to which it points. The plants and animals with whom we live teach us about birth, growth, maturation, and death, about the need for gentle care, and especially about the importance of patience and hope. And even more profoundly, water, oil, bread, and wine all point beyond themselves to the great story of our re-creation.

One of the sad features of our day is that we no longer believe in the ministry of nature to us. We easily limit ministry to work for people by people. I wonder if the sheer artificiality and ugliness with which many people are surrounded is not as bad or worse than their interpersonal problems.

I found this painfully true in ministry to the elderly. Many old people suffer from the ugliness of their environment. Much healing could be offered to older people by helping them to make their home and room a little more beautiful. With real plants who grow and die as they do and ask for care and attention as they do, their lives might be less lonely. Real flowers about which and to which we can speak can have more healing power than well-chosen words about the meaning of life and death.

Here we see how a deeper contemplation of nature can broaden our ministry of teaching, healing and worship.

Time

A second relationship in which the contemplative life requires the ongoing movement from opaqueness to transparency is our relationship to time. Time constantly threatens to become our great enemy. In our contemporary society it often seems that not money but time enslaves us. We say, "I wish I could do all the things that I need to do, but I simply have no time. Just thinking about all the things I have to do today makes me tired: writing five letters, visiting a friend, practicing my music, making a phone call, going to class, finishing a paper, doing my meditation." Indeed it seems that many people feel that they no longer have time, but that time has them; they have become victims of an ongoing pressure to meet deadlines. The most frequently heard excuse is, "I am sorry, but I have no time." The most common request is, "I know how busy you are, but do you have a minute?" And the most important decisions are often made over a quick lunch, or, to use an even more catching phrase, "while grabbing a bite."

A strange sense of hurry has entered many people's lives. We wonder, "Who or what is pushing me? It seems I am so busy that I have no time left to live."

All this suggests that time has become opaque, dark and impenetrable. It is the experience of time as chronology, a randomly collected series of incidents and accidents over which we have no control and which gives us a sense of fatalism. This fatalism often manifests itself in the guise of boredom. Boredom does not mean that we have nothing to do or that there is not enough going on to entertain us, but that we are gnawed by the feeling that whatever we do or say makes no real difference. It is the feeling that the real decisions are made independently of our words or actions.

The contemplative life is the life in which time slowly loses its opaqueness and becomes transparent. This is often a very difficult and slow process, but full of re-creating power. To start seeing that the many events of our day, week, or year are not in the way of our search for a full life, but the way to it, is a real experience of conversion. If we discover that writing letters, attending classes, visiting people and cooking food are not a series of random events which prevent us from realizing our deepest self, but contain in themselves the transforming power we are looking for, then we are beginning to move from time lived as *chronos* to time lived as *kairos*. *Kairos* means *the* opportunity. It is the right time, the real moment, the chance of our lives. When our time becomes *kairos*, it opens up to endless new possibilities, and offers us a constant opportunity for a change of heart.

In Jesus' life every event has become opportunity. He opens his public ministry with the words, "The time has come" (Mark 1:15) and lives every moment of it as an opportunity. Finally, he announces that his time is near (Matthew 26:18) and enters into his hour as *the* opportunity, liberating history from its fatalistic chronology.

This really is good news. Now we know that all events of life, even such dark events as war, famine and flood, violence and murder, are not irreversible fatalities but carry within them the possibility to become *the* moment of change. We no longer need to run from the present in search of the place where we think life is really happening. We can see in the center of the present the first manifestation of the kingdom. Now boredom can no longer exist, since every moment is filled with infinite meaning. Time becomes transparent.

The contemplative life is not a life that offers a few good movements among many bad ones; it transforms all of our time into a window which makes the invisible world visible.

It hardly needs to be said that it belongs to the core of all ministry to make time transparent for each other such that in the most concrete circumstances of life we can see that our hour is God's hour and that all time is therefore opportunity. All who suffer, especially the elderly, the poor, and those who are physically, mentally, or spiritually imprisoned are tempted by fatalism. When we break the chains of this fatalism and help others see the real nature of what takes place in their lives, then we really are bringing good news to the poor, new sight to the blind, and liberty to the captives.

People

The third relationship that invites the contemplative to move from opaqueness to transparency is our relationship with people. Here, more than in the two previous relationships, the importance of contemplation as seeing the real connection becomes manifest. One of our greatest temptations is to relate to people as interesting characters, as individuals who strike us as worthy of special attention because of their special qualities.

We are always intrigued by interesting characters, whether they are film stars or criminals, sports heroes or killers, Nobel Prize winners or perverts. Magazines such as *People* make millions of dollars exploiting human curiosity about humans, and the front pages of most newspapers give less and less news and more and more reports about new records in human irregularities, whether they lead to praise or blame.

As long as people are little more than interesting characters to us, they remain opaque. We can be quite sure that no one who is approached as an interesting character is going to reveal to us his or her secret. On the contrary, characterization is often so narrowing and limiting that it makes people close themselves and hide.

Especially in the field of the helping professions, the temptation to label people with easy characterizations is great, since it gives us the illusion of understanding. Not only psychiatric labels such as "neurotic," "psychopathic," or "schizophrenic," but also religious labels such as "unbeliever," "pagan," "sinner," "progressive," "conservative," "liberal," and "orthodox," can give us a false sense of understanding. They explain more about our own insecurities than about the real nature of our neighbor.

Our great task is to prevent our fears from boxing our fellow human beings into characterizations and to see them as persons. The word "person" comes from *personare* which means "sounding through." Our vocation in life is to "sound through" to each other a greater reality than we ourselves fully know. As persons we sound through a love greater than we ourselves can grasp, a truth deeper than we ourselves can articulate, a beauty richer than we ourselves can contain. As persons we are called to be transparent to each other, pointing far beyond our character to him who has given us his love, truth, and beauty.

Contemplation as seeing what is really there has a very significant meaning in the context of interpersonal relationships. Although we cannot hear ourselves sounding through, we are sounding through to each other. This implies that our real gifts only become known to us when they are recognized and affirmed by those who receive them.

Here we can begin to see the intimate connection between contemplation and ministry. Contemplation enables us to see the gifts in those to whom we minister. And ministry is first of all the reception and affirmation of what we hear sounding through them, so that they themselves may recognize their own giftedness. What more beautiful ministry is there than the ministry by which we make others aware of the love, truth, and beauty they reveal to us? Ours is a time in which many people doubt their self-worth and are often on the verge of self-condemnation, not seldom leading to suicide. We can indeed save lives by seeing in the eyes of those in need, and hearing in their words, the story which speaks of the gifts they have to share.

How beautiful, then, is the ministry by which we can call forth the hidden gifts of people and celebrate with them the love, truth and beauty they give us. Ministry and contemplation, therefore, enrich each other and lead to an always-increasing joy, since God keeps revealing himself to us in the ever-changing lives of people.

Contemplation requires a constant movement from opaqueness to transparency: from nature as a property to be possessed to nature as a gift to be received with admiration and gratitude; from time as a randomly thrown together series of incidents and accidents, to time as a constant opportunity for a change of heart; from people as interesting characters to people as persons sounding through more than they themselves can hold. This does not mean that nature is never property, that time is never random succession, and that people are never interesting characters. It does mean that when these become the dominant modes of relating to our world, then our world remains opaque and we never see how things really hang together. When, however, we are slowly able to peel away our blindfolds and see nature as a gift, time as opportunity, and people as persons, we will also see that our whole world is a sacrament constantly revealing to us the great love of God.

The practice of contemplative prayer is the discipline by which we begin to see God in our heart. It is a careful attentiveness to him who dwells in the center of our being so that through the recognition of his presence we allow him to take possession of all our senses. Through the discipline of prayer we awaken ourselves to the God in us and let him enter into every aspect of our lives.

It is by being awake to this God in us that we can see him in the world around us. The great mystery of the contemplative life is not that we see God in the world, but that God in us recognizes God in the world. It is the divine Spirit praying in us who makes our world transparent and opens our eyes to the presence of the divine Spirit in all that surrounds us. This explains the intimate relationship between contemplation and ministry.

As ministers of the word of God, we urgently need a discipline of contemplative prayer. For us mind-minded people, the two main characteristics of contemplative prayer seem to be simplicity and obedience.

Our contemplation should first of all be simple, very simple. Contemplative prayer lets the word of God descend from our mind into our heart where it can become fruitful. It is a becoming flesh *in* us of the word of God. This is why it is important to avoid all long inner reasoning and inner speeches and to focus quietly and patiently on a word or a sentence—to ruminate on it, murmur it, chew it, eat it—so that its power can be sensed in our innermost self. Thus our overstimulated minds and our overextended bodies can find rest and peace.

Secondly, our prayer should be obedient. The word obedience includes the word *obaudire*, which means to listen. Contemplative prayer requires us to listen, to let God speak to us, when he wants and in the way he wants. This is so difficult for us precisely because it means allowing God to say what we might not want to hear. But if we listen long and deeply, God will reveal himself to us as a soft breeze or a still, small voice; he will offer himself to us in gentle compassion. Without this obedience, this listening to the God of our heart, we remain deaf and our life grows absurd. The word absurd includes the term *surdus*, which means deaf. The absurd life is the opposite of the obedient life.

Simple and obedient and contemplative prayer is the way in which we come to know our God by heart. When we know him by heart, we will recognize him in our world, its nature, its time, and its people. The discipline of contemplative prayer is the basis of the contemplative life and of all ministry.

According to Evagrius, the discipline of prayer and the contemplative life find their culmination in the direct knowledge of God. Here we go beyond the practice of the contemplative prayer and even beyond the vision of the nature of things, and enter into the most intimate communion with God himself. This direct knowledge is the greatest gift of all, the grace of complete unity, rest, and peace. It is the highest degree of spiritual life, in which the created world is transcended and we experience directly our being lifted up into God's inner life. In this experience, the distinction between ministry and contemplation is no longer necessary; there are no longer blindfolds to remove and all has become seeing.

This direct knowledge is the Mount Tabor experience in our lives. It is an experience which is given to only a few and even they must return to the valley without permission to tell others what they have seen. For most of us, the greater part of our lives are spent not on the mountaintop, but in the valley. And in this valley we are called to be contemplative ministers.

Reprinted with permission from *Sojourners*, 2401 15th Street Northwest, Washington, D.C. 20009; (202) 328-8842 or 800-714-7474.

Your Money or Your Life:
The Place of Money in Modern Life

In truth, all human beings are called to be saints, but that
just means called to be fully human, to be perfect—that is,
whole, mature, fulfilled. The saints are simply those men
and women who relish the event of life as a gift and
who realize that the only way to honor such a gift is
to give it away.

—*William Stringfellow*

Spending Money as if Life Really

by Evy McDonald

Evy McDonald is co-founder of the New Road Map [
all-volunteer nonprofit organization dedicated to help___ people
shift to low-consumption, high-fulfillment lifestyles. Their primary
educational tool is the national bestseller, *Your Money or Your Life*,
by Joe Dominguez and Vicki Robin. This book provides practical
strategies for reducing expenses, increasing savings and improving
quality of life.

McDonald was born and raised in Nebraska. With both an RN
and MS degree, she has taught neurosurgical nursing and directed
Intensive Care and Coronary Care units. After leaving paid
employment, she directed an all-volunteer medical research project
on psychological differences in short-term and long-term survivors
of a neuromuscular disease. An internationally known expert on
quality-of-life issues, she lectures widely on how financial stresses
affect our health and well-being, and on ways of handling money
that can bring more time for the things in life that really matter.
McDonald, studying to become an ordained Methodist minister, is
active in a Methodist congregation in her hometown of Seattle.

This is a powerful personal story and at the same time a thought-
provoking piece on the place of money and possessions in our lives.
Into this story McDonald weaves discussion of American consumer
habits (shopping whenever we feel sad or lonely...), our level of
happiness, and the way in which she brought her spending habits
and relationship with money into alignment with her values as a
Christian. McDonald emphasizes that aligning her spending habits
with her values had "nothing to do with deprivation" and everything to do with a life of fulfillment and "immeasurable wealth."

∞

The alarm sounds, feet hit the floor and we're up for the start of another day.
We slip into store-bought clothes and eat breakfast bought at the neighborhood
grocery. Our day begins with consuming. Consuming is not wrong; in fact it is necessary for life.

What concerns me and many others is over-consumption. Our affluence has
shifted our focus from consuming only what we need to consuming for the sake of
consuming. Consumption has become a habit, a hobby and a sport. A survey of

girls in the United States discovered that 93% of them identified store-
ping as their favorite activity.

Most North Americans recognize the problem. A recent Merck Family Fund
Poll indicated that 82% of North Americans say we consume too much. Overflow-
ing landfills and neighborhoods lined with stuffed garbage cans witness to our patterns of excess.

Overconsumption has not always been a pattern of life in the United States.
Though history shows that there was a constant tension between material acquisition and spiritual transcendence, most households until the twentieth century were
not consumers but producers and manufacturers. People grew their own food, built
their own homes, barns and furniture, poured their own candles and sewed their
own clothes.

Then a complex series of events moved our country into the consumer society.
Just before the Great Depression, social innovators were planning self-sufficient
communities that would give people a sense of belonging and integrate urban and
rural towns. As David Shi said in his book *The Simple Life*, an "organic simplicity"
would evolve. With the collapse of the economy these dreams disappeared.

As the United States got back on its feet the American Boom Era began. Leading
economists felt that perpetual economic growth was possible. We, the public, only
needed to be taught to want and consume more and more. In 1955 economist Victor Lebow wrote, "We seek our spiritual satisfaction or ego satisfaction in consumption...We need things consumed, burned up, worn out, replaced and discarded at an
ever-increasing rate." Industry flourished as long as planned obsolescence reigned.

A theology of consumption began to invade our culture—and our churches.
Slowly, almost imperceptively, we wandered away from the foundational teachings
of Jesus—sharing our wealth, identifying with the marginalized, living a life of
grateful stewardship—and began to identify our worth with how much money we
made or how many possessions we owned.

Today many modern shopping malls evoke the image of a cathedral, with towers
of glass rising upward and lighting effects suggestive of the second coming. On any
given Sunday more people visit shopping centers than centers of worship. Rituals
of communion have been replaced with rituals of consumption. We need to ask
ourselves: What do we worship? The Gospel of Matthew warns us that "Where
your treasure is, there your heart will be also" (Mt. 6:21). All too often our treasures lie tucked away in the department store sale.

Our identity has changed: from being American citizens to being American consumers. We now produce very little for ourselves. We have become voracious consumers of not only goods but services, all in an attempt to increase our quality of
life.

But has our affluence and consumption given us more fulfilling, happier and just
ways of living? Today, people admit to feeling stressed and tired with little time to
care for and nurture relationships, family, friends or the environment. Since 1970

our quality of life (as measured by the Index of Social Health) has dropped by 51%, even though our standard of living (per capita consumption) rose by 45%. We have luxuries beyond the dreams of previous generations, we can enjoy ecotours, wilderness adventure trips and weekend retreats, yet we are not happier.

We need to take a look at our patterns of consumption and reevaluate the ways we use that resource called money. In addition, as Christians we are compelled to see if these patterns align with Biblical teachings and living a Christian life.

For many years my life reflected typical mainstream Christianity. I attended church on Sundays, sang in the choir and at times assisted with Sunday school. These church activities fit into and around my professional activities and busy life as director of intensive care and coronary care units. I was a "convenience Christian." When church activities fit into my schedule, I was willing to participate—but I was unwilling to inconvenience myself or my routine. My life was centered not around God but on work, professional goals, money, promotions, looking good and proving myself.

One day, browsing through the newspaper, a simple list caught my eye. All it said was "God, Family, Exercise and Work." The article told the story of a successful business man who described the hectic work days that gave him no time to go to ball games with his children, be home for meals or spend quality time with his wife. Every morning he looked at that list. One day, in a flash of insight, he realized that he was living life upside down. The list represented his heart-felt priorities but the everyday reality of his life was: Work, Exercise, Family, God. Family and God fit in around the edges of his life. This realization transformed his thinking, which in turn led to significant lifestyle changes. He began to live his priorities, to make that list a reality in his life. Soon he was spending less time at work and more time with his family, and he was participating in projects that brought joy, purpose and meaning to his life.

This was the kind of life I was seeking, the kind I suspect all of us long for at some level. Social researcher Alan Durning, in his book *How Much is Enough*, tells us that the percentage of Americans reporting they are "very happy" was no larger in 1991 than in 1957. In the 1950's the average home was 1,100 square feet, in 1993 it was over 2,000 square feet. We can choose from over 25,000 supermarket items, including 200 kinds of cereal. We live in larger homes and have more choices, yet are not any happier or more fulfilled. Marcus Borg in *Meeting Jesus Again for the First Time* eloquently states that: "Our culture's secular wisdom does not affirm the reality of the spirit... It looks to the material world for satisfaction and meaning. Its dominant values are what I call the three A's—Achievement, Affluence and Appearance. We live our life in accord with these values. We have the experience of being satiated and yet we are still hungry."

Satiated at the physical level, yet starved at the spiritual level—that was an accurate description of me in the late 1970's. At that time my primary goal was to become the youngest female hospital administrator in the country. By 1980 I had a

Master's degree and had taught neurosurgical nursing, had been Director of Education at one of the first three Hospices in our country and had directed intensive care and coronary care units. I was rapidly headed towards my goal.

My life appeared successful. As a young and vibrant woman I seemed a natural for reaching my goals. As I ascended the ranks of hospital administration, I adjusted my lifestyle to each new position. I quickly grew dissatisfied with my "old" car, my rented apartment and the "shabby" condition of my material possessions. To rise above this "second-class" lifestyle I bought a home, a new car, better clothes and upgraded my kitchen appliances. I was making more and more money and couldn't understand why I felt I had less.

Only after reflection did I realize that as my income had increased so had my spending. Work was the center of my life—at the hospital by 4 AM and not home until 8-9 PM, always on call and ready to respond to any emergency. Enthralled and exhilarated by the adrenalin surges that came with encountering life and death situations, I saw no reason to change my life's direction. In all probability this hectic, exciting yet ultimately unfulfilling life would have continued indefinitely if a serious illness had not entered the picture.

In the summer of 1980 my world was turned upside down. It was a sweltering southwest day and I was lying in a hospital bed a thousand miles from home, waiting for the doctor to tell me what was wrong. It was morning when he walked in, fully armored in his white labcoat, otoscope protruding from his pocket, stethoscope hung around his neck.

Exuding an air of cool calmness, he crossed his arms and said, "Well, you already know what's going on and I'm here to confirm it. You'll probably die within the year. There's no treatment so I suggest you go home, make out your will and prepare for the inevitable." With that proclamation he turned quickly and left. I lay there in stunned silence, my mind numb, my emotions in limbo.

A few hours later the phone rang. It was the Director of Nursing at the hospital where I worked. After a few moments of polite conversation she asked me if I would be coming back to work in the next two or three days. A cold fear gripped me. I knew that intensive care and coronary care needed daily leadership; and I had been gone for nearly three weeks. When I said No, she continued with a concerned voice and said, "The units need leadership. I'm sorry, Evy, but we will need to replace you immediately. We have someone in mind who is willing to step in. When you can come back to work we'll find some type of position for you."

The day was surreal, nothing was sinking in. I had lost the job that gave me my identity, my purpose in life and my sense of self-worth, and I had been told that I was going to die. But the day was not over yet. In the evening my housemate called. Hesitantly, she asked if I had home-owners' insurance because the house had been burglarized and most of my possessions stolen. This was the capper, an ironic conclusion to the day my world ended. In the course of 12 hours I had lost almost everything I identified with. Gone was the dream of being the youngest female hospital administrator. Gone were the material possessions that let others know my status. Gone was the sense of power that came from being a leader in nursing. Gone was the sense of success that came not only from my position but also from the quality and amount of my possessions. Gone were my "idols."

The only place for me to turn—the only source left of comfort, solace and meaning for my life—was God. There was nothing else. Returning home I ran into a wall of anger and hurt inside me. Through the emotional pain I touched a deeper spiritual pain—my life was not rooted in my faith. God only existed for me at times of crisis or convenience. The values I professed to hold dear—the ones I preached as necessary to a love-filled, God-filled life—were not the values I lived.

I professed to act with the well-being of others in mind. I boldly stated that everyone had the right to enough food, decent clothes, adequate shelter and acceptable health care. But before the robbery I had 70 pairs of shoes and closets full of clothes (many hardly worn). I began to question myself deeply. What did these objects represent to me? Meaning? Success? Status?

A Bible verse I had learned as a child kept haunting me. Proverbs 30:8-9. "Give me neither riches nor poverty, let me be fed with the food that is needful for me. Lest I be full and deny thee and say, Who is the Lord? Lest I be poor and steal and profane the name of my God." The meaning of this verse emerged like new leaves after a warm spring rain. Contentment, fulfillment and joy come from knowing how much is enough. If I wanted to see all my sisters and brothers in my town, in my world, have enough to be fed, clothed and sheltered then I needed to discover just how much of the material world I needed to possess in order to be truly content and fulfilled.

I'd been told I would die soon. Why in the world, then, was I bothering to look at my relationship with money? It began one cool November morning. I was reading a book by Tolbert McCarroll, *Notes From the Song of Life*, a book about being at peace. Yet, my inner turmoil raged. I was at war with myself and about as far from inner peace as Australia is from the Arctic Circle. A question suddenly popped into my mind: Who did I want to be when I died? The answer appeared just as quickly: I wanted to be a person who lived her values, understood what service was about and could love herself enough to accept God's love and love her neighbor. My self-centered and unhealthy relationship with money was a logical place to start learning how to live my values.

Almost immediately, as if in response to my intention, my friend Karen invited me to attend a seminar given by Joe Dominguez called "Transforming Your Relationship with Money and Achieving Financial Independence." "Not interested," was my reply. "It's probably just another get-rich-quick seminar." Karen, worried that I was spending too much time alone and inside, assured me otherwise and said that I would at least enjoy the evening. Somewhat reluctantly I decided to go. It was a pivotal night for me. This person, Joe Dominguez, was not talking about making a million dollars but about aligning your spending habits with your values.

He spoke to my heart. (Eventually he co-authored with Vicki Robin a best-selling book, *Your Money or Your Life,* based on these seminars.)

Two key points from that night stood out for me: (1) identifying how much is enough and (2) understanding the true definition of money.

I had no idea how much was enough for me at the material level. It seemed that enough was always a little bit more than I had. How could I discern whether or not a purchase was necessary, fulfilling or even in alignment with my values? I didn't have a clue.

Joe led us through an exercise to identify our own unique point of enough. He asked us to recall a purchase that was fulfilling at every level. I recalled my first car. I loved that car. It was sleek, fast and red with a white interior. Most important, I purchased that car as a college freshman with money I had earned and saved. It might have been five years old when I bought it but it was a beautiful 1965 red Mustang—and it was mine. No car since, and I doubt any car in the future, will match the thrill, the excitement and the fulfillment I received for my $500. My second, third and fourth cars were a lot more expensive and loaded with fancy options like rear window wipers or a sun roof, but they were just cars, just transportation—functional but not fulfilling.

We went on to look at our inherited and learned notions about money and consuming. I soon discovered a pattern of purchasing something whenever I felt sad or insecure or had had a difficult week at work. A new pair of shoes was the most common purchase that momentarily raised my spirits. How many times have you thought that a second computer, a jet ski, or some other purchase would make you happier? Maybe an espresso machine or a crock pot would ease this uneasy feeling. It goes on and on and on. We've been taught to have a never-ending list of wants and desires that can be filled by something external—a product for every need.

Most of us, including myself, spend a lot of time shopping. Recent research shows that on average we spend six hours a week shopping and only forty minutes a week in interactive play or conversation with our children. We buy more and more stuff, spend more and more money, and get less and less fulfillment.

Most of the stuff I bought and brought into my home was clutter. After all, how many pairs of shoes can I really wear? It's clutter. Clutter in the drawers. Clutter in the closets. Clutter in the mind. Clutter in the soul. Unconsciously, as a culture, we've internalized the belief that material possessions will fill the spiritual vacuum in our souls.

The inflation of our desires has resulted in "poverty consciousness"—where we think we're poor when our salaries are twenty-, thirty-, forty-, or even one hundred-thousand dollars a year. This is a crisis of perception. We have continued to confuse our standard of living with quality of life. Vera Shaw, a Christian writer and a wise woman, once said, "We need to become more concerned about raising the standard of loving instead of the standard of living."

But how does this lead to identifying the point of enough? Joe, first in his seminar and later in the book *Your Money or Your Life*, defined "enough" as having our sur-vival needs met (food, clothing, shelter), having possessions that bring joy and com-fort and even having those few special luxuries that add to the quality of our life.

In examining how much was enough for me I began to cherish, respect and be grateful for everything I owned. I came to realize that every transaction with money is also a transaction with the earth. The items I buy are made from raw materials and resources from the sacred earth. Since I was taking the earth's resources for my pleasure, I felt commanded to use them consciously and carefully. Helen Keller once said, "Not until we can refuse to take without giving can we create a society in which the chief activity is the common welfare." It became clear that my choices about what items to buy and what resources to use needed to be in alignment with my values of giving, as well as taking, so that everyone in the world could not only survive but thrive.

As I came to know that point of "enough" I experienced a new sense of freedom and a growing power. I was no longer subject to the dictates of our consumer cul-ture to buy more, more, more. The quality of my life rose higher and higher while I was spending less and less. (This happened, incidentally, while I was still ill.)

The second major part of that lecture involved learning a new definition of money. Money for me had been power, prestige, status and a way to identify where I stood in relation to other people in my profession. For Joe, the definition was much simpler. Money is something for which you trade your life energy—your time. Think about it.

During the years I worked for pay I traded those hours of my life spent on the job for money. What a revolutionary definition! This definition takes on an even deeper meaning when you figure out your true hourly wage. I learned that in reality I didn't make $20 per hour, as I thought: because there were both job-related expenses and job-related activities that had to be factored in.

For example, it took time for me to get dressed and ready for my job, drive to work and "decompress" at the end of the day. And there were job-related expenses to consider—uniforms, lunches out, medical equipment for work. When I did the entire calculation my real hourly wage was closer to $5 per hour. Now I was begin-ning to have a reality-based relationship with money.

Every purchase could be seen in terms of the number of hours I would need to work to pay for it. The real cost of a $100 blouse, therefore, would be the 20 hours on the job needed to make the money to buy it. Would I receive satisfaction from that blouse equal to 20 hours of my life? I began to apply that question to all my purchases.

In addition I asked myself if this expenditure of money and time was in align-ment with my values. If not I put the blouse back on the rack and felt good about myself. If the answer was yes, the purchase remained fulfilling and I felt good about myself.

Aligning my values and spending habits had nothing to do with deprivation. It was about being comfortable, not satiated. I began to see the difficulty in creating a world that reflects the social justice teachings of Jesus if we, as a nation, are unwilling to confront our own levels of consumption, our own gluttony. In about 600 BCE the Greek philosopher Thales said, "Only if there is *neither* wealth nor immoderate poverty in a nation, can justice be said to prevail."

This alignment between my values and my money was the first building block in creating a life of integrity—it was one way of moving God back into the center of my life. Jesus never said don't have possessions. He *did* say you can't serve two masters—God and Mammon. He *did* tell us to treasure God, not the finite.

> "Do not store up for yourselves treasures on earth where
> moth and rust consume and where thieves break in and steal;
> but store up for yourselves treasures in heaven where
> neither moth nor rust consume and where thieves do not break
> in and steal."
>
> —Matthew 6:19-21

As Marcus Borg said in *A New Vision*, "One may treasure the finite or one may treasure God—center in Spirit above all else."

After losing everything, my journey became one of discovering how to have my life reflect love for God and creation. Gradually my actions became more aligned with my values. I discovered the truth of graceful simplicity: having a few pairs of shoes, not 70; a few blouses, not a hundred; books that are read instead of lining the shelves. Through this process I reclaimed the most precious gift God gave me—the hours of my life—and I could begin to discover how God wanted those hours used. In defining how much was enough for me I found time for serving, reading, watching sunsets, singing, going for a walk with friends, enjoying a concert and listening in silent prayer. In short, a life of immeasurable wealth.

I still consume. We all consume. The critical step is to move from being conspicuous consumers to being conscious consumers.

Discovering what was enough for me allowed me to make that shift. Our task now is to return to a life based on feeding the hungry, clothing the poor, raising healthy loving children, and stewarding and preserving creation. Perhaps then each act of consumption will become a hymn of thanksgiving. And the following pledge will be our prayer:

> *I pledge to discover how much is enough for me to be truly fulfilled,*
> *neither rich nor poor, and to consume only that.*
>
> *I pledge to be part of the discovery of how much would be enough for*
> *everyone—not only to survive but to thrive—and to find ways for them*
> *to have access to that.*
>
> *Through this commitment to restraint and justice, I am living the teachings of Jesus, healing my life and am part of the healing of the world.*

Money

by William Stringfellow

William Stringfellow does not easily fit into any one category.
That he was a prophet, however, does seem clear. Educated at Harvard Law School he served as a street lawyer in East Harlem, New
York City. Yet he did not see himself primarily as a lawyer or social
activist. During the eminent theologian Karl Barth's visit to the
United States, Stringfellow was one of eight theologians chosen to
question and dialogue with Barth. Yet he did not see himself primarily as a theologian. And author of sixteen books, he did not see
himself primarily as an author. His vocation, according to editor
Kellermann, was, "to be William Stringfellow, nothing more and
nothing less. He understood all human beings to enjoy a comparable vocation: to be who they were called in the Word of God to
be…to offer their gifts renewed."

All of us struggle with the place of money in our lives. There are no
easy answers. Yet whether rich or poor, by either American or global standards, money is surely one of our culture's most prevalent
and powerful idols: promising that which it cannot finally deliver.
Ultimately, the issue is "whether a person trusts money more than
God." Stringfellow closes his article with the liberating notion that
freedom from the idolatry of money comes through seeing money
as a sacrament. He says that all of life, including money, is a great
and wonderful gift; saints are simply those who recognize that the
only way to "honor such a gift is to give it away."

Idolatry, whatever its object, represents the enshrinement of any other person or
thing in the very place of God. Idolatry embraces some person or thing, instead of
God, as the source and rationalization of the moral significance of this life in the
world for, at least, the idolater, though not, necessarily, for anybody else at all.
Thus human beings, as idolaters, have from time to time worshipped stones and
snakes and suns and fire and thunder; their own dreams and hallucinations, images
of themselves and of their progenitors; they have had all the Caesars, ancient and
modern, as idols; others have fancied sex as a god; for many, race is an idol; some
worship science, some idolize superstition. Within that pantheon, money is a most
conspicuous idol.

The idolatry of money means that the moral worth of a person is judged in terms
of the amount of money possessed or controlled. The acquisition and accumulation

of money in itself is considered evidence of virtue. It does not so much matter how money is acquired—by work or invention, through inheritance or marriage, by luck or theft—the main thing is to get some. The corollary of this doctrine, of course, is that those without money are morally inferior—weak, or indolent, or otherwise less worthy as human beings. Where money is an idol, to be poor is a sin.

This is an obscene idea of justification, directly in contradiction with the Bible. In the gospel none are saved by any works of their own, least of all by the mere acquisition of money. In fact, the New Testament is redundant in citing the possession of riches as an impediment to salvation when money is regarded idolatrously. At the same time, the notion of justification by acquisition of money is empirically absurd, for it oversimplifies the relationship of the prosperous and the poor and overlooks the dependence of the rich upon the poor for their wealth. In this world human beings live at each other's expense, and the affluence of the few is proximately related to, and supported by, the poverty of the many.

This interdependence of rich and poor is something Americans are tempted to overlook, since so many Americans are in fact prosperous, but it is true today as it was in earlier times: the vast multitudes of people on the face of the earth are consigned to poverty for their whole lives, without any serious prospect whatever of changing their conditions. Their hardships in great measure make possible the comfort of those who are not poor; their poverty maintains the luxury of others; their deprivation purchases the abundance most Americans take for granted.

That leaves prosperous Americans with frightful questions to ask and confront, even in customs or circumstances that are regarded as trivial or straightforward or settled. Where, for instance, do the profits that enable great corporations to make large contributions to universities and churches and charity come from? Do they come from the servitude of Latin American peasants working plantations on seventy-two-hour weekly shifts for gross annual incomes of less than a hundred dollars? Do they depend upon the availability of black child labor in South Africa and Rhodesia? Are such private beneficences in fact the real earnings of some of the poor of the world?

To affirm that we live in this world at each other's expense is a confession of the truth of the Fall rather than an assertion of economic doctrine or a precise empirical statement. It is not that there is in every transaction a direct one-for-one cause and effect relationship, either individually or institutionally, between the lot of the poor and the circumstances of those who are not poor. It is not that the wealthy are wicked or that the fact of malice is implicit in affluence. It is, rather, theologically speaking, that all human and institutional relationships are profoundly distorted and so entangled that no person or principality in this world is innocent of involvement in the existence of all other persons and all institutions...

The idolatry of money has its most grotesque form as a doctrine of immortality. Money is, then, not only evidence of the present moral worth of a person but also the way in which a life gains moral worth after death. If someone leaves a substantial estate, death is cheated of victory for a while, if not ultimately defeated, because the money left will sustain the memory of the person and of the fortune. The poor just die and are at once forgotten. It is supposed important to amass money not for its use in life but as a monument in death. Money thus becomes the measure of a person's moral excellence while alive and the means to purchase a certain survival of death. Money makes people not only moral but immortal; that is the most profound and popular idolatry of money.

To the Christian conscience, all ideas of immortality—along with all notions of self justification including that of the mere acquisition of money or other property—are anathema. The gospel of Jesus Christ is not concerned with immortality but with the resurrection from death; not with the survival of death either in some "afterlife" or in the memorialization of life after death. The gospel is, instead, distinguished by the transcendence of the power of death here and now within the precincts of life in this world. The gospel discerns and exposes *all* forms of idolatry as the worship of death, and thus, the gospel recognizes and publicizes the idolatry of money or property in any form as both false and futile. False because where money is an idol—that is, where money is thought to impute great or even ultimate moral significance to the one who holds it—it preempts the place of God; futile because money, and everything whatsoever that money can buy or build or do, along with those who lust after or gain money, dies. Where money is beheld as an idol, in truth the idol that is secreted in such worship is death. The gospel is about resurrection and it is that which unmasks the fraudulent association of all promissory doctrines of immortality with idolatry in one or another fashion. The gospel, in other words, has to do with the readily available power of God's grace to emancipate human beings in this life from all idols of death, even money—and even in America.

It is the freedom from idolatry of money that Christ offers the rich young man in the parable. Remember, it is not that money is inherently evil or that the possession of money as such is sin. The issue for the Christian (and ultimately, for everyone) is whether a person trusts money more than God and comes to rely on money rather than on grace for the assurance of moral significance, both as an individual and in relationship with the whole of humanity.

As a Christian I am aware—with more intimate knowledge and, therefore, with even greater anguish than those outside the church—that the churches in American society nowadays are so much in the position of that rich young man in the parable that they are rarely in a position to preach to prosperous Americans, much less to the needy. Even where the churches are not engaged in deliberate idolatry of money, the overwhelming share of the resources in money and other property inherited by and given to the trust of the churches ends up being utilized just for the upkeep of the ecclesiastical establishment. Appeals are still being made that to give money to the churches is equivalent to giving money to God. Of course anyone who cares to, or who is free to do so, can see through such a claim: it is just a modern…sale of indulgences, an abuse against which there is a venerable history of protest beginning with Jesus himself when he evicted the moneychangers from the temple.

Freedom from idolatry of money, for a Christian, means that money becomes useful only as a sacrament—as a sign of the restoration of life wrought in this world by Christ. The sacramental use of money has little to do with supporting the church after the manner of contributing to conventional charities and even less with the self-styled stewardship that solicits funds mainly for the maintenance of ecclesiastical salaries and the housekeeping of churchly properties. The church and the church's mission do not represent another charity to be subsidized as a necessary or convenient benevolence, or as a moral obligation, or in order to reassure the prosperous that they are either generous or righteous. Appeals for church support as charity or for maintenance commonly end up abetting the idolatry of money.

Such idolatry is regularly dramatized in the offertory, where it is regarded as "the collection" and as an intermission in the worship of the people of the congregation. Actually, the offertory is integral to the sacramental existence of the church, a way of representing the oblation of the totality of life to God. No more fitting symbol of the involvement of Christians in the everyday life of the world could be imagined, in American society at least, than money, for nearly every relationship in personal and public life is characterized by the obtaining or spending or exchange of money. If then, in worship, human beings offer themselves and all of their decisions, actions, and words to God, it is well that they use money as the witness to that offering. Money is, thus, used sacramentally within the church and not contributed as to some charity or given because the church, as such, has any need of money.

The sacramental use of money in the formal and gathered worship of the church is authenticated—as are all other churchly sacramental practices—in the sacramental use of money in the common life of the world.

No end of ways exist in which money can be so appropriated and spent, but, whatever the concrete circumstances, the consistent mark of such a commitment of money is a person's freedom from idolatry of money. That includes not simply freedom from an undue affection for money but, much more than that, freedom from moral dependence upon the pursuit, acquisition, or accumulation of money for the sake of justifying oneself or one's conduct or actions or opinions, either to oneself or to anybody else. It means the freedom to have money, to use money, to spend money without worshiping money, and thus it means the freedom to do without money, if need be, or, having some, to give it away to anyone who seems to need money to maintain life a while longer.

The charity of Christians, in other words, in the use of money sacramentally— in both the liturgy and in the world—has no serious similarity to conventional charity but is always a specific dramatization of the members of the Body of Christ losing their life in order that the world be given life. For members of the church, therefore, it always implies a particular confession that their money is not their own because their lives are not their own but, by the example of God's own love, belong to the world.

That one's own life belongs to the world, that one's money and possessions, talents and time, influence and wealth, all belong to the whole world is, I trust, why the saints are habitues of poverty and ministers to the outcasts, friends of the humiliated and, commonly, unpopular themselves. Contrary to many legends, the saints are not spooky figures, morally superior, abstentious, pietistic. They are seldom remembered, much less haloed. In truth, all human beings are called to be saints, but that just means called to be fully human, to be perfect—that is, whole, mature, fulfilled. The saints are simply those men and women who relish the event of life as a gift and who realize that the only way to honor such a gift is to give it away.

From *Dissenter in a Great Society*, pp. 40-47. Used with permission of the trustees of William Stringfellow.

How Much Is Enough?: Lifestyles, Global Economics, and Justice

The richest billion people in the world have created a form of civilization so acquisitive and profligate that the planet is in danger...of course, the other extreme from overconsumption—poverty—is no solution to environmental or human problems: it is infinitely worse for people and equally bad for the environment... Answering [how much is enough] definitively is impossible, but for each of us in the world's consuming class, seeking answers may be a prerequisite to transforming our civilization into one the bio-sphere can sustain.

The biblical authors never gave an abstract definition of justice but keep pointing to the poor, the oppressed, and the vulnerable as those whom God is especially concerned to protect and restore. Justice, we find, means standing with the lowest neighbor, rejecting the worship of wealth or power, and creating structures supportive of all...

— *from* Reformed Faith and Economics, *ed. by Robert Stivers*

The Big Economy, The Great Economy

by Michael Schut

One significant goal of this book is to help explore how poverty
and ecological degradation are connected to consumption levels in
affluent countries. While these connections are on the one hand
intricate and complex, they are on the other simple and direct: the
human (global, monetary) economy spreading throughout the
world does not see itself as embedded within nature's economy.
The ramifications of this one characteristic are profound, its influence on our lives far-reaching. This article provides a framework
for thinking about these two economies in the context of relationships and faith. Can we make a difference as we confront the
global economy, poverty and ecological degradation?

Shortly after graduating from college, I packed a couple of suitcases and flew to
Washington D.C. For a year I volunteered as an Innkeeper (resident manager) with
Samaritan Inns, a ministry of Church of the Savior. I lived in a nicely remodeled
brick row-house with 10 formerly homeless men.

It was an impossible job, really—to relate with and participate in community
with that group of men. It was an intense job, too: intensely boring at times as I
needed to be present and available, yet conversations were usually short, perfunctory and interrupted by the ever-present TV; intensely difficult when I smelled
alcohol on someone's breath and could not let them stay the night; and intensely
funny, educational (and sad), like the time I decided to cut up a healthy snack of
carrots and celery only to find that most of my housemates could not eat them
because they had so few teeth remaining.

I was seriously out of place. Most of the men were twice my age, of another race,
from the East coast, addicted to drugs or alcohol, and had spent part of their lives
on the streets. What they had survived I could only imagine.

I was 22 years old, white, the grandson of Dutch farmers with family roots in
Minnesota and Iowa; I had never known homelessness, and though the case could
be made for an addiction to Ben and Jerry's New York Super Fudge Chunk, I had
never so much as tried drugs.

And yet I was an authority figure in that house. The incongruity of the situation
was sometimes painfully obvious. One man in particular threw the realities of the
situation back in my face as he slammed the door on me one day. What business
did I have...even being there? I had nothing to say.

I remember, about six months after arriving, on one of those oven-like D.C.
days, asking myself just what in the heck I was doing there. I realized that what I

really wanted was to share love, to show love to these men. Up until that point in my life I'd done a lot of striving, trying to know God, trying to know love and be loving. But, and it hit me like the day's hammering heat, most all that effort had been motivated by duty and obligation. I knew next to nothing of love, so could not very well share it. I can still recall that very moment—crossing Columbia Road after lunch at Christ House—for it was a turning point for me. I started over.

Living at Samaritan Inns, I was definitely in relationship with "the other," with people I might otherwise not have seen as my neighbor. While those relationships were anything but easy, they were transformative. They are a sign to me of healing, evidence that if we open ourselves up to others, we may begin to see we are more connected than separate. When I return to D.C., I sometimes see one of those men. We exchange a handshake or a hug, chat about our lives, and go on our way—nothing out of the ordinary. However, I know that man's story, know how he helped me, and can no longer see myself as separate from homeless men and women as I otherwise might.

Linkages Not Immediately Apparent

I introduce this article by way of a story. Do you have similar stories? Ones that perhaps surprised you, which for a moment swept away a sense of separateness and revealed a relationship with someone, with some place or animal? This essay asks you to consider connections that may not be immediately apparent as well: connections between overconsumption, poverty and ecological degradation.

The links between these all-pervasive cultural problems are simple and direct. The reason they do not necessarily appear so is also simple: our economic system does not see itself as embedded in the larger world of nature. Our economic system does not take the natural world's cycles as its model. As a result our waste leads to ecological degradation. Those with power and wealth (over)consume resources from anywhere on the globe, directly contributing to the inability of others simply to sustain themselves.

Consider nature's cycles (the "Great Economy," as defined by Wendell Berry in *Home Economics*, p. 56). The symbol that comes to mind is a circle with three distinct characteristics. First, circles represent ongoing cycles where "waste equals food" (Hawken, *The Ecology of Commerce*, p. 12). The Great Economy is the first and most efficient recycler. All sloughed off life-forms become food for another life-form. Nothing is wasted and there is no "away" (as in "throw it away"). Death brings on new life.

Second, a circle signifies a closed system; except for solar energy, earth's economy operates solely on the limited bounty of earth's "one-time endowment" (Rasmussen, *Earth Community, Earth Ethics*, p. 113).

Third, the Great Economy thrives on local resources. A tree grows in the soil and feeds off the nutrients of a certain place. It does not and cannot usurp nutrients from soil thousands of miles away. Earth's economy thus creates and is dependent on its own diversity. Healthy systems within the Great Economy are "highly varied and specific to time and place" (Hawken, p. 12). Every plant, every animal is uniquely adapted to its place, its surroundings. We can envision each of these unique places as a community.

Now consider our economic system (the "Big Economy," Rasmussen, p. 111), the dominant global economy as it has developed in Western culture (and spread through the world). Rather than a circle, we might envision a line. At one end, capital, labor, and natural resources are input. Along the way "things" are produced, advertising creates a desire for those things, which we then consume. Along the way, some people reap profits. But, also along the way, a lot of waste is produced.

The Big Economy, however, does not see waste as food. The Big Economy hopes that the Great Economy will somehow assimilate all waste, a hope we now know is futile; the waste generated each year in the United States would fill a convoy of 10-ton garbage trucks 145,000 miles long—over halfway to the moon ("All Consuming Passion," New Road Map Foundation, p. 8). "Each person in the United States generates twice his or her weight per day in household, hazardous or industrial waste, and an additional half-ton of gaseous wastes such as carbon dioxide" (Rasmussen, p. 113). These wastes are not reused, but are simply "released."

We can now begin to compare and contrast the Big and Great Economies. First of all, note that the "line" of the Big Economy, whether we realize it or not, is wholly dependent on and contained within the circle of the Great Economy. All inputs (including capital and labor, which are also ultimately dependent on a healthy natural world) come from the Great Economy, and all wastes return to it. Yet the Big Economy refers to its effects on the natural world as "externalities;" that is, these effects are not taken into account within our monetary economy. Examples of externalities include water pollution, soil erosion, ozone depletion and toxic waste.

Externalities Affect People

These externalities profoundly affect people and places—in our own backyards and around the world. For example, consider toxic and hazardous waste sites ("externalities of the Big Economy"). In 1987 the United Church of Christ's Commission for Racial Justice published a landmark report titled "Toxic Waste and Race in the United States." Among this report's more important findings were the following:

- Although economic status plays an important role in the location of toxic waste sites, race is the leading factor;
- Sixty percent of both the total U.S. black and Hispanic populations live in communities with one or more uncontrollable toxic waste sites;
- In Los Angeles, the higher the concentration of Hispanics in an area, the higher the concentration of uncontrolled waste sites in that area.

Since 1987 it has become clear that "people-of-color communities are also disproportionately exposed to lead poisoning, pesticide contamination, and a host of other air, land, and water pollution. As a consequence, there is a sharp rise in the incidence of infant mortality, cancer, respiratory disease, and other public health problems in these communities" (*The Egg: An Ecojustice Quarterly*, Spring 1993, p. 5).

Notice the linkages: the Big Economy produces waste for which it does not take responsibility; waste leads to ecological degradation, the effects of which are more pronounced for poor and minorities; people's health and human communities suffer.

Consider one other "externality story" about a common, everyday product of our global economy—the french fry:

> "*The potato (for my fries) was grown in one-half square foot of sandy soil in the upper Snake River valley of Idaho...the growing season was 150 days; my potato was watered repeatedly...from the Snake River. Eighty percent of the Snake's original streamside habitat is gone, most of it replaced by reservoirs and irrigation canals. Dams have stopped 99 percent of salmon from running up the Snake River...*
>
> "*My potato was treated with fertilizers to ensure that its shape and quality were just like those of other potatoes. These chemicals accounted for 38 percent of the farmer's expenses. Much of the fertilizer's nitrogen leached into ground water; that, plus concentrated salts, made the water unfit even for irrigation.*
>
> "*Freezing the potato slices required electrical energy which came from a hydroelectric dam on the Snake River. Frozen foods require 10 times more energy to produce than their fresh counterparts...My fries were frozen using hydrofluorocarbons, carbon coolants which have replaced chlorofluorocarbons (CFCs) that harm the ozone layer.*
>
> "*Some coolants escaped from the plant. They rose 10 miles up into the stratosphere, where they depleted no ozone, but they did trap heat, contributing to the Greenhouse Effect. A refrigerated 18-wheeler brought my fries to my hometown. They were fried in corn oil from Nebraska, sprinkled with salt mined in Louisiana, and served with catsup made in Pittsburgh of Florida tomatoes.*"
>
> (Quoted from *Stuff: The Secret Lives of Everyday Things*, by John Ryan and Alan Durning, Northwest Environment Watch.)

Notice the (unaccounted for) externalities: the loss of stream habitat resulting in a precipitous decline in the salmon population, heavily impacting the livelihood of salmon fishers; or the pesticide- and fertilizer-contaminated groundwater. The dollar or so we pay for those french fries certainly will not cover the costs of these externalities. The costs are borne by salmon fishers losing their jobs, by rural families with contaminated drinking water; and, lest we forget, by the salmon themselves.

There Is No "Away"

These two examples of french fries and toxic waste sites reveal what the Great Economy already knows—there is no "away." That which we treat as waste ends up adversely affecting "the other." The "other" are most often those with no effective voice, those discriminated against due to skin color or lack of wealth, those species—like salmon—and those elements—like the soil—of this earth.

This discussion of externalities leads to a second characteristic of the Big Economy: it sees itself as an open system. It sees earth as one giant "resource." Any resource from anywhere may be taken and plugged into the Big Economy's production line with no thought to the effects such actions have on local communities (both human and non-human).

In contrast, the Great Economy respects each place in its uniqueness; in response, unique communities form in those places. The Big Economy treats these communities as resources to fuel production, then as markets for consumption, and then finally as sinks for externalities such as pollution, toxic waste, soil loss, ozone depletion, species extinction…The list goes on, as does the number of adversely affected communities.

By some measures, of course, the Big Economy is incredibly successful. Many people can and do live in relative comfort. A few of us have become fabulously wealthy, and by the world's standards, most Americans are very well off. (With 5 percent of the world's population we consume anywhere from 25 to 30 percent of the world's resources.) However, that same economic system has also created vast inequities of power and wealth. Contrary to many economic optimists, wealth rarely filters down and is increasingly consolidated in fewer and fewer hands.

What Can We Do?

In the face of a global economy that treats all communities as potential "resource," in the face of such inequity and injustice, in the face of numbers too large or discouraging to comprehend, what can we do? As followers of Christ, who came to "preach good news to the poor, to proclaim freedom for the prisoners… and to release the oppressed" (Luke 4:18), what can we do? How can we enflesh an abundant life, one which calls us to a simpler, less consumptive lifestyle?

Each one of us can and does make a difference, but first we must wake up! We must wake up to the advertising industry's manufacturing of needs. In 1990 that industry spent $256 billion to convince us to buy the Big Economy's products. The average American teenager watches 20,000 TV commercials a year (Athanasiou, *Divided Planet*, p. 43, quoting Durning). We must resist being sold this "bill of goods" and wake up to the fact that the global economy is dependent upon our consuming its products. What we buy, how we eat, and our means of transportation are, in a very real sense, votes that can move us toward or away from abundant living.

As an example, consider food choices. In America our food travels, on average, 1,200 miles to reach our plate (Ryan and Durning, *Stuff*, p. 57). We can eat bananas, oranges, and kiwi any time of the year. The ecological and social wake of such a global food system is much larger than that of most of our parents' or grandparents' generations (where most food came from within 50 miles or so).

To begin to imagine the size of this wake, simply consider all the fossil fuels necessary to transport our food those 1,200 miles. Or, consider the working conditions of many migrant or tenant farmers. Worldwide, 40,000 children die of hunger-related disease or malnutrition every day. If we Americans ate 10 percent less meat (it takes 12 pounds of grain to produce one pound of red meat), enough grain would be saved to more than feed those children (Robbins and Patton, *May All Be Fed*, chapter 2).

Thus, our everyday food choices are one way we can make a significant difference. Try eating lower on the food chain (eating less meat) more often. Discover ways to buy local fruit and vegetables; support local farmers.

Given the presence and increasing strength of the Big Economy, we cannot, even if we wanted to, immediately cease consuming its products. However, if the Big Economy were modeled after the Great Economy (nature's cycles), what would be the implications for our daily lives?

Draw on Local Resources

First, we would endeavor to draw on local resources for local consumption. Second, we would seek to recycle the "waste" caused by the harvesting, production and consumption of those resources; waste would also be seen as a resource, as "food." Third, we would grow in our awareness of the impacts our lifestyles have on our local communities.

Maintaining the integrity of each community (human and non-human) and its ability to sustain itself over the long term would be a natural and primary priority of that economy. Thus, to the extent that we do support local businesses, farmers, retailers—local economies—we will simultaneously move incrementally toward mirroring the Great Economy.

The above examples pertaining to food make clear the importance of individual choice and action. Individuals must also work together, though, to create the political will to change unjust systems. As an example, I find it difficult not to have an automobile. As much as possible I can try to bike, walk, or take public transportation. However, when the bus requires one hour, as opposed to 10 minutes by car, I am much more likely to drive my car. In that case I can join my voice and vote with others to advocate politically for more efficient public transportation or for safer bike lanes, or I can join community groups lobbying for such systemic changes. We all can take similar actions to advocate for changes in the food system: to increase access, affordability and availability of local, organic food.

Both individual action and political change aimed at creating just institutions are important and valid. The debate between advocates for one versus the other seems fruitless.

Ultimately, we must realize that we are all (all humans, all animals, all ecosystems) in this together. There is no "away." The pollution our consumptive habits create today shows up tomorrow as increased cancer rates, birth defects, and oil-soaked birds. What we throw away comes back to harm us (especially minorities), our earth and other creatures. Finally, to the extent that we see God as not only transcendent but also immanent, our waste, our pollution, damages that part of God's image that we see in God's creation.

In many ways, then, the Big Economy is a reflection of brokenness, of separation from each other, from the earth, and from our very selves. We can pray for the healing of relationships—that we might see these connections, that we might "love our neighbor as ourselves." In the Kingdom of God there is no unredeemed "waste." As in the Great Economy, all waste equals food, and death nurtures new life.

Moving Against Cultural Messages

However, if we are to change we will need the support of others. Moving toward simplicity, toward an abundant life pregnant with meaning and healing relationships, toward lowering our rates of consumption, requires moving against dominant cultural (and often ecclesiastical) messages. Swimming upstream against these messages is never easy, but the way is smoother and more enjoyable when shared with others.

In my own life God's love and grace are most often mediated through people with whom I am in community and through God's creation. Those experiences of "meeting" fill me with hope and energy to continue to open myself to relationships with "the other."

One of the primary ways we can seed compassion within us is to open ourselves to developing relationships with those we seldom recognize as part of our community, as a neighbor. Such opportunities can once again reveal that we are all interconnected and part of God's wondrous gift of this earth.

Adapted from "The Great Economy/The Big Economy," *Christian Social Action*, June, 1997; published by the General Board of Church and Society of the United Methodist Church. Used by permission.

Christian Faith and the Degradation of Creation

by John B. Cobb, Jr.

John Cobb, Jr. has become one of our culture's most eloquent and respected eco-theologians. He has also played a central role in developing process theology (integrating Whitehead's process philosophy and theology). In the late '60s, his son, Cliff, first pushed John to reading about ecological issues. Convinced that our relationship with, and treatment of, the natural world were theological and ethical issues, Dr. Cobb focused his attention on environmental issues. His attention came to bear on the intimate connection between ecology and economics. Ever since then he has been a strong voice for justice and sustainability. He is the author of over 20 books including *For the Common Good* (with Herman Daly); *Sustainability; Is It Too Late? A Theology of Ecology; and Sustaining the Common Good.*

A retired United Methodist minister, John received his M.A. and Ph.D. from the University of Chicago's Divinity School. From 1958 to 1990 he taught at Claremont School of Theology and Claremont Graduate School. He also co-directed the Center for Process Studies. He and his wife have four grown children.

In today's world, nothing more significantly impacts the health of human and non-human communities than the global economic system. Cobb reveals one of that system's core assumptions, its view of human nature: we are individuals-in-a-market rather than persons-in-community. He discusses the profound implications of this assumption. And while he recognizes the positive aspects of the current economic system, he provides a very clear Christian critique as well and suggests paths we might follow to create alternative economies that value community.

...The growth of human population that accompanies civilization has almost always accelerated degradation... While various systems of belief have helped to protect the environment against human ravages, none have been very effective over long periods of time once cities are built and the population has grown. Taoism, for example, could not protect the Chinese mountains from deforestation, despite its sensitivity to nature.

The modern degradation of the earth, in some respects, may be considered simply a continuation of this long human history. The rapid growth of human population has its inevitable consequences regardless of the accompanying beliefs. Nevertheless, there are qualitative differences between the degradation of the planet in recent times and that which preceded it.

Previously, human effects on the earth were local; now they are planetary. Previously, most of them were gradual and largely unplanned; now the changes are rapid, and many are under conscious human control. Previously, the long-term consequences of human actions were poorly understood; now we continue the process of degrading the earth with our eyes open. Previously, the system of belief on which civilizations operated had only sporadic and secondary effect on the extent of their despoliation of their environment; now we confront decisions that clearly involve fundamental commitments.

We are free as a species to continue to accelerate the degradation of the earth or to slow and finally reverse this process. Our decision depends on the deepest convictions and fundamental commitments that constitute the religious level of our being. For many people this level is not expressed in their official involvement in a traditional religious community. Especially in the West since the Enlightenment, explicitly religious traditions have been assigned more limited roles, with the basic belief structure being determined elsewhere.

In the past few decades, the religious fervor with respect to environmental concerns has been largely disconnected from traditional religious institutions. Many of the most deeply religious people have felt the need for a new vision attuned to the realities of the world and free from the destructive baggage of the great traditions. They hoped this new religious community would arise from the debris of the great traditions, rallying the energies of all humanity for the salvation of the earth.

However, hope for such a new religion has faded, and even those most estranged from the religious traditions have become more interested in their potential for support of the healing of the earth. Some of us have believed all along that the current situation calls for the repentance and renewal of these traditions, and specifically of Christianity, rather than the effort to produce a religion disconnected from the great traditions. Although it is already very late, there are increasing signs that repentance and renewal are occurring, and that the major traditions will shift from being enemies of the earth to being its friends.

Before we ask directly what the stance of Christianity should be, it is important to examine the dominant ideology out of which the most determinative decisions about the fate of the earth are now being made. Many Christians still support that ideology, and critical evaluation of it will give a healthy dose of realism to theological reflection.

The ideology in question is that of the European Enlightenment, which found its purest expression in the eighteenth century. In the history of thought it was severely criticized in the nineteenth century. Academic philosophy and theology today are far removed from the deism associated with the Enlightenment, as are contemporary painting and literature. Thus it may seem strange to identify that ideology as the currently determinative one, but the decisions that determine how we act in relation to the natural world are only sporadically and secondarily affected by these developments in intellectual history.

From the beginning, the economy has determined how human beings have dealt with their environment, and this is still true. But in modern times, the actual economy is deeply affected by economic theory, as expressed in eighteenth-century Enlightenment thinking. The connection between the Enlightenment and economic theory is no mystery. Every textbook on the history of economics points to the views of Scottish philosopher Adam Smith as the turning point in economic thought.[23] What happened before him is viewed as prescientific anticipation of the science of economics, and Smith initiated the line of thinking that has become contemporary economics. In spite of the great advances since his time, he established the basic assumptions, and no one can doubt that Smith was an Enlightenment thinker.

Much of what needs to be understood about economic theory follows from Smith's view of the human being. Smith knew that human beings can be deeply affected by sympathy for others. But he saw that this operated in quite narrow circles. In the economic order people provide us the goods and services we need, whether they feel sympathy for us or not, because it is in their interest to do so. If all act according to their best interest, it turns out, goods and services flow in the most favorable way.

Smith knew that the self-interested individual is an abstraction from the fullness of human beings, especially from the human capacity for sympathy. But he was convinced that this abstraction clarifies the way human beings function in economic relationships. Hence the abstractness of this model could be largely ignored for purposes of understanding the economic order. Smith himself, in fact, showed awareness of other dimensions of human beings, such as patriotism, as relevant to the functioning of the economy, but because he did not make these his theme, the science of economics ignored them. His individual actor in the market became *Homo economicus.*

Homo economicus as worker wants to procure as many goods and services as possible in exchange for as little work as possible. *Homo economicus* as owner of capital wants to invest in the way that will bring the largest possible returns. Obviously he will pay as little as possible to his workers. Much of the reflection of the early economists was on this situation and its effects on wages and profits.

The quest for maximum returns on investments has another effect, however. It leads to specialization. Instead of one skilled artisan making a product, such as a pin, from raw materials, a group of workers, each performing just one simple operation, produces pins on an assembly line. Total production is vastly increased. Specialization dramatically improves productivity, which is the total product divided by the number of hours of human labor.

One such pin factory can produce far more pins than are needed in the local community. Hence, rather than each community having its own pin factory, it is better for the neighboring community to specialize in something else, perhaps hats. A third community will specialize in shoes, and so forth. The result is that the same total number of hours of labor will produce far more goods, and hence the people of these communities collectively will be more prosperous. (Unfortunately, there is no assurance of equitable distribution of the new wealth.) The size of the market, that is, of the area in which goods and services can flow freely, determines how far specialization can go. The larger the market, the greater the specialization possible, and the greater the productivity. The greater the productivity, the greater the prosperity.

The economic system works best when left to itself. Competition leads investors to supply what is most wanted and keeps the prices as low as possible. Specialization is encouraged, also to keep prices low, and is accompanied by an increase in productivity and the supply of goods. Government interference can only hamper this positive working of the market. The economic ideal is laissez-faire within each country and the elimination of national boundaries as barriers to trade. Free trade in this sense is a central goal of most economists.

Through most of the two centuries in which economic theory has been developed, economic nationalism in fact remained strong. Hence free trade was constantly restricted by perceived national interests. In the late twentieth century, however, nationalism has subsided to a remarkable degree, and other economic considerations have become dominant. The Reagan and Bush administrations pushed free trade with impressive single-mindedness as the solution to economic problems everywhere. The Clinton administration shows no signs of disputing the basic theory, although it is more concerned with labor conditions and the environment...

How should a Christian respond to this system of beliefs that shapes the activity of so many committed and idealistic people? Let us consider first what is attractive in it and then its limitations.

Adam Smith did not write as a Calvinist theologian, but his view of the human being is not far removed from that of many Scottish Calvinists of his day. They, too, were suspicious of expecting too much from human sympathy or love. They recognized with Smith that most people's actions were basically selfish. They differed, of course, in that they deplored this selfishness and sought forgiveness for it. But it was easy for them to accept that a realistic account of the economic order would describe it, not in terms of love, but in terms of self-interest. The brilliant success of economists in describing market activity in these terms is further confirmation of the fruitfulness of the model. The Christian can hardly dispute this.

Secondly, most Christians rejoice in the success of the economy in producing more goods and services and eventually bringing affluence to a high percentage of the people in the First World. We may admire poverty when it is chosen by the saint for the fulfillment of a particular vocation, but we regard imposed and inescapable poverty as a degradation to be fought. Hence, the increase of material wealth is a great good, and economic theory deserves credit for its contribution to the attainment of affluence.

Third, Christians, who for several centuries have feared nationalism as the greatest idolatry of the modern world, can only rejoice at the role played by economics in overcoming its limitations. Knowing that human beings constitute one great family under God, that God cares alike for all, Christians have sought to extend human concern across national boundaries. The erosion of these boundaries and of the nationalism associated with them is surely something to be celebrated.

Nevertheless, from a Christian point of view, the model is seriously flawed, and the effects of shaping the economy according to the model have been severely damaging. If the policies derived from this model are continued much longer they will be disastrous. Hence, the full application of the economic ideal that we are now witnessing forces us to think clearly about the Christian ideal.

The economic model describes how production increases with the increase of specialization and the growth of the size of the market. It does not take into account the input of raw materials in the production process or the emission of wastes into the environment. From a Christian point of view, it limits itself to human production and ignores the creation. This feature of the model has had damaging effects from the beginning, but they were on the whole local and sporadic. Now the scale of human production is so large that these damaging effects are global and catastrophic. The goal of increasing production still more, the only goal to which the dominant economic model is adapted, encourages the further, and intensified, degradation of creation.

The aim at unceasing growth and the understanding of *Homo economicus* are closely connected. While the doctrine of human sinfulness supports the view of *Homo economicus* as aiming only at individual advantage, this does not exhaust Christian anthropology even in its most extreme Calvinist forms. Another feature of human beings as understood by Christians is that they belong to one another in communities. Roman Catholic economic thinking has kept this point alive, and Christians in general believe that human beings are more adequately and realistically understood as persons-in-communities rather than as individuals-in-markets. From the Christian point of view, therefore, participation in a healthy community is more important to human well-being than consumption of goods and services beyond what are essential for biological health. But the notion of human community is absent from the economic model. As a result, economic theory has supported economic practice that has long been, and still is, engaged in an extended and global assault on human communities.

The most dramatic instances of this assault are to be found in what until recently we have called the Second and Third Worlds. Communists were dedicated to destroying traditional communities of all sorts so as to attain a rational world oriented to efficient production and equality in consumption. Development models for the less-industrialized nations saw traditional community as a major obstacle; for example, the idea of community nurtured values that made workers reluctant to leave their people even when higher wages were available elsewhere. Thus, programs of development based on these models have in fact destroyed much of that community.

However, one need not look outside the United States to see how the economy, guided by the model sketched above, has assaulted community. Owners of factories are encouraged by the approved model to remain always alert to the possibility that their capital could be invested more profitably elsewhere. When such an opportunity is found, the theory declares it desirable that the factory be closed and the money be invested in another way. This mobility of capital keeps the economy as a whole growing. The destructive effects of factory closings on the communities in which they are located do not appear in the economic equations. Consideration of them is viewed as sentimentality that inhibits economic growth.

Rural America also illustrates the effects of the economic model. Since World War II the dominant economic theory as applied to U. S. agriculture has resulted in dramatically increased productivity—again, as measured by total product divided by hours of human labor. This has been achieved by specialization and mechanization, involving vastly increased use of fossil fuels, chemical fertilizers, pesticides, and herbicides, and vastly decreased labor. Farming thus has been reshaped according to the industrial model, and thousands of rural communities have been destroyed. This has resulted in mass migrations into the inner cities and suburban areas, where the quality of community established is likely to be inferior to what was destroyed in the countryside.

This example shows the intimate connection between the degradation of the biosphere and the destruction of human community. Small family farms were quite capable of degrading the earth; of that there is no question. But in many parts of the world they have operated in sustainable ways for millennia. In the United States, also, they could be reformed along sustainable lines. In any case, their use of exhaustible resources and their pollution of the environment were small in comparison to the factory farming that has replaced them. The Amish, for example, have shown that a far superior form of farming—both for the sake of human community and for the sake of the environment—is possible.

The above critique has been limited to two quite simple, and quite basic, points. Christians, in general, believe that the earth is God's and that to degrade it is evil, implying that as we structure our economic life we should aim to meet human needs without further degradation of the planet. Christians, in general, also believe that our relationships with one another are at least as important as our consumption of goods and services, implying that we should find ways of meeting our needs that do not continue to destroy human communities. Indeed, if we are persons-in-communities rather than individuals-in-markets, the goal of the economy should be the building up of communities rather than the expansion of markets.

These points may seem quite simple, but their implications are very radical. They require that Christians help envisage and implement a profoundly different economic order. Otherwise, the situation will continue much as in the past, when, almost regardless of avowed religious beliefs, economic practices led to the continuing despoliation of the earth...The two points above can help illustrate how [a different economic order] would differ from the one that embodies the presently dominant ideals.

First, placing economic activity in the context of the whole earth requires attention to the question of scale. Bigger is obviously not necessarily better, so the optimum scale of the human economy in relation to the total economy becomes basically a question of sustainability. When the effects of the economy on the environment undercut the possibility of its own continuance, the scale is too large.

The determination of the optimum scale of the global economy will inevitably have disturbing consequences, especially when viewed with now-dominant assumptions. Already the present scale of the economy is clearly unsustainable. Yet three-fourths of the world's people are extremely poor, and even the affluent fourth are far from satisfied with their present level of consumption. Very few are prepared to cut their consumption drastically in order to share with those who have more urgent needs. We seem to have no choice but to increase production greatly in order to respond to these needs.

The dilemma is a real and difficult one, but it is not wholly insuperable. The issue of scale needs to be formulated more exactly to examine not how many goods and services are available to people, but how much pressure the production of these goods and services places on the environment. Human ingenuity needs to be directed toward meeting more human needs with less disruptive impact on the environment. We are already making some progress in this direction. For example, automobiles and appliances can be designed to require far less energy without any reduction in service to the consumer. Houses can be built so as to require little or no energy for heating and cooling other than that from the sun. And crops can be grown organically with greatly reduced use of oil-based products.

Another, and essential, step in meeting more needs with less impact on the environment is shortening supply lines. Compare two scenarios for putting tomatoes on your dining table. In the first scenario, they have been machine harvested, packaged, and shipped an average of twelve hundred miles. More energy goes into packaging and shipping them than into growing and harvesting, and the total environmental stress is considerable. In the extreme opposite scenario, you would raise tomatoes organically in your own garden. Any resultant environmental stress would be negligible, and one might even participate in the regeneration of the soil that is so badly needed. (I am not dwelling here on the superior taste and food value of the homegrown tomato.) Obviously there are intermediate scenarios. With produce bought at the local farmers' market or at roadside stands, much of the cost of packaging and shipping is eliminated, and often the tomatoes are grown in less energy-consumptive and soil-destructive ways.

Some of these means of providing goods in ways that place less pressure on the environment are in only modest tension with dominant economic theory. More efficient use of energy is often profitable to the companies that adopt new technologies for that purpose. Nevertheless, much of the progress that has been made, even at that level, has involved government intervention, and most of the rest has resulted from the committed work of persons who care for the whole earth enough to demonstrate the advantages of energy efficiency.[24] Left to themselves, those acting chiefly by the standard model have been slow to adopt the needed changes.

Advocacy of small family farms and shorter supply lines, on the other hand, directly opposes the implications drawn from the dominant model. These proposals, which shift the concern from the growth of the market to the well-being of the whole earth, will be rejected as long as that growth is the primary aim of policymakers. The contrast is especially clear between the goal of shortening supply lines and the now-dominant economic model, which calls for greater and greater specialization over larger and larger regions, making each region dependent on trade for most of its needs. Supply lines grow longer and longer. Costs of packaging and transportation increase and inevitably involve costs to the environment as well. The system is inherently unsustainable. The sustainable alternative is one in which smaller and smaller regions produce more and more of the goods they need closer and closer to where they are consumed. These economies will contribute little to the greenhouse effect and will survive the exhaustion of oil.

This leads directly to the second theological principle enunciated above in criticism of the dominant version of *Homo economicus*. Shorter supply lines mean more economic self-reliance and relative stability in smaller regions. Instead of economic forces breaking up community as at present, they would encourage it. Communities would have considerable power over their own economies rather than being at the mercy of distant deciders or impersonal market forces.

Indeed, from a Christian point of view, this is just as important a reason for redirecting the economy as is the concern for the earth. If people are more accurately understood as persons-in-community than as individuals-in-markets, then the economy should serve community rather than the growth of markets, even apart from the unsustainability of policies aimed at endless market growth. Healthy communities require that people through their communities have basic control over the means of livelihood, which is possible only when there are relatively self-sufficient economies in small regions.

People living in healthy communities may be less preoccupied with increased consumption. For example, when faced with a choice between more enjoyment of work and more goods and services, many of them may choose the former. There may be increased willingness in the First World to live more frugally so as to share the earth more fairly with others. Many people may find this different lifestyle more satisfying, and biblical teaching about possessions may take on a meaning it has almost lost in most of our churches. Thus, in addition to ordering society so that less pressure on the environment can accompany increasing production, we may have a society in which people measure their well-being less by their possessions and consumption and more by their contribution to the well-being of others.

The Christian teachings to which I have appealed thus far are simple and basic ones. They have been rhetorically present throughout Christian history. Unfortunately, in practical effect they have often been subordinated to other emphases. Especially since the Enlightenment, many Protestants have identified their faith with a very individualistic relation to God and to neighbor. The rest of creation has either dropped out of the picture, been viewed sentimentally, or been seen as a field of conquest. This form of Christianity has lent itself to cooperation with the dominant economic order and the theory that supports it.

For this reason, the fact that these teachings are simple and basic ones does not mean that the theological task of repentance and transformation is an easy one. The deep separation Protestants have often made between creation and redemption must be overcome. Without losing the important truth in individualism, Protestants must recover an authentic doctrine of the church and also of the wider human community. Without ceasing to appreciate the distinctiveness of human beings as made in the image of God, Protestants must overcome the modern dualism between human beings and the remainder of the created order that modern hermeneutics has imposed on the Bible. There is much work to be done.

Further, Protestants need to build on the best in the modern social teaching of the church. This teaching has called us to be responsible in and for the world, which has never been more important. We have learned not to impose simple ideals naively on complex situations but to analyze them thoroughly and then find ways to move toward Christian goals within them. Yet there has been a widespread movement in the church to reject those leaders who engage in such analysis of social issues. When they make pronouncements and take actions guided by that analysis, they are accused of imposing their private political views on the church. If we are to be responsible in relation to the global crisis, the church as a whole must commit itself to Christian thinking and to having its actions informed by that thinking. If instead we allow ourselves to be easily swayed by attractive slogans, our good intentions will be directed to ends that are at best harmless and too often supportive of the forces that are degrading the earth.

For example, we are inclined to celebrate interdependence. In our opposition to individualism and to nationalism, we affirm that we as individuals need one another and that nations, too, need one another, as we all need God. Interdependence is a central mark of healthy community. Hence, as economic development makes all dependent on others for survival, our immediate response is that this is a great gain.

The free trade that makes this possible seems equally admirable. However, careful analysis shows that interdependence as it develops out of free trade means the dependence of all on those who control the movement of capital and the terms of trade. They act according to the laws of the market, which dictate that they seek maximum profit. Meanwhile, decisions made thousands of miles away on the basis of quite impersonal principles can wreak havoc in a village, a city, or even a whole country.

On the other hand, people who participate together in a real human community experience a desirable form of interdependence. In such a community, everyone is concerned with the fate of all the others, and everyone shares in making the decisions that determine their fate. There are risks in depending even on such a community, but these are the risks that faith encourages. They are very different from the total surrender of personal control to the impersonal forces of the market.

Similarly, when we examine free trade carefully, we see that it is often not free at all. Companies are free to ignore national boundaries and the well-being of the people of the nation. But once whole peoples have become dependent on imports for their survival, they are no longer free not to trade. They must sell what they have at whatever price others set in order to import what they need. Trade is truly free only when those who trade are free to trade or not to trade. That is possible only when they are basically self-sufficient and can base their decisions on what truly benefits them. Christians can affirm and celebrate this kind of free trade. The global community we want is a community of free peoples, not the subordination of all to a few transnational corporations.

If the church finds it difficult to reform its own teaching and practice in light of some of its central convictions, how much more difficult will it be to seek a change in the direction of public policy and economic theory and practice? The ideal of free trade is deeply entrenched, while the ideal of relative self-reliance or self-sufficiency has a modest foothold at the fringes of Christian economic thinking. Even if Christians and other religious groups throw their support in this direction, they will still not win the day. But it may force a serious discussion that will show the futility of the effort to heal the world's sickness by more of the medicine that has already so degraded the planet.

Excerpt pp. 1-17 from *Sustaining the Common Good: A Christian Perspective on the Global Economy* by John B. Cobb, Jr. Copyright © John B. Cobb, Jr., 1994. Permission granted by Pilgrim Press.

How Much Is Enough?

by Alan Durning

While studying trombone at Oberlin College, Alan Durning heard an Earth Day lecture by David Orr. Orr said the challenge for our generation was "not to create more consumer products, but to create a new culture—one that could survive." Durning blames Orr for "most of what has come since." After college, Durning went to work as a research assistant for the Worldwatch Institute in Washington, D.C. After promotion to senior researcher, he wrote his first book *How Much Is Enough: The Consumer Society and the Future of the Earth* in 1992.

In 1993 Durning and his family returned to his childhood home, Seattle, where he founded Northwest Environment Watch (NEW). NEW is a wholly independent, not-for-profit research and publishing organization. With Durning as the executive director NEW has become an important voice in developing plans for an ecologically sustainable future. He is the author of *This Place on Earth* and co-author of *Stuff: The Secret Lives of Everyday Things*. As a father of small children, he has added incentive to work for sustainable development and improved environmental conditions.

Durning's essay asks the important question, "How Much Is Enough?" in a global context—and his approach reveals increasing inequity and costs to human and ecological health.

∞

Early in the post-World War II age of affluence, a U.S. retailing analyst named Victor Lebow proclaimed, "Our enormously productive economy ...demands that we make consumption our way of life, that we convert the buying and use of goods into rituals, that we seek our spiritual satisfaction, our ego satisfaction, in consumption... We need things consumed, burned up, worn out, replaced, and discarded at an ever increasing rate." Americans have risen to Mr. Lebow's call, and much of the world has followed.

Since 1950, American consumption has soared. Per capita, energy use climbed 60 percent, car travel more than doubled, plastics use multiplied 20-fold, and air travel jumped 25-fold.

We are wealthy beyond the wildest dreams of our ancestors; the average human living today is four-and-a-half times richer than his or her great-grandparents, and the factor is larger still among the world's consuming class. American children under the age of 13 have more spending money—$230 a year—than the 300 million poorest people in the world.

The richest billion people in the world have created a form of civilization so acquisitive and profligate that the planet is in danger. The lifestyle of this top echelon—the car drivers, beef eaters, soda drinkers, and throwaway consumers—constitutes an ecological threat unmatched in severity by anything but perhaps population growth. The wealthiest fifth of humankind pumps out more than half of the greenhouse gases that threaten the earth's climate and almost 90 percent of the chlorofluorocarbons that are destroying the earth's protective ozone layer.

Ironically, abundance has not even made people terribly happy. In the United States, repeated opinion polls of people's sense of well-being show that no more Americans are satisfied with their lot now than they were in 1957. Despite phenomenal growth in consumption, the list of wants has grown faster still.

Of course, the other extreme from overconsumption—poverty—is no solution to environmental or human problems: it is infinitely worse for people and equally bad for the environment. Dispossessed peasants slash-and-burn their way into the rain forests of Latin America, and hungry nomads turn their herds out onto fragile African rangeland, reducing it to desert. If environmental decline results when people have either too little or too much, we must ask ourselves: How much is enough? What level of consumption can the earth support? When does consumption cease to add appreciably to human satisfaction?

Answering these questions definitively is impossible, but for each of us in the world's consuming class, seeking answers may be a prerequisite to transforming our civilization into one the biosphere can sustain.

The Compulsion to Consume

"The avarice of mankind is insatiable," declared Aristotle 23 centuries ago, setting off a debate that has raged ever since among philosophers over how much greed lurks in human hearts. But whatever share of our acquisitiveness is part of our nature, the compulsion to have more has never been so actively promoted, nor so easily acted upon, as it is today.

We are encouraged to consume at every turn by the advertising industry, which annually spends nearly $500 per U.S. citizen, by the commercialization of everything from sporting events to public spaces, and, insidiously, by the spread of the mass market into realms once dominated by family members and local enterprises. Cooking from scratch is replaced by heating prepared foods in the microwave; the neighborhood baker and greengrocer are driven out by the 24-hour supermarket at the mall. As our day-to-day interactions with the economy lose the face-to-face character that prevails in surviving communities, buying things becomes a substitute source of self worth.

Traditional measures of success, such as integrity, honesty, skill, and hard work, are gradually supplanted by a simple, universally recognizable indicator of achievement—money. One Wall Street banker put it bluntly to the *New York Times*: "net worth equals self worth." Under this definition, there is no such thing as enough. Consumption becomes a treadmill with everyone judging their status by who's ahead of them and who's behind.

Technologies of Consumption

In simplified terms, an economy's total burden on the ecological systems that undergird it is a function of three factors: the size of the human population, people's average consumption level, and the broad set of technologies—everything from mundane clotheslines to the most sophisticated satellite communications systems—the economy employs to provide for those consumption levels.

Transformations of agricultural patterns, transportation systems, urban design, energy use, and the like could radically reduce the total environmental damage caused by the consuming societies, while allowing those at the bottom of the economic ladder to rise without producing such egregious effects.

Japan, for example, uses one-third as much energy as the Soviet Union to produce a dollar's worth of goods and services, and Norwegians use half as much paper and cardboard apiece as their neighbors in Sweden, though they are equals in literacy and richer in dollar terms.

Eventually, though, technological change will need to be complemented by curbing our material wants. Robert Williams of Princeton University and a worldwide team of researchers conducted a careful study of the potential to reduce fossil fuels consumption through greater efficiency and use of renewable energy.

The entire world population, Williams concluded, could live with the quality of energy services enjoyed by West Europeans—things like modest but comfortable homes, refrigeration for food, and ready access to public transit, augmented by limited auto use.

The study had an implicit conclusion, however. The entire world population decidedly could *not* live in the style of Americans, with their larger homes, more numerous electrical gadgets, and auto-centered transportation systems.

The details of such studies will stir debate among specialists for years to come. What matters for the rest of us is the lesson to hope and work for much from technological and political change, while looking to ourselves for the values changes that will also be needed.

Consuming Drives

The realities of current consumption patterns around the world point toward quantitative answers to the question of how much is enough.

For three of the most ecologically important types of consumption—transportation, diet, and use of raw materials—the world's 5.3 billion people are distributed unevenly over a vast range. Those at the bottom clearly fall beneath the "too little line," and those at the top, the cars-meat-and-disposables class, clearly consume too much. But where in the larger middle class does "enough" lie?

About one billion people do most of their traveling—aside from the occasional donkey or bus ride—on foot. Many in the walking class never go more than 100 miles from their birthplaces. Unable to get to work easily, attend school, or bring their complaints before government offices, they are severely hindered by the lack of transportation options.

The massive middle class of the world, numbering some three billion people, travels by bus and bicycle. Mile for mile, bikes are cheaper than any other vehicle, costing under $100 in most of the Third World and requiring no fuel. They are also the most efficient form of transportation ever invented and, where not endangered by polluted air and traffic, provide their riders with healthy exercise.

The world's automobile class is relatively small: only 8 percent of humans, about 400 million, own cars. The auto class's fleet of four-wheelers is directly responsible for an estimated 13 percent of carbon dioxide emissions from fossil fuels worldwide, along with air pollution and acid rain, traffic fatalities numbering a quarter million annually, and the sprawl of urban areas into endless tract developments lacking community cohesion.

The auto class bears indirect responsibility for the far-reaching impacts of their chosen vehicle. The automobile makes itself indispensable: cities sprawl, public transit atrophies, shopping centers multiply, employers scatter. Today, working Americans spend nine hours a week behind the wheel. To make these homes-away-from-home more comfortable, 90 percent of new American cars are air-conditioned, which adds emissions of gases that aggravate the greenhouse effect and deplete the ozone layer.

Around the world, the great marketing achievement of automobile vendors has been to turn the machine into a cultural icon. As French philosopher Roland Barthes writes, "cars today are almost the exact equivalent of the great Gothic cathedrals...the supreme creation of an era, conceived with passion by unknown artists, and consumed in image if not in usage by a whole population which appropriates them as purely magical objects."

Ironies abound: more "Eagles" drive America's expanding road network, for instance, than fly in the nation's polluted skies, and more "Cougars" pass the night in its proliferating garages than in its shrinking forests.

Some in the auto class are also members of a more select group: the global jet set. The four million Americans who account for 41 percent of domestic trips, for example, cover five times as many miles a year as average Americans. Furthermore, because each mile traveled by air uses more energy than a mile traveled by car, jet setters consume six-and-a-half times as much energy for transportation as ordinary car-class members.

Eat, Drink, and Be Sustainable

On the food consumption ladder, people of the world fall into three rungs reflecting calories eaten and the richness of diet. The world's 630 million poorest people lack the resources necessary to provide themselves with sufficient calories for a healthy diet, according to the latest World Bank estimates.

The 3.4 billion grain eaters of the world's middle class get enough calories and plenty of plant-based protein, giving them the healthiest basic diet of the world's people. They typically receive no more than 20 percent of their calories from fat, a level low enough to protect them from the consequences of excessive dietary fat.

The top of the ladder is populated by the meat eaters, those who obtain about 40 percent of their calories from fat. These 1.25 billion people eat three times as much fat per person as the remaining 4 billion, mostly because they eat so much red meat. The meat class pays the price of their diet in high death rates from the so-called diseases of affluence—heart disease, stroke, and certain types of cancer.

In fact, the U.S. government, long beholden to livestock and dairy interests, now recommends a diet in which no more than 30 percent of calories come from fat. California heart specialist Dr. Dean Ornish, credited with creating the first non-drug therapy proven to reverse clogging of the arteries, prescribes a semi-vegetarian diet virtually indistinguishable from that eaten daily by peasants in China, Brazil, or Egypt.

Indirectly, the meat-eating quarter of humanity consumes almost half of the world's grain—grain that fattens the livestock they eat. They are also responsible for many of the environmental strains induced by the present global agricultural system, from soil erosion to over-pumping of underground water.

In the extreme case of American beef, producing a pound of steak requires five pounds of grain and the energy equivalent of a gallon of gasoline, not to mention the associated soil erosion, water consumption, pesticide and fertilizer runoff, groundwater depletion, and emissions of the greenhouse gas methane.

Beyond the effects of livestock production, the affluent diet rings up an ecological bill through its heavy dependence on shipping goods over great distances. One-fourth of grapes eaten in the United States are grown 7,000 miles away in Chile, and the typical mouthful of food travels 1,300 miles from farm field to dinner plate. America's far-flung agribusiness food system is only partly a product of agronomic forces. It is also a result of farm policies and health standards that favor large producers, massive government subsidies for Western irrigation water, and a national highway system that makes trucking economical by transferring the tax burden from truckers onto car drivers.

The thousands of small farms, bakeries, and dairies that once encircled and fed the nation's cities cannot supply chain supermarkets with sufficient quantities of perfectly uniform products to compete with the food industry conglomerates. Their lot is to slide ever closer to foreclosure while hauling their produce to struggling weekend "farmers' markets."

Processing and packaging add further resource costs to the affluent diet, though those costs remain largely hidden. Even relatively familiar prepared foods are surprisingly energy consumptive. Ounce for ounce, getting frozen orange juice to the consumer takes four times the energy (and several times the packaging) of providing fresh oranges. Likewise, potato chip production has four times the energy budget of potatoes.

The resource requirements of making the new generation of microwave-ready instant meals, loaded as they are with disposable pans and multi-layer packaging, are about ten times larger than preparing the same dishes at home from scratch.

Mirroring food consumption, overall beverage intake rises little between poor and rich. What changes is what people drink. The 1.75 billion people at the bottom of the beverage ladder have no option but to drink water that is often contaminated with human, animal, and chemical wastes.

Those in the next group up, in this case nearly two billion people, take more than 80 percent of their liquid refreshment in the form of clean drinking water. The remainder of this class's liquids come from commercial beverages such as tea, coffee, and, for the children, milk. At the quantities consumed, these beverages pose few environmental problems. They are packaged minimally, and transport energy needs are low because they are moved only short distances or in a dry form.

In the top class are the billion people in industrial countries. At a growing rate, they drink soft drinks, bottled water, and other prepared commercial beverages that are packaged in single-use containers and transported over great distances—sometimes across oceans.

Ironically, where tap water is purest and most accessible, its use as a beverage is declining. It now typically accounts for only a quarter of drinks in developed countries. In the extreme case of the United States, per capita consumption of soft drinks rose to 47 gallons in 1989 (nearly seven times the global mean), according to the trade magazine *Beverage Industry*. Americans now drink more soda pop than water from the kitchen sink.

The Stuff of Life

In consumption of raw materials, about one billion rural people subsist on local biomass collected from the immediate environment. Most of what they consume each day—about a pound of grain, two pounds of fuelwood, and fodder for their animals—could be self-replenishing renewable resources. Unfortunately, because they are often pushed by landlessness and population growth into fragile, unproductive ecosystems, their minimal needs are not always met.

If these billion are materially destitute, they are part of a larger group that lacks many of the benefits provided by modest use of nonrenewable resources—particularly durable things like radios, refrigerators, water pipes, high-quality tools, and carts with lightweight wheels and ball bearings. More than two billion people live in countries where per-capita consumption of steel, the most basic modern material, falls below 100 pounds a year.

Though similar international data are not available for most other basic raw materials, energy consumption can serve as a substitute indicator since most processes that use lots of raw materials also use lots of energy. In those same countries, per-capita consumption of all types of energy (except subsistence fuelwood) is lower than 20 gigajoules per year.

Roughly one-and-a-half billion live in the middle class of materials users. Providing them with durable goods each year uses between 100 and 350 pounds of steel per-capita and between 20 and 50 gigajoules per-capita. At the top of the heap is the throwaway class, which uses raw materials like they're going out of style. A typical resident of the industrialized world uses 15 times as much paper, 10 times as much steel, and 12 times as much fuel as a resident of the developing world. The extreme case is again the United States, where the average person consumes most of his or her own weight in basic materials each day.

In the throwaway economy, packaging is the essence of the product. It is at once billboard, shipping container, and preservative. Seven percent of consumer spending in the United States goes for packaging. Yet, it all ends up in the dump. Disposable goods proliferate in America and other industrial countries. Each year, Japan uses 30 million "disposable" single-roll cameras, and Americans toss away 18 billion diapers and enough aluminum cans to make about 6,000 DC-10 jet airplanes.

In throwaway economics, even "durable" goods are not particularly durable, nor are they easy to repair. Technological improvement would be expected to steadily raise the average working life of goods. Yet, over time, new items have fallen dramatically in price relative to repair costs, according to data compiled by the Organization for Economic Cooperation and Development. The average life span of most household appliances has stayed level. The reason is that manufacturers have put their research dollars into lowering production costs, even if it makes repair more difficult.

Tinkerer-filmmaker Tin Hunkin spent two years poking around waste sites in England studying discarded household appliances. His findings, reported in the British magazine *New Scientist*, reveal the prevailing trend toward planned obsolescence and disposability.

"The machines that date back to the 1950s are very solid, made mostly of metal with everything bolted or welded together," observes Hunkin. "As the years passed, machines have become more flimsy. More parts are now made of plastic, and they are glued together rather than welded or bolted....Many parts are now impossible to repair....New machines are so cheap that it frequently does not pay to have a faulty appliance repaired professionally."

Where disposability and planned obsolescence fail to accelerate the trip from purchase to junk heap, fashion sometimes succeeds. Most clothing goes out of style long before it is worn out, but lately, the realm of fashion has colonized sports footwear, too. Kevin Ventrudo, chief financial officer of California-based L.A. Gear, which saw sales multiply fifty times in four years, told the *Washington Post*, "If you talk about shoe performance, you only need one or two pairs. If you're talking fashion, you're talking endless pairs of shoes."

In transportation, diet, and use of raw materials, as consumption rises on the economic scale so does waste—both of resources and of health. Bicycles and public transit are cheaper, more efficient, and healthier transport options than cars. A diet founded on the basics of grains and water is gentle to the earth and the body. And a lifestyle that makes full use of raw materials for durable goods without succumbing to the throwaway mentality is ecologically sound while still affording many of the comforts of modernity.

Ethics for Sustainability

When Moses came down from Mount Sinai, he could count the rules of ethical behavior on his fingers. In the complex global economy of the late 20th century, in which the simple act of turning on an air conditioner affects planetary systems, the list of rules for ecologically sustainable living could run into the hundreds.

The basic value of a sustainable society, the ecological equivalent of the Golden Rule, is simple: Each generation should meet its needs without jeopardizing the prospects of future generations. What is lacking is the practical knowledge—at each level of society—of what living by that principle means.

In a fragile biosphere, the ultimate fate of humanity may depend on whether we can cultivate a deeper sense of self-restraint, founded on a widespread ethic of limiting consumption and finding non-material enrichment.

Those who seek to rise to this environmental challenge may find encouragement in the body of human wisdom passed down from antiquity. To seek out sufficiency is to follow the path of voluntary simplicity preached by all the sages from Buddha to Mohammed. Typical of these pronouncements is this passage from the Bible: "What shall it profit a man if he shall gain the whole world and lose his own soul?"

Living by this credo is not easy. As historian David Shi of Davidson College in North Carolina chronicles, the call for a simpler life is perennial through the history of the North American continent: the Puritans of Massachusetts Bay, the Quakers of Philadelphia, the Amish, the Shakers, the experimental utopian communities of the 1830s, the hippies of the 1960s, and the back-to-the-land movement of the 1970s.

None of these movements ever gained more than a slim minority of adherents. Elsewhere in the world, entire nations have dedicated themselves to rebuilding human character—sometimes through brutal techniques—in a less self-centered mold, and nowhere have they succeeded with more than a token few of their citizens.

It would be hopelessly naive to believe that entire populations will suddenly experience a moral awakening, renouncing greed, envy, and avarice. The best that can be hoped for is a gradual widening of the circle of those practicing voluntary simplicity. The goal of creating a sustainable culture—that is, a culture of permanence—is best thought of as a challenge that will last several generations.

Voluntary simplicity, or personal restraint, will do little good, however, if it is not wedded to bold political steps that confront the forces advocating consumption. Beyond the oft-repeated agenda of environmental and social reforms necessary to achieve sustainability, such as overhauling energy systems, stabilizing population, and ending poverty, action is needed to restrain the excesses of advertising, to curb the shopping culture, and to revitalize household and community economics as human-scale alternatives to the high-consumption lifestyle.

For example, if fairly distributed between the sexes, cooking from scratch can be dignified and use fewer resources than the frozen instant meal. Just so, communities that turn main streets into walking zones where local artisans and farmers display their products while artists, musicians, and theater troupes perform can provide a richness of human interaction that shopping malls will never match.

There could be many more people ready to begin saying "enough" than prevailing opinion suggests. After all, much of what we consume is wasted or unwanted in the first place. How much of the packaging that wraps products we consume each year—462 pounds per-capita in the United States—would we rather never see? How many of the distant farms turned to suburban housing developments could have been left in crops if we insisted on well-planned land use inside city limits?

How many of the unsolicited sales pitches each American receives each day in the mail—37 percent of all mail—are nothing but bothersome junk? How much of the advertising in our morning newspaper—covering 65 percent of the newsprint in American papers—would we not gladly see left out?

How many of the miles we drive—almost 6,000 a year apiece in the United States—would we not happily give up if livable neighborhoods were closer to work, a variety of local merchants closer to home, streets safe to walk and bicycle, and public transit easier and faster? How much of the fossil energy we use is wasted because utility companies fail to put money into efficient renewable energy systems before building new coal plants?

In the final analysis, accepting and living by sufficiency rather than excess offers a return to what is, culturally speaking, the human home: the ancient order of family, community, good work and good life; to a reverence for excellence of craftsmanship; to a true materialism that does not just care *about* things but cares *for* them; to communities worth spending a lifetime in.

Maybe Henry David Thoreau had it right when he scribbled in his notebook beside Walden Pond, "A man is rich in proportion to the things he can afford to let alone."

Reprinted with permission from Worldwatch Institute, 1776 Massachusetts Avenue Northwest, Washington, D.C. 20036. (202)452-1992.

Word and Flesh

by Wendell Berry

Wendell Berry is a modern-day prophet. Terry Tempest Williams writes, "he is our nation's conscience." Edward Abbey has called him "the best essayist working in America." Berry received his M.A. from the University of Kentucky, was awarded a Wallace Stegner Writing Fellowship at Stanford and a Guggenheim Fellowship to study in Europe. At the age of 31, he returned to Henry County, Kentucky, where he was born in 1934. He and his wife Tanya have farmed with horses the 70 acres of Lanes Landing Farm since then. The recipient of six honorary doctorates, Berry is the acclaimed writer of poetry, short stories, novels and essays. Some of his books include *The Unsettling of America: Culture and Agriculture; Home Economics; The Wild Birds;* and *Fidelity.* He and his wife have two children, Mary and Pryor.

In light of global economic relationships, Berry's article draws attention to the appropriate scale of our response. He calls "preposterous" the suggestion that anybody can "do anything to heal a planet." The scale of our competence, according to Berry, is to work to preserve each of our "humble households and neighborhoods." Were all such neighborhoods preserved, many planetary problems would disappear. Risking being called an idealist, Berry nonetheless appeals to love as the only power able to accomplish such a movement: toward the scale of our competence; toward loving our neighbors, human and non-human; and toward loving the neighborhoods we all call home.

Toward the end of *As You Like It*, Orlando says: "I can live no longer by thinking." He is ready to marry Rosalind. It is time for incarnation. Having thought too much, he is at one of the limits of human experience, or human sanity. If his love does put on flesh, we know, he must sooner or later arrive at the opposite limit, at which he will say, "I can no longer live without thinking." Thought—even consciousness—seems to live between these limits: the abstract and the particular, the word and the flesh.

All public movements of thought quickly produce a language that works as a code, useless to the extent that it is abstract. It is readily evident, for example, that you can't conduct a relationship with another person in terms of the rhetoric of the civil rights movement or the women's movement—as useful as those rhetorics may initially have been to personal relationships.

The same is true of the environment movement. The favorite adjective of this movement now seems to be "planetary." This word is used, properly enough, to refer to the interdependence of places, and to the recognition, which is desirable and growing, that no place on earth can be completely healthy until all places are.

But the word "planetary" also refers to an abstract anxiety or an abstract passion that is desperate and useless exactly to the extent that it is abstract. How, after all, can anybody—any particular body—do anything to heal a planet? The suggestion that anybody could do so is preposterous. The heroes of abstraction keep galloping in on their white horses to save the planet—and they keep falling off in front of the grandstand.

What we need, obviously, is a more intelligent—which is to say, a more accurate—description of the problem. The description of a problem as "planetary" arouses a motivation for which, of necessity, there is no employment. The adjective "planetary" describes a problem in such a way that it cannot be solved. In fact, though we now have serious problems nearly everywhere on the planet, we have no problem that can accurately be described as "planetary." And, short of the total annihilation of the human race, there is no planetary solution.

There are also no national, state, or country problems, and no national, state, or country solutions. That will-o'-the-wisp, the large-scale solution to the large-scale problem, which is so dear to governments, universities, and corporations, serves mostly to distract people from the small, private problems that they may, in fact, have the power to solve.

The problems, if we describe them accurately, are all private and small. Or they are so initially.

The problems are our lives. In the "developed" countries, at least, the large problems occur because all of us are living either partly wrong or almost entirely wrong. It was not just the greed of corporate shareholders and the hubris of corporate executives that put the fate of Prince William Sound into one ship; it was also our demand that energy should be cheap and plentiful.

The economies of our communities and households are wrong. The answers to the human problems of ecology are to be found in economy. The answers to the problems of economy are to be found in culture and in character. To fail to see this is to go on dividing the world falsely between guilty producers and innocent consumers.

The "planetary" versions—the heroic versions—of our problems have attracted great intelligence. But these problems, as they are caused and suffered in our lives, our households, and our communities, have attracted very little intelligence.

There are some notable exceptions. A few people have learned to do a few things better. But it is discouraging to reflect that, though we have been talking about most of our problems for decades, we are still mainly *talking* about them. The civil rights movement has not given us better communities. The women's movement has not given us better marriages or better households. The environment movement has not changed our parasitic relationship to nature.

We have failed to produce new examples of good home and community economies, and we have nearly completed the destruction of the examples we once had. Without examples, we are left with theory and the bureaucracy and meddling that come with theory. We change our principles, our thoughts, and our words, but these are changes made in the air. Our lives go on unchanged.

For the most part, the subcultures, the countercultures, the dissenters, and the opponents continue mindlessly—or perhaps just helplessly—to follow the pattern of the dominant society in its extravagance, its wastefulness, its dependencies, and its addictions. The old problem remains: How do you get intelligence *out* of an institution or an organization?

My small community in Kentucky has lived and dwindled for a century at least under the influence of four kinds of organization: governments, corporations, schools, and churches—all of which are distant (either actually or in interest), centralized, and consequently abstract in their concerns.

Governments and corporations (except for employees) have no presence in our community at all, which is perhaps fortunate for us, but we nevertheless feel the indifference or the contempt of governments and corporations for communities such as ours.

We have had no school of our own for nearly thirty years. The school system takes our young people, prepares them for "the world of tomorrow," which it does not expect to take place in any rural area, and gives back "expert" (that is, extremely generalized) ideas.

The church is present in the town. We have two churches. But both have been used by their denominations, for almost a century, to provide training and income for student ministers, who do not stay long enough even to become disillusioned.

For a long time, then, the minds that have most influenced our town have not been *of* the town, and so have not tried to even perceive, much less to honor, the good possibilities that are there. They have not wondered on what terms a good and conserving life might be lived there. In this my community is not unique but is like almost every other neighborhood in our country and in the "developed" world.

The question that *must* be addressed, therefore, is not how to care for the planet, but how to care for each of the planet's millions of human and natural neighborhoods, each of its millions of small pieces and parcels of land, each one of which is in some precious way different from all the others. Our understandable wish to preserve the planet must somehow be reduced to the scale of our competence—that is, to the wish to preserve all of its humble households and neighborhoods.

What can accomplish this reduction? I will say again, without overweening hope but with certainty nonetheless, that only love can do it. Only love can bring intelligence out of the institutions and organizations, where it aggrandizes itself, into the presence of the work that must be done.

Love is never abstract. It does not adhere to the universe or the planet or the nation or the institution or the profession, but to the singular sparrows of the street, the lilies of the field, "the least of these my brethren." Love is not, by its own desire, heroic. It is heroic only when compelled to be. It exists by its willingness to be anonymous, humble, and unrewarded.

The older love becomes, the more clearly it understands its involvement in partiality, imperfection, suffering, and mortality. Even so, it longs for incarnation. It can live no longer by thinking.

And yet, to put on flesh and do the flesh's work, it must think.

In his essay on Kipling, George Orwell wrote: "All left-wing parties in the highly industrialized countries are at bottom a sham, because they make it their business to fight against something which they do not really wish to destroy. They have internationalist aims, and at the same time they struggle to keep up a standard of life with which those aims are incompatible. We all live by robbing Asiatic coolies, and those of us who are 'enlightened' all maintain that those coolies ought to be set free; but our standard of living, and hence our 'enlightenment,' demands that the robbery shall continue."

This statement of Orwell's is clearly applicable to our situation now; all we need to do is change a few nouns. The religion and the environmentalism of the highly industrialized countries are at bottom a sham, because they make it their business to fight against something that they do not really wish to destroy. We all live by robbing nature, but our standard of living demands that the robbery shall continue.

We must achieve the character and acquire the skills to live much poorer than we do. We must waste less. We must do more for ourselves and each other. It is either that or continue merely to think and talk about changes that we are inviting catastrophe to make.

The great obstacle is simply this: the conviction that we cannot change because we are dependent upon what is wrong. But that is the addict's excuse, and we know that it will not do.

How dependent, in fact, are we? How dependent are our neighborhoods and communities? How may our dependencies be reduced? To answer these questions will require better thoughts and better deeds than we have been capable of so far.

We must have the sense and the courage, for example, to see that the ability to transport food for hundreds or thousands of miles does not necessarily mean that we are well off. It means that the food supply is more vulnerable and more costly than a local food supply would be. It means that consumers do not control or influence the healthfulness of their food supply and that they are at the mercy of people who have the control and influence. It means that, in eating, people are using large quantities of petroleum that other people in another time are almost certain to need.

Our most serious problem, perhaps, is that we have become a nation of fanta-sists. We believe, apparently, in the infinite availability of finite resources. We persist in land use methods that reduce the potentially infinite power of soil fertil-ity to a finite quantity, which we can then proceed to waste as if it were an infinite quantity. We have an economy that depends not upon the quality and quantity of necessary goods and services, but on the moods of a few stockbrokers. We believe that democratic freedom can be preserved by people ignorant of the history of democracy, and indifferent to the responsibilities of freedom.

Our leaders have been for many years as oblivious of the realities and dangers of their time as were George III and Lord North. They believe that the difference between war and peace is still the overriding political difference—when, in fact, the difference is diminished to the point of insignificance. How would you describe the difference between modern war and modern industry—between, say, bombing and strip mining, or between chemical warfare and chemical manufacturing? The difference seems to be only that in war the victimization of humans is directly intentional and in industry it is "accepted" as a "trade-off."

Were the catastrophes of Love Canal, Bhopal, Chernobyl, and the *Exxon Valdez* episodes of war or peace? They were, in fact, peacetime acts of aggression, inten-tional to the extent that the risks were known and ignored.

We are involved unremittingly in a war not against "foreign enemies," but against the world, against our freedom, and indeed against our existence. Our so-called industrial accidents should be looked upon as revenges of Nature. We forget that Nature is necessarily party to all our enterprises, and that she imposes condi-tions of her own.

Now she is plainly saying to us: "If you put the fates of whole communities or cities or regions or ecosystems at risk in single ships or factories or power plants, then I will furnish the drunk or the fool or the imbecile who will make the neces-sary small mistake."

Social and Environmental Impacts of Everyday Food Choices

Eating with the fullest pleasure—pleasure, that is,
that does not depend on ignorance—is perhaps the
profoundest enactment of our connection with the
world. In this pleasure we experience and celebrate
our dependence and our gratitude, for we are
living from mystery, from creatures we did not
make and powers we cannot comprehend.

—*Wendell Berry*

The Pleasures of Eating

by Wendell Berry

Eating is certainly one of life's greatest gifts and pleasures. Whether offering hospitality, celebrating significant life-passages, or gathering for a rich potluck with friends, we understand food as not only a necessity but a symbol of communion. Wendell Berry extends the pleasure that can come from eating. Because "how we eat determines, to a considerable extent, how the world is used," he suggests that a significant element in the pleasure of eating is "in one's accurate consciousness of the lives and the world from which food comes." He provides seven practical suggestions for increasing one's consciousness of the ways our everyday food choices impact people and the land and how to go about supporting local, sustainable agriculture.

∞

Many times, after I have finished a lecture on the decline of American farming and rural life, someone in the audience has asked, "What can city people do?"

"Eat responsibly," I have usually answered. Of course, I have tried to explain what I meant by that, but afterwards I have invariably felt that there was more to be said than I had been able to say. Now I would like to attempt a better explanation.

I begin with the proposition that eating is an agricultural act. Eating ends the annual drama of the food economy that begins with planting and birth. Most eaters, however, are no longer aware that this is true. They think of food as an agricultural product, perhaps, but they do not think of themselves as participants in agriculture. They think of themselves as "consumers." If they think beyond that, they recognize that they are passive consumers. They buy what they want—or what they have been persuaded to want—within the limits of what they can get. They pay, mostly without protest, what they are charged. And they mostly ignore certain critical questions about the quality and the cost of what they are sold: How fresh is it? How pure or clean is it, how free of dangerous chemicals? How far was it transported, and what did transportation add to the cost? How much did manufacturing or packaging or advertising add to the cost? When the food product has been manufactured or "processed" or "precooked," how has that affected its quality or price or nutritional value?

Most urban shoppers would tell you that food is produced on farms. But most of them do not know what farms, or what kinds of farms, or where the farms are, or what knowledge or skills are involved in farming. They apparently have little doubt that farms will continue to produce, but they do not know how or over what obstacles. For them, then, food is pretty much an abstract idea—something they do not know or imagine—until it appears on the grocery shelf or on the table.

The specialization of production induces specialization of consumption. Patrons of the entertainment industry, for example, entertain themselves less and less and have become more and more passively dependent on commercial suppliers. This is certainly true also of patrons of the food industry, who have tended more and more to be *mere* consumers—passive, uncritical, and dependent. Indeed, this sort of consumption may be said to be one of the chief goals of industrial production. The food industrialists have by now persuaded millions of consumers to prefer food that is already prepared. They will grow, deliver, and cook your food for you and (just like your mother) beg you to eat it. That they do not yet offer to insert it, prechewed, into your mouth is only because they have found no profitable way to do so. We may rest assured that they would be glad to find such a way. The ideal industrial food consumer would be strapped to a table with a tube running from the food factory directly into his or her stomach.

Perhaps I exaggerate, but not by much. The industrial eater is, in fact, one who does not know that eating is an agricultural act, who no longer knows or imagines the connections between eating and the land, and who is therefore necessarily passive and uncritical—in short, a victim. When food, in the minds of eaters, is no longer associated with farming and with the land, then the eaters are suffering a kind of cultural amnesia that is misleading and dangerous. The current version of the "dream home" of the future involves "effortless" shopping from a list of available goods on a television monitor and heating precooked food by remote control. Of course, this implies and depends on a perfect ignorance of the history of the food that is consumed. It requires that the citizenry should give up their hereditary and sensible aversion to buying a pig in a poke. It wishes to make the selling of pigs in pokes an honorable and glamorous activity. The dreamer in this dream home will perforce know nothing about the kind or quality of this food, or where it came from, or how it was produced and prepared, or what ingredients, additives, and residues it contains—unless, that is, the dreamer undertakes a close and constant study of the food industry, in which case he or she might as well wake up and play an active and responsible part in the economy of food.

There is, then, a politics of food that, like any politics, involves our freedom. We still (sometimes) remember that we cannot be free if our minds and voices are controlled by someone else. But we have neglected to understand that we cannot be free if our food and its sources are controlled by someone else. The condition of the passive consumer of food is not a democratic condition. One reason to eat responsibly is to live free.

But if there is a food politics, there are also a food esthetics and a food ethics, neither of which is dissociated from politics. Like industrial sex, industrial eating has become a degraded, poor, and paltry thing. Our kitchens and other eating places more and more resemble filling stations, as our homes more and more resemble motels. "Life is not very interesting," we seem to have decided. "Let its satisfactions be minimal, perfunctory, and fast." We hurry through our meals to go to work and hurry through our work in order to "recreate" ourselves in the evenings and on weekends and vacations. And then we hurry, with the greatest possible speed and noise and violence, through our recreation—for what? To eat the billionth hamburger at some fast-food joint hellbent on increasing the "quality" of our life? And all this is carried out in a remarkable obliviousness to the causes and effects, the possibilities and the purposes, of the life of the body in this world.

One will find this obliviousness represented in virgin purity in the advertisements of the food industry, in which food wears as much makeup as the actors. If one gained one's whole knowledge of food from these advertisements (as some presumably do), one would not know that the various edibles were ever living creatures, or that they all come from the soil, or that they were produced by work. The passive American consumer, sitting down to a meal of pre-prepared or fast food, confronts a platter covered with inert, anonymous substances that have been processed, dyed, breaded, sauced, gravied, ground, pulped, strained, blended, prettified, and sanitized beyond resemblance to any part of any creature that ever lived. The products of nature and agriculture have been made, to all appearances, the products of industry. Both eater and eaten are thus in exile from biological reality. And the result is a kind of solitude, unprecedented in human experience, in which the eater may think of eating as, first, a purely commercial transaction between him and a supplier and then as a purely appetitive transaction between him and his food.

And this peculiar specialization of the act of eating is, again, of obvious benefit to the food industry, which has good reasons to obscure the connection between food and farming. It would not do for the consumer to know that the hamburger she is eating came from a steer who spent much of his life standing deep in his own excrement in a feedlot, helping to pollute the local streams, or that the calf that yielded the veal cutlet on her plate spent its life in a box in which it did not have room to turn around. And, though her sympathy for the slaw might be less tender, she should not be encouraged to meditate on the hygienic and biological implications of mile-square fields of cabbage, for vegetables grown in huge monocultures are dependent on toxic chemicals—just as animals in close confinement are dependent on antibiotics and other drugs.

The consumer, that is to say, must be kept from discovering that, in the food industry—as in any other industry—the overriding concerns are not quality and health, but volume and price. For decades now the entire industrial food economy, from the large farms and feedlots to the chains of supermarkets and fast-food restaurants, has been obsessed with volume. It has relentlessly increased scale in order to increase volume in order (presumably) to reduce costs. But as scale increases, diversity declines; as diversity declines, so does health; as health declines, the dependence on drugs and chemicals necessarily increases. As capital replaces

labor, it does so by substituting machines, drugs, and chemicals for human workers
and for the natural health and fertility of the soil. The food is produced by any
means or any shortcut that will increase profits. And the business of the cosmeti-
cians of advertising is to persuade the consumer that food so produced is good,
tasty, healthful, and a guarantee of marital fidelity and long life.

It is possible, then, to be liberated from the husbandry and wifery of the old
household food economy. But one can be thus liberated only by entering a trap
(unless one sees ignorance and helplessness as the signs of privilege, as many people apparently do). The trap is the ideal of industrialism: a walled city surrounded
by valves that let merchandise in but no consciousness out. How does one escape
this trap? Only voluntarily, the same way that one went in: by restoring one's consciousness of what is involved in eating; by reclaiming responsibility for one's own
part in the food economy. One might begin with the illuminating principle of Sir
Albert Howard's The Soil and Health, that we should understand "the whole problem of health in soil, plant, animal, and man as one great subject." Eaters, that is,
must understand that eating takes place inescapably in the world, that it is inescapably an agricultural act, and that how we eat determines, to a considerable extent,
how the world is used. This is a simple way of describing a relationship that is inex-
pressibly complex. To eat responsibly is to understand and enact, so far as one can,
this complex relationship. What can one do? Here is a list, probably not definitive:

1. Participate in food production to the extent that you can. If you have a yard or
   even just a porch box or a pot in a sunny window, grow something to eat in it.
   Make a little compost of your kitchen scraps and use it for fertilizer. Only by
   growing some food for yourself can you become acquainted with the beautiful
   energy cycle that revolves from soil to seed to flower to fruit to food to offal to
   decay, and around again. You will be fully responsible for any food that you grow
   for yourself, and you will know all about it. You will appreciate it fully, having
   known it all its life.
2. Prepare your own food. This means reviving in your own mind and life the arts
   of kitchen and household. This should enable you to eat more cheaply, and it
   will give you a measure of "quality control": you will have some reliable knowledge of what has been added to the food you eat.
3. Learn the origins of the food you buy, and buy the food that is produced closest
   to your home. The idea that every locality should be, as much as possible, the
   source of its own food makes several kinds of sense. The locally produced food
   supply is the most secure, the freshest, and the easiest for local consumers to
   know about and to influence.
4. Whenever possible, deal directly with a local farmer, gardener, or orchardist. All
   the reasons listed for the previous suggestion apply here. In addition, by such
   dealing you eliminate the whole pack of merchants, transporters, processors,
   packagers, and advertisers who thrive at the expense of both producers and
   consumers.

5. Learn, in self-defense, as much as you can of the economy and technology of industrial food production. What is added to food that is not food, and what do you pay for these additions?
6. Learn what is involved in the best farming and gardening.
7. Learn as much as you can, by direct observation and experience if possible, of the life histories of the food species.

The last suggestion seems particularly important to me. Many people are now as much estranged from the lives of domestic plants and animals (except for flowers and dogs and cats) as they are from the lives of the wild ones. This is regrettable, for these domestic creatures are in diverse ways attractive; there is much pleasure in knowing them. And farming, animal husbandry, horticulture, and gardening, at their best, are complex and comely arts; there is much pleasure in knowing them, too.

It follows that there is great *dis*pleasure in knowing about a food economy that degrades and abuses those arts and those plants and animals and the soil from which they come. For anyone who does know something of the modern history of food, eating away from home can be a chore. My own inclination is to eat seafood instead of red meat or poultry when I am traveling. Though I am by no means a vegetarian, I dislike the thought that some animal has been made miserable in order to feed me. If I am going to eat meat, I want it to be from an animal that has lived a pleasant, uncrowded life outdoors, on bountiful pasture, with good water nearby and trees for shade. And I am getting almost as fussy about food plants. I like to eat vegetables and fruits that I know have lived happily and healthily in good soil, not the products of the huge, bechemicaled factory-fields that I have seen, for example, in the Central Valley of California. The industrial farm is said to have been patterned on the factory production line. In practice, it looks more like a concentration camp.

The pleasure of eating should be an *extensive* pleasure, not that of the mere gourmet. People who know the garden in which their vegetables have grown and know that the garden is healthy will remember the beauty of the growing plants, perhaps in the dewy first light of morning when gardens are at their best. Such a memory involves itself with the food and is one of the pleasures of eating. The knowledge of the good health of the garden relieves and frees and comforts the eater. The same goes for eating meat. The thought of the good pasture and of the calf contentedly grazing flavors the steak. Some, I know, will think it bloodthirsty or worse to eat a fellow creature you have known all its life. On the contrary, I think it means that you eat with understanding and with gratitude. A significant part of the pleasure of eating is in one's accurate consciousness of the lives and the world from which food comes. The pleasure of eating, then, may be the best available standard of our health. And this pleasure, I think, is pretty fully available to the urban consumer who will make the necessary effort.

I mentioned earlier the politics, esthetics, and ethics of food. But to speak of the

pleasure of eating is to go beyond those categories. Eating with the fullest pleasure—pleasure, that is, that does not depend on ignorance—is perhaps the profoundest enactment of our connection with the world. In this pleasure we
experience and celebrate our dependence and our gratitude, for we are living from
mystery, from creatures we did not make and powers we cannot comprehend.
When I think of the meaning of food, I always remember these lines by the poet
William Carlos Williams, which seem to me merely honest:

> There is nothing to eat,
>   seek it where you will,
>   but the body of the Lord.
> The blessed plants
>   and the sea, yield it
>   to the imagination intact.

"The Pleasures of Eating," from *What are People For?* by Wendell Berry. Copyright 1990 by Wendell Berry. Reprinted
by Permission of North Point Press, a division of Farrar, Straus and Giroux, Inc.

The Great Hunter-Gatherer Continuum
by James T. Mulligan

Jim Mulligan currently serves as Earth Ministry's Executive Director. He, along with his wife, Ruth, and Carla Berkedal, co-founded
this ecumenical, Christian, environmental nonprofit organization
in 1992. Ordained as a Presbyterian minister, Mulligan spent 23
years as a Pastoral Counselor with the Presbyterian Counseling
Service in Seattle, Washington. Mulligan is a skilled photographer
and woodworker, and he enjoys long walks and poking around
Puget Sound in his kayak. He and his wife are both fine cooks.
They have two children and two grandchildren.

In this essay Mulligan constructs a "hunter-gatherer continuum."
The continuum presents, and discusses implications of, seven different food-purchasing pathways. Where do you see yourself?

∞

We all eat. What we eat, where it comes from, and the process of our obtaining
it all leave their impact on us and on the earth. In the earliest times hunting and

gathering were the chief pathways. From what we are able to learn of those times, these methods had the least detrimental impacts on both land and people. Later, as domestication and agriculture arose, people began to make increasing impacts on the natural environment. Here in this country we are not that far removed historically from a time when far more of our population actively farmed. Many of us need look back only to our parents' or grandparents' generation to find examples of people living "close to the land."

Now, at the close of the 20th century, we in this country think nothing of buying pineapple from the Philippines, cocoa from Africa, coffee from Brazil, kiwi from New Zealand, and oranges from Florida, in the middle of winter, at the mall only minutes away. In the US our food travels an average of 1,200 miles before it reaches our home. Our patterns of obtaining food have changed remarkably in a relatively short time, considering the long sweep of human history.

The environmental "footprint" of such a global food economy is many times greater than that of even our parents' generation. Are there practical steps we can take as individuals and families to mitigate the impact of such a vast system? One place to begin is to consider where and how we personally purchase our food. In this reading we will examine a framework to organize and think about our range of options. It is presented in the form of a continuum. Harking back to our ancestors, I have called it the Hunter-Gatherer Continuum. In the weekly process of making shopping lists, planning which stores to stop at, in which order, anticipating traffic, and fitting this all into the rest of my schedule, I often feel like a modern day hunter-gatherer, in the forest of urban life.

The Continuum

We can envision a spectrum of options for how we shop for the food we buy. You might well be aware of other options, and where they might fit in to this simple model. The purpose of presenting this continuum is to help us to recognize as clearly as possible the range of choices we have, and to thoughtfully consider the larger impact of these choices upon our communities and the earth.

Such a continuum might be graphically represented like this:

Culturally Normative						Most Earth Friendly
Supermarket Only	Selective Supermkt.	Some Specialized	Both	Exclusively Specialized	Farmers' Market	Subscription Farm

The basic assumption in organizing this continuum is as follows: it begins with the most common options, widely available in our society. As you move along the continuum toward the right, you move progressively away from the culturally normative pathways, towards those which are more earth friendly, but also rarer. This means options will be fewer; so, choosing these options usually requires more time and longer commutes. Why would we want, then, to choose such options? Because they are more earth friendly; that is, they are much more likely to sell organically grown, chemically-free products, from farmers who are more likely to be sensitive about their impact on the land. In addition, these options are also more supportive of the local agricultural community and local food economies, as well as more healthy for ourselves and our families. Let us consider for a moment each of these "steps" along the continuum.

Supermarket Shopping

Perhaps the most common food-purchasing pattern in our society is to simply shop at the closest supermarket, buying the brands we trust or those items that are on sale. Here, our choices are limited to those foods available through supermarket chains—almost exclusively products of the vast agribusiness complex. Our choices are often influenced by the constant blitz of advertising, in the media as well as in the store. In this position on the continuum, we are in the mainstream of our society's economy. We are functioning as a consumer within the most pervasive and accessible pathway. Our national economic system spends considerable time and money to try to shape our awareness of and sensibilities about this step on the continuum. The vast bulk of the information readily available to most people assumes that we will be shopping at conventional supermarkets in just this way. Advertisers will assume that our sole objective is to find the items we want in the freshest condition, with the widest possible selection of choices, for the best price, at the most convenient location (with plenty of accessible parking), from retailers whose reputations we have come to know and to trust. As far as they go, these are not bad considerations. These criteria are central not only for shoppers, but also for the retailers themselves. However, other considerations (e.g. locally produced, organically grown, minimal packaging and shipping) are of only secondary importance in most of these stores. Therefore, this step on the continuum can be seen as the easiest, but also the least likely to be environmentally friendly or to support the local food economy of our region.

Selective Supermarket Shopping

The next step along this continuum would be to continue to shop at the local supermarket, but to make a concerted effort to shop as selectively as possible. Buy as many local products and produce as possible. Ask the management to stock local brands. Seek out minimal and recycled packaging. Buy bulk items in containers you bring from home. Ask about the produce: where was it grown, is it organic, what chemicals were used? Request that the manager stock products you have learned about from other sources. In short, use your influence to both buy locally and to encourage the supermarket chains to stock more local and, earth-friendly goods.

In this option you are taking the initiative, both to become a more conscientious consumer and to exert your influence within the mainstream economy. The more people asking for local organic produce, the more likely the store will be to develop a section featuring these choices. Your efforts can make a difference. However, your influence, and that of other like-minded consumers, is not the only factor which helps to shape the mainstream food economy. Supermarket chains, wholesale distribution systems, and large advertising and marketing organizations are all part of the even larger agribusiness complex. Consumer pressure, even highly organized and orchestrated consumer pressure (such as national boycotts), are only one factor in a much larger field. The central concerns of the agribusiness complex are often far more influential. So while you can thus be a force within the mainstream for change, you should not over-estimate the possible impact of these efforts. Therefore, you might want to consider other steps along the continuum as well.

Occasional Shopping at Specialized Retailers

A next step would be to shop occasionally at specialized retailers who focus on local, organic, and earth-friendly products: such as co-ops, natural food stores, and produce stands. As there are considerably fewer of these retailers than there are supermarkets, you may well have to go somewhat out of your way to patronize them. Perhaps you could go there once a month and stock. Often, with such specialized retailers, some of the job of learning about the origin and production of the food has been done for you. More consumer education is incorporated into the organization of the store. There are still decisions to make, but the whole array of choices is generally much more earth friendly; produce is more often locally grown. The larger of such retailers (here in Seattle, Puget Consumers Co-Op would be a good example) may offer a wide array of specialized educational materials and classes to help you become a much more informed consumer and to learn how to cook with some products which have not been a part of our culture's mainstream diet. These businesses are significantly less tied in to the agribusiness economy and more supportive of the local economy and local community efforts towards bioregional self-sufficiency. Products you can't find at these selective retailers you still buy at the local supermarket on regular shopping trips. You have to think and plan ahead to shop successfully in this way or you will find yourself needing to go to two stores every week instead of one.

Regular Shopping at Both Specialized Retailers and Supermarkets

A next step along the continuum would be to consciously do just that, shop at both regularly. On the whole you will probably purchase more food from the specialized stores than when you shop there less frequently. Here you need not plan ahead as elaborately. But, you will be doing more commuting. While the impact on your time and fuel is a factor you will need to consider, you most likely will be also exerting increasing levels of your financial influence to support the regional food economy, and eating more food which is healthy for yourself and for the earth.

Buying Almost Exclusively at Specialized Retailers

A next step would be to bite the bullet and buy as exclusively as you can at such specialized stores. Here your consumer economic weight is maximally influencing the local retail economy towards supporting such green businesses. However, the range of choices for products will most likely be decreased. These smaller, local retailers simply cannot match the large supermarket chains for their vast array of choices, or their comprehensiveness of non-food choices. (Thus far, at least, few co-ops and produce stands have branch offices of banks, video rentals, bakeries, and pharmacies on the premises, thank heavens!) So, even the most dedicated earth-friendly shoppers often find that they will make occasional forays to the supermarket to pick up some hard-to-find items. In this step the bulk of your "consumer power" is being used to support the viability of the local food economy.

Shop at Farmers' Markets

A related step, usually available only from summer through fall, is to buy food at community farmers' markets. The bonus here is significant. You get the freshest produce, all of your money goes directly to the local producer, and you have an opportunity to interact directly with the farmer. As there are fewer Farmer's Markets than there are specialized retailers and they are usually open far fewer hours per week, this step increases your shopping complexity. You are now exerting a focused economic influence on the local farming community, helping to keep small family farming alive in your area. Many of these farmers' markets are developing a real community of support, and often include booths for local crafts people and artists, a truly festive atmosphere. So shopping at them can be an enriching experience in itself, making the old supermarket seem rather sterile by comparison.

Subscribe to a "Community Supported Agriculture" Farm

The final step in this continuum, requiring the greatest commitment, is to become a subscriber to a (community supported agriculture) "subscription farm." Here farmers contract directly with their customers, who are then their "subscribers." You pay a lump sum (in advance of the growing season) for a share of that years' produce. Then regularly, at a designated time each week of the growing season, you pick up your portion of that week's harvest. Your life in some measure will need to be coordinated with that of the farmer. You will get more food in bulk (i.e. lots of corn at one time, lots of tomatoes at another), much like having your own garden. You might want to put up some of the food for the winter. (Remember when people lived closer to the land, and everyone canned or froze the produce from their gardens?) Clearly this option requires the most planning, just as using the produce from your own garden. And, as with your own garden, the food could not be fresher. This step will, of course, require that you continue to purchase (at some retailer) all those other food items which a small farm cannot be expected to produce (staples, dairy, crops not grown in this local region, etc.). It is also clearly seasonal; in winter you are back at the grocery store full time.

Another advantage to subscribing to such a farm is that you can maintain a close connection with the grower, even helping with the harvesting if you like. In this step you play a significant part in insuring the continued economic viability of local organic farms, as the farmer and subscriber both share in the risks of production: in good years you get more produce, in lean years, less. By your participation you have guaranteed that another farmer will not go bankrupt, and contributed to keeping one more farm and one more farmer an active part of the local food economy. You and the farmer are truly working partners.

Gardening as an Adjunct

In addition to the steps along this continuum, you can also have your own garden and grow some of your own food. This is not really a "step" along the continuum itself, as you can garden as an adjunct to your hunting and gathering from any position along the continuum. Here you invest considerable time and effort, but you learn first-hand about the complex issues and joys of "living off the land." It is one thing to read about the complexities of organic farming: the vicissitudes of soil, weather, and sunshine, the foraging habits of numerous insects, the marvels of composting. It is quite another to experience them firsthand. In addition, it has been scientifically demonstrated that no corn tastes sweeter, no tomatoes are juicier, no herbs are fresher, and certainly no zucchini more exuberantly plentiful than your own! You've become a mini-farmer yourself, directly involved in both the labor and the miracle of "life sustaining life."

Social Structures and the Politics of Simplicity

...insofar as it is apolitical, simple living risks being
conservative in its political implications, focusing
inordinately on the ability and responsibility
of the individual for the quality of his/her life.
If the simple living idea remains largely
individualistic, it will not only be irrelevant
to most Americans—in the end it will
disappear under the influence of the
dominant forces in American life. It
is as a form of politics, a politics
that is both personal and social, that
simple living has enormous potential for deeply and lastingly
transforming life in America.

—*Jerome Segal*

Christian Existence in a World of Limits

by John B. Cobb, Jr.

John B. Cobb, Jr.'s essay begins with a discussion of the various limits we face today: the finitude of our planet and its ability to assimilate waste; our limited ability to even conceive of a new way of living; and Earth's limited ability to support (carrying capacity) the burgeoning human population. Most of us are familiar with the public discussion of these limits and how facing such limits can lead to profound despair. Cobb reminds the reader, though, that "the Christian faith has been one important way in which people have lived with hope in the midst of conditions that appeared objectively hopeless." And while "Christianity does not underestimate the strength of tendencies which in the course of history have become anti-human and now threaten our survival, we discover that there is a power at work in us that can transform even our distorted wills. This transformation comes as a gift. We call it grace."

As a discussion of limits appears elsewhere in this collection (see Weiskel, page 161), we pick up Cobb's article with his presentation of five "images of appropriate Christian response." These images provide a helpful historical, yet contemporary, framework for envisioning a public/political response to the realities of today's world. While there is some tension between these responses, and Cobb recognizes that "none of us is called to enter equally into all of them," it is his hope that we "can support one another in our varied Christian decisions."

∞

Christian Realism

By Christian realism I mean to point to that style of action described so brilliantly by Reinhold Niebuhr. Niebuhr knew that the quest for justice in human affairs would not be consummated by the achievement of a just society. Every attainment of relative justice produces a situation in which new forms of injustice arise. There is no assurance that any amount of effort will lead to a society that is better than our own, and, even if it does, there is no assurance that the improvement will last. But this is no reason to relax our efforts. The maintenance of relative justice requires constant struggle.

In this struggle moral exhortation is of only limited use. People in large numbers are motivated by self-interest or group interest. Relative justice is obtained only as the competing groups within society arrive at relatively equal strength. Thus, organized labor now received relative justice in American society because labor unions had power comparable to that of capital.

Christian realists do not appeal to the United States on idealistic grounds alone to supply food to a world food bank. They form alliances with those groups that stand to gain financially by such an arrangement or see political advantages to be won. Furthermore, they realize the fragility of any agreement on the part of the United States that is not clearly in its self-interest, and they work accordingly to strengthen the political power of those countries most in need of American largesse.

Christian realists know that influencing government policy requires hard work and shrewdness. They employ the best lobbyists they can find and bring as much sophisticated understanding as possible to bear on issues while exerting pressure through influencing public opinion. They know that the problems we are dealing with will be with us for the foreseeable future, and hence, they settle in for the long haul rather than rely on a quadrennial emphasis on hunger or a special plea for compassionate action.

Christian realists see that the church itself has its own independent capacity to deal with global issues and that there are other nongovernmental organizations with which it needs to work closely. Rightly directing the energies of these private institutions may be as important as directly influencing government policy. Often government policy will follow directions pioneered by other institutions.

The Eschatological Attitude

Although Christian realism is a more appropriate response for American Christians than either moral exhortation or revolution, it has limitations. Its maximum achievement will be ameliorative. Since it accepts the existing structures of power, and since these structures are part of the total world system that moves toward catastrophe, Christian realism alone is not an adequate Christian response. Although any direct attempt to overthrow the existing system would be counterproductive, that system may well collapse of its own weight. It would be unfortunate if Christians became so immersed in a "realistic" involvement in existing institutions that they could not respond creatively to the opportunity that may be offered to build different ones.

Some Christians may elect to live now in terms of what they envision as quite new possibilities for human society even when they do not know how to get from here to there. We may not know how to bring about a society that uses only renewable resources, but we can experiment with lifestyles that foreshadow that kind of society. We may not know how to provide the Third World with space and freedom to work out its own destiny, but in the name of a new kind of world we can withdraw our support from the more obvious structures of oppression. We may not know how to shift from a growth-oriented economy to a stationary-state economy, but we can work out the principles involved in such an economy.

To exert energies in these ways is not to live in an irrelevant world of make-believe. It is to live from a hopeful future. It may not affect the course of immediate events as directly as will the policy of Christian realism, but it may provide the stance that will make it possible, in a time of crisis, to make constructive rather than destructive changes. Even if the hoped-for future never comes, the choice of living from it may not be wrong. The Kingdom expected by Jesus' disciples did not arrive, but the energies released by that expectation and the quality of lives of those who lived from that future deeply affected the course of events in unforeseen and unintended ways. To live without illusion in the spirit of Christian realism may turn out in the long run to be less realistic than to shape our lives from visions of a hopeful future.

To live eschatologically in this sense is not simply to enjoy hopeful images from time to time. The hope for the Kingdom freed early Christians from concern for success or security in the present order. Similarly, for us today to live from the future will mean quite concretely that we cease to try to succeed and to establish our security in the present socio-economic order. For most of us that would be a radical change, and many would say it is unrealistic. But unless there are those Christians who have inwardly disengaged themselves from our present structures, we will not be able to offer leadership at a time when there might be readiness for such leadership.

The Discernment of Christ

Most dedication to social change has involved the belief that history is on the side of the change. Christians have made the stronger claim that they were working to implement God's will. When God is understood as omnipotent, Christians have an assurance of ultimate success for their causes regardless of the most immediate outcome of the efforts. But, today, we do not perceive God as forcing divine decisions upon the world. Every indication is that the human species is free to plunge into catastrophes of unprecedented magnitude if it chooses to do so.

If we no longer think of God as on our side, ensuring the success of our undertakings, we can and should seek all the more to discern where Christ as the incarnate Logos is at work in our world. When we look for Christ we do not seek displays of supernormal force but quiet works of creative love, or the still small voice. Dietrich Bonhoeffer did well when he pointed away from a controlling deity and spoke of the divine suffering. But he was dangerously misleading when he spoke of the divine as powerless. The still small voice and the man on the cross have their power, too, but it is a different sort of power from that of the thunderbolt and the insurance company's "acts of God."

If our eyes are opened by faith, we see Christ wherever we look. We see Christ in the aspirations for justice and freedom on the part of the oppressed and in the glimmering desire of the oppressor to grant justice and freedom. Christ appears most strikingly in the miracle of conversion when something radically new enters a person's life and all that was there before takes on changed meaning. But we see Christ less fully formed in a child struggling to understand, or in a gesture of sympathy to an injured dog. Wherever human beings are reaching out from themselves, wherever there is growth toward spirit, wherever there is hunger for God, wherever, through the interaction of people, a new intimacy comes into being, we discern the work and presence of Christ. Equally, we experience Christ in challenges that threaten us and in opportunities we have refused. Christ appears also in the emergence of new ideas and insights, in the creativity of the artist, and in the life of the imagination, for Christ is that which makes all things new, and without newness there can be no thought, art, or imagination.

In a situation where habits, established institutions, social and economic structures are leading us to destruction, Christ is our one hope. In quietness and in unexpected places Christ is bringing something new to birth, something we cannot foresee and build our plans upon. As Christians we need to maintain an attitude of expectancy, open to accepting and following the new work of Christ. It may even be that Christ wants to effect some part of that important work in us, and we must be open to being transformed by it. We cannot produce that work, but we can attune ourselves and practice responsiveness to the new openings that come moment by moment.

The attitude I am now describing is different from Christian realism and Christian eschatology, but it is contradictory to neither. Ultimately, we should adopt the realist or eschatological stance only as we are led to do so by Christ, and we should remain in those postures only as we find Christ holding us there. That is to say, to live by faith is to live in readiness to subordinate our past plans and projects, even those undertaken in obedience to Christ, to the new word that is Christ today.

In the discernment of that word we need one another. It is easy to confuse Christ with our own desires or impulses or even our fears. Our ability to discriminate Christ is heightened by participation in a community which intends to serve him and which remembers the failures as well as the achievements of the past. But, finally, Christians know that they stand alone with Christ responding or failing to respond to the offer of new life through which they may also mediate Christ to others.

The Way of the Cross

Jurgen Moltmann followed up his great book *The Theology of Hope* with another entitled *The Crucified God*. He rightly recognized that, for the Christian, hope stands in closest proximity to sacrifice. Whereas in the sixties it was possible for some oppressed groups to believe that the forces of history were on their side and that they had suffered enough, the course of events has reminded us all that hope is not Christian if it is tied too closely to particular events and outcomes. We cannot circumvent the cross. Now, as we face more clearly the limits of the human situation and the fact that poverty and suffering cannot be avoided even by the finest programs we devise, we are forced to look again at the meaning of the cross for us. Have affluent middle-class American Christians been avoiding the cross too long?

I am not suggesting that affluent Christians should court persecution or adopt ascetic practices in order to suffer as others do. There is enough suffering in the world without intentionally inflicting it upon ourselves. Whatever the future, we are called to celebrate all life, including our own, not to repress it. But the celebration of life does not involve participation in the luxury and waste of a throwaway society that exists in the midst of world poverty. More important, it does not mean that Christians can float on down the stream because the current carries us effortlessly along. We are all called to swim against the stream, at personal cost, and without expectation of understanding and appreciation. That is a serious and authentic way of bearing a cross.

Furthermore, in a world in which global poverty is here to stay, we are called as Christians to identify with the poor. That has always been Christian teaching, but when we thought that our own affluence contributed to the spread of affluence around the world, we could evade that teaching. Now we know that riches can exist in one quarter only at the expense of the poverty of others. In a world divided between oppressor and oppressed, rich and poor, the Christian cannot remain identified with the oppressor and the rich.

The rhetoric of identification with the poor and the oppressed has been around for some time. We have to ask what it means, and here diversity is legitimate. For some, it means functioning as advocates for the cause of the poor; for a few, joining revolutionary movements; for others, embracing poverty as a way of life. I believe this third meaning needs to be taken by Christians with increasing seriousness. The one who actually becomes poor will be a better advocate for the cause of the poor and freer to respond to other opportunities for identification.

I do not have in mind that we should dress in rags, go around with a begging bowl, or eat inferior food. That, too, may have its place, but I mean by poverty two things: first, and chiefly, disengagement from the system of acquiring and maintaining property and from all the values and involvements associated with it; and second, frugality. The Catholic church has long institutionalized poverty of this sort. Protestants tried to inculcate frugality and generosity as a form of poverty to be lived in the world, but that experiment failed. Today we need to reconsider our earlier rejection of special orders so as to develop new institutions appropriate for our time. We can learn much from the Ecumenical Institute as well as from Taize.

I believe that the actual adoption of poverty as a way of life, supported by the churches, would strengthen the capacity of Christians to respond in all the ways noted above. The Christian realist is limited not only by the political powers with which he or she must deal but also by involvement in a way of life that the needed changes threaten. The Christian voice will speak with greater clarity and authenticity when it speaks from a life situation that is already adapted to the new condition that is needed. Although a life of poverty is not by itself a sufficient definition of living from the hoped-for future, it is an almost essential element in such a life. Our capacity to be sensitive to the call of Christ can be enhanced when we do not nurse a secret fear that Christ will speak to us as to the rich young ruler. Of course, there will be danger of self-righteousness and otherworldliness, but we have not escaped these dangers by abandoning special orders.

Prophetic Vision

"Where there is no vision, the people perish" (Proverbs 29:18). That proverb has a frighteningly literal application to our time. We simply will not move forward to the vast changes that are required without an attracting vision. But such vision is in short supply. There are still proposed visions of a future of increasing global affluence, but they are irrelevant to our present situation and encourage the wrong attitudes and expectations. There are catastrophic images aplenty, but they breed a despair that is worse than useless. We need a prophetic vision of a world into which God might transform ours through transforming us.

This means that one particularly important response to our situation is openness to the transformation of our imagination. We live largely in and through our images. Where no adequate images exist, we cannot lead full and appropriate lives. In recent centuries church people have not been in the forefront of image making. We have increasingly lived in and from images fashioned by others. Our traditional Christian images have been crowded into special corners of our lives. Recognizing our poverty, we need to find Christ at work in other communities in the new creation of images by which we can be enlivened. We can hope also that as we confess our nakedness and gain a fresh appreciation for the creative imagination, the sickness of the church in this respect may be healed and our Christian faith can be released to share in the fashioning of the images so urgently needed.

Concretely, we in the United States need a prophetic vision of an economic order that is viable and humane with respect to our own people without continuing economic imperialism and environmental degradation. We need a vision of a global agriculture that can sustain the health of an increased population in the short run without worsening the opportunities of future generations or decimating other species of plants and animals. We need a vision of urban life that maximizes the social and cultural opportunities of cities while minimizing the destructive impact of our present cities both upon their inhabitants and upon the environment. We need a vision of personal existence in community that brings personal freedom into positive relation with mutual intimacy and individual difference into positive relation with mutual support. We need a vision of how the finest commitments of one generation can be transmitted to the next without oppression and so as to encourage free responsiveness to new situations.

Bits and pieces of the needed vision exist. In my personal search I have found the most impressive breakthrough in the work of Paolo Soleri. But in all areas most of the work remains to be done. Vision in no sense replaces the need for rigorous reflection on details of both theory and practice. Instead, it gives a context in which hard work of mind and body takes on appropriate meaning.

Without vision the other types of response I have mentioned degenerate into legalism and self-righteousness. As the bearer of prophetic vision, the church could again become a center of vitality in a decaying world. But to bear prophetic vision is costly. It is not possible apart from some of the other responses noted above.

Conclusion

Perhaps for affluent Christians the deepest level of response to the awareness of limits is the recognition that we cannot free ourselves from guilt. We are caught in a destructive system, and we find that even our will to refuse to identify with that system is mixed with the desire to enjoy its fruits. None of us is innocent, either in intention or behavior. At most we ask that we may be helped to open ourselves to re-creation by God, but we also depend on grace in another sense. It is only because we know ourselves accepted in our sinfulness that we can laugh at our own pretenses, live with a measure of joy in the midst of our halfheartedness, and risk transformation into a new creation.

Used with permission of John Cobb, Jr.

Structural Changes

by Cecile Andrews

For simplicity to reach its prophetic potential and help create a more compassionate society, not only must individuals change, but structures and institutions must change in such a way as to promote compassion. Cecile Andrews' essay is a good overview of "the politics of simplicity." She summarizes some of today's best and most important ideas and policies to help move us toward a "new society": from developing new standards of economic health (such as the Genuine Progress Indicator rather than the current Gross Domestic Product) to developing new kinds of taxation. Andrews also discusses ways to limit advertising and regulate the power of corporations.

∞

It is a mistake—as so many over-centralized socialist societies have discovered—to try to eliminate money as an incentive. Money is one incen-

> *tive among many, and has its place. But to put no limits on the impulse
> to accumulate money obsessively is as destructive as to place no limits on
> the impulse to commit violence. A viable democratic society needs a ceil-
> ing and a floor with regard to the distribution of wealth and assets.*

—Philip Slater

∞

Creating a New Cultural Vision

We want to create a society in which the quality of life both for people and for the planet are more important than the attainment of wealth....We need to create a belief system that makes the welfare of people and the planet a higher priority than the belief in the right of a few people to get rich. What are the characteristics of an ecocentric society?

Caring

We want to create a society that is caring. Lack of caring is at the root of the people's despair and the planet's devastation. When you care for people and the planet, you won't sell them down the road. We have seen that in order to be caring, we need to experience caring. So we need structural changes that allow people to behave in a caring way.

Security

As long as people feel insecure about their ability to survive, they will stay in the old system of striving for more. As long as people are worried that they'll be left behind, they'll keep on the treadmill of work and spend. We need structural changes that give people security.

Equality

Sometimes, when I'm driving on a freeway and marvel at the fact that we're all out there careening along without crashing into each other, I see our traffic system as a metaphor for life. We're pretty much following the rules, and we usually reach our destination without an accident. The reason? Of course there are the structures of licenses, laws, and punishments, but more important is the fact that on the highway, we're all pretty much equal. If someone runs into me, it will probably hurt him or her as much as it will hurt me.

It's easy to see that inequality hurts people, but perhaps it is the system of hierarchy and dominance that is at the root of our environmental problems—when dominance over people is acceptable, we feel it's acceptable to dominate and exploit the planet.

Participatory Democracy

As Philip Slater shows in his book, *A Dream Deferred*, democracy is the only system that is flexible enough to manage our problems. All theories about change show that change does not succeed unless there is participation by people who are affected. We need structures that encourage participation.

Critical Thinking

People need access to accurate information and a way to talk over what they have learned in order to understand what is in their long-term best interest. We need systems that encourage critical thinking.

Concrete Proposals for a New Society

Finding structures that encourage caring, security, equality, democracy, and critical thinking requires a lot of creativity, talking, and study. I am going to describe some of the [exciting] solutions....This list is not comprehensive and is meant mainly to spark conversations....Giving consideration to some of these ideas is a good start.

Develop a New Standard of Economic Health

In trying to develop a new vision of societal well-being, we need to have a new way to measure what is going on in the economy and society.

The current measurement used by the government and academics, the Gross Domestic Product (which used to be the Gross National Product before multinational organizations made that an inaccurate measure), reflects that we are doing well. Yet 70 percent of the American public feels unhopeful about the future.

Many groups are urging our government to adopt a different way of measuring progress. For instance, some recommend that we adopt a standard called the Genuine Progress Indicator, a measurement that would more accurately reflect reality. Put simply, the GDP measures all money that changes hands. If money is involved, the GDP goes up. That means negative activities as well as positive activities make our economy look like it's growing.

Even though the *Exxon Valdez* oil spill was bad, it boosted the GDP. Crime is a great booster because of a huge crime-prevention industry. Pollution can count twice—once as a part of an industry that produced it and another as part of an industry to clean it up.

If no money changes hands, the activity is ignored: the unpaid work of caring for family and friends or volunteering in community projects isn't counted, so it is not valued.

The GPI, the Genuine Progress Indicator, includes factors ignored by conventional measurements, such as the value of home and community work. Things such as pollution and crime, resource depletion and degradation of the habitat are included as the negatives that they truly are.

Not surprisingly, the GPI shows things are getting worse. It shows an upward curve from the early fifties until about 1970, and then a decline of about 45 percent to the present. What that means is that costs of our economic activities are starting to outweigh the benefits.

If we begin to see things in more realistic terms, we can more easily argue for the following changes.

Develop New Kinds of Taxation

Taxation brings in money to run the government, but it also sets policy. The way we tax affects people's behavior. For instance, when people advocate a "sin" tax, they are trying to discourage things like smoking by making cigarettes very expensive.

Reducing Consumption through Taxation

Although there are a variety of policies that could reduce consumption, some argue that the only way to get people to quit using up resources is to price things out of range through taxation. Thus in Denmark, the tax markup on cars is so high that people buy fewer cars. The taxes that are collected can be used to provide public transportation.

In Europe as a whole, there is a growing movement advocating green taxes or ecological tax reform. Basically, green taxes cut income taxes and payroll taxes and, at the same time, tax activities that create pollution and use up natural resources.

This approach is also popular with the public because it reduces unemployment: by lowering payroll taxes, companies can afford to hire more people. By lowering income taxes, more people can afford to work part time—further helping unemployment by spreading the jobs around.

What we would really be doing with green taxes is reflecting the true costs of production: the costs of pollution and the use of resources. In the long run, someone pays for pollution, and we know who that is.

Limiting Wealth Accumulation

If we are thinking of true well-being and health....we must limit the ability to acquire great wealth.

Economist Juliet Schor, author of *The Overworked American*, advocates a more simple and fair tax system: there should be more exemptions for low-income people and higher taxes for the rich. There should be more taxes on corporations and higher inheritance taxes.

Create Security by Setting a Minimum Level of Support

As long as people have both the possibility of great wealth or the possibility of dire poverty, the desire for more will dominate us. We not only need to set an upper limit on wealth, but a lower limit. Europe is beginning to discuss what it calls a Basic Income Grant (BIG) where everyone would receive a minimum income from the government that would allow them to live modestly. It would allow people to periodically opt out of the labor market to pursue studies, raise children, create their own business, or live as artists.

Ironically, we want to cut the welfare rolls and promote workfare at a time when there just are not enough jobs to go around. In fact, when unemployment drops, the stock market often takes a dive, because the market worries that low unemployment will cause inflation causing interest rates to rise. Perhaps it will be Wall Street who supports a basic income grant.

Because we have so many problems of addiction and mental illness, giving money outright to people might not be possible. However, we can give people the things they need money for in the first place: food to eat, a place to live, and basic medical care. Access to these necessities should be a right.

Provide Work

Few politicians are going to recommend a basic income grant. But if we don't do that, then we had better guarantee people jobs. But is this possible? Our jobs are disappearing as companies continue to automate and transport jobs overseas.

One of the most often-mentioned ways to provide more work is to reduce the work week and spread jobs around. This can be done in a way that both employees and employers benefit.

For instance, some companies find that people will accept a lower salary if their hourly wage goes up. Since productivity tends to rise when people work shorter hours, both the people and the company would benefit: there would be higher productivity for the company and a higher hourly wage for the people.

Juliet Schor found that only 23 percent of adults say that if they had enough income to live comfortably, they would prefer to work full-time. Schor advocates tax policies that would induce employers to offer a variety of options such as trading income for time off, jobsharing, and the upgrading of part-time work. She recommends policies that would prohibit mandatory overtime, policies that would replace overtime pay with comp time (including salaried workers), and policies giving all American workers a guaranteed four week vacation. All of these policies would create more jobs and give overworked Americans a chance to have a full life.

Jeremy Rifkin suggests taxing companies with high profits and giving grants to nonprofit organizations to hire people to expand their work. With this plan, we need not expand the government and we could ensure quality of work by giving grants only to agencies that have proven their effectiveness over the years. This plan would employ more people and attack our social problems at the same time.

Cut Back on Defense Spending

One way to find more money to make these changes is to cut back on defense spending. It not only would generate a great deal of money, but the defense industry is one of the biggest polluters—war is the biggest polluter of all.

Reform Campaign Financing

None of the above will be accomplished until our Congress is freed from its bondage to corporations. Both parties are held hostage by corporate contributions.

Part of election reform is finding ways to increase voter turnout. Some advocate making voting mandatory as it is in Australia, where, if you fail to vote, you are fined. There should be universal registration, which could be done by the post office or the IRS. And voting should be on the weekend.

Create an FDA-Type Commission to Reduce Consumption

Before he died, Erich Fromm wrote a book called *To Have or to Be* in which he grappled with our extreme consumerism. He came up with several very interesting ideas. For instance, he advocated creating a government structure similar to the Food and Drug Administration to encourage what he called "sane consumption." This commission would use a variety of experts such as scientists and sociologists, but would also include theologians, psychologists, and representatives from environmental groups, nonprofits, and social organizations. They would work together to develop a program to reduce consumption and encourage people to consume green products, products that minimize their impact on the earth.

The commission would encourage what is "life-furthering" and discourage what is "life-damaging," developing programs to educate and inspire the public to change. It would think not only in terms of what products and behaviors harm the environment, but what products and behaviors harm people by encouraging passivity, boredom, and destructiveness instead of creativity, participation, and community....

Expand National Service Programs

Related to this could be an expanded national service program, a chance for people to work on solutions to our problems. Jobs would be low paying, but with good benefits, including housing, health care, and educational opportunities. It would be an expanded version of Vista and the Peace Corps, and it could work at educating people about how to live sustainably, helping people to learn to garden organically or develop plans to use fewer household resources.

Continue Efforts Toward Establishing Justice

Although we need new policies, we can't neglect what we have started in this century in trying to bring equity and justice to groups without power like women, people of color, old people, people with handicaps, and gays and lesbians. We must continue to support affirmative action and laws that prevent discrimination.

Transform the Global Economy

Focusing on our country is not enough, though. We can never again ignore the global aspects of change. If we make changes in our country, the corporations will move to another country. As we continue to accept the poverty of the rest of the world, we are laying a foundation for future disaster—either through mass starvation and sickness or war. Organizations such as the World Bank must support projects that benefit the poor people of the world without devastating the environment.

Attacking the Giants

It wouldn't be easy to bring about these changes. You need a mass social movement with people demanding change. There are two things that stand in the way of such a movement: advertising and corporations. Many feel that we cannot reduce consumption unless we put restraints on corporations and the kind and amount of advertising they do.

Reducing Consumption By Limiting Advertising

In making an argument for the reduction of advertising, we must realize that there are more costs to advertising than meet the eye:

- We pay for advertising in higher prices: $150 billion, or almost $600 per person. Ten percent or more of the price of goods is for promotional costs.
- We lose taxes because advertising costs are considered tax-deductible business expenses. Some estimate that the federal government loses up to $35 billion a year.
- Makers of cigarettes and alcoholic beverages spend $5 billion a year on their advertising, while cigarettes and alcohol kill over 500,000 people each year. Drinking causes traffic fatalities and plays a direct role in violence, particularly domestic violence.
- Advertising supports violence on television, with hundreds of studies linking television violence to violence in real life.
- Advertising undermines parental control as it is increasingly directed toward kids. Schools are one of the latest territories to be invaded by commercialism....
- Freedom of the press is undermined. The press is not free to say what it wants for fear of advertising being withdrawn. Advertisers threaten to pull out their money when there are stories and programs that they don't like....
- With the takeover of news networks by entertainment corporations such as Disney, the news gets watered down or programs censored. Almost 90 percent of newspaper editors said, in a 1992 Marquette University study, that advertisers had tried to influence story content, and 37 percent said the newspapers had complied. In another study, half of the business editors surveyed said that advertising pressure had influenced their editorials....
- Our right to privacy is being undermined. Not only is our privacy invaded by the telemarketers' annoying calls at dinner, marketers have volumes of information on all of us....

In their book, *Marketing Madness*, Michael Jacobson and Laurie Mazur recommend several steps we could take:

- Tax advertising and use the money for consumer information programs such as anti-smoking campaigns.
- Stop advertising aimed at children. (Several European countries have banned TV and radio advertising directed at children.)

- Expand restrictions on alcohol and tobacco advertising. (Canada has banned all cigarette advertising in all media.)
- Restrict telemarketing and direct mail. (Great Britain forbids companies to rent or exchange customer lists unless the customer is told prior to purchasing a product.)
- Expand restrictions on billboards. (This could be done on highways financed with federal funds.)
- Reduce the volume of advertising. (Make it more expensive by raising taxes on it, set time limits on the airwaves, and revitalize the Federal Trade Commission so that it could do its job.)
- Expand Public Broadcasting. (Compared to the United States, Japan spends eighteen times as much per person, Canada spends thirty-two times as much, and Great Britain thirty-eight times as much. Ralph Nader has called for laws that would require all stations to give an hour of prime time daily to community groups.)

Of course, corporations would fight all of this, first by claiming that any curbs would inhibit freedom of speech. But we have always limited speech whenever the damages outweigh the benefits; and, in this case, the damage done through the promotion of a consumerist lifestyle is one of the greatest, and most threatening, we have ever faced.

But if we are going to touch advertising, we are going to have to find a way to regulate and reform corporations.

Regulate Corporations

Corporations bring together all the elements of greed that I described earlier. They are run by hierarchy and competition and their goal is to get you to consume by manipulating you with advertising. They are devoted to greed. There is no shilly-shallying; it is only the bottom line that concerns them. This is the primary institution responsible for people's despair, for the destruction of the planet....

Jerry Mander, in his book, *In The Absence of the Sacred*, portrays the way corporations have reached into all corners of our lives:

- With the exception of the government, corporations are the largest landowners in the United States. They are the major financial backers of electoral campaigns, and the major lobbyists for laws that benefit corporate goals.
- ...The basic rule of corporate operation is that it must produce income and show a profit over time. Among publicly held companies there is another basic rule: it must make *a lot* of money. Nothing else counts—the welfare of people and the planet are nothing.

Finally, though, people are beginning to feel that corporate domination isn't fair. Some people fight back by attending shareholder meetings to try to influence corporate policies, but persistent critics of corporate policy have often been faced with legal action. Schor proposes a Corporate Democracy Act that would require corporations to have boards filled with representatives of various stakeholder groups as well as stockholders. In other words, the boards of directors would have to represent the interests of people in general instead of just people who make money from the company.

Ensure Public Participation

To bring about policy changes, we need public participation. We must find ways to help people band together to work for change. We need simplicity circles. We need to support unions and democratically controlled enterprises such as consumer cooperatives, employee-owned firms, and community-owned businesses.

Excerpt from "Structural Changes" as submitted from *The Circle of Simplicity* by Cecile Andrews. Copyright © 1997 by Cecile Andrews. Reprinted by permission of HarperCollins Publishers, Inc.

The Lifestyle of Christian Faithfulness

by William Gibson

Born in Alton, Illinois in 1921, William Gibson has always been interested in the issues of social and economic justice. In the early 1970s, Gibson began to see that justice issues were inseparable from ecological concerns. Since then, he has been one of the Church's leading voices for eco-justice. An ordained Presbyterian minister, Gibson graduated from Princeton Theological Seminary and later from Union Theological Seminary with a Ph.D. in Christian Ethics. In 1974 he became the Founding Director of Cornell University's Eco-Justice Project.

Gibson and his wife, Judy, have three children and four grandchildren. They enjoy hiking and swimming in New York's state parks. In recent years Gibson has served on various working groups of the National Council of Churches, the World Council of Churches, and the Presbyterian Church (USA). He was the principal author of an excellent study book, *Keeping and Healing the Creation*, published by the Presbyterian Eco-Justice Task Force.

Gibson's essay was written over twenty years ago—his words are still prophetic today. He maintains that a Christian lifestyle begins with "sharing the servanthood of Jesus and standing…with the poor and all the victims of cruelty and injustice. Faith, therefore, begins with repentance, the acceptance of judgment, the confession that one has denied the inescapable claim of every neighbor to be respected and loved. If we are comfortable and privileged, we confess that we are numbered with the oppressors."

These are hard words. For in order for everyone to enjoy "enough of the things that are needed for a reasonably secure and fulfilling life"—sufficiency—many Americans would need to make radical lifestyle changes. Gibson recognizes that individual cutbacks in consumption, however, will do little to help the poor "attain sufficiency unless they are synchronized with political activities directed toward redistribution." He discusses the variety of ways Christians might be called to political activity as a pathway to justice. Gibson then returns to the theme of how community can satisfy the void we often attempt to fill with consumption.

∞

Sufficiency as the Norm of Justice

…In the modern industrial world, people have been beguiled into the assumption that unlimited economic growth makes justice cheap. The hard questions about justice have been finessed. In a growth economy the rich get richer still; but at the same time, if the growth rate is high enough, the poor (or some of them anyway) climb slowly out of poverty. The inequality may be huge, but this is not supposed to matter because there will be prosperity enough to include everybody, finally, in some semblance of the "good life." According to capitalist ideology, the public good is furthered by the competitive pursuit of private gain; justice is the by-product of the pursuit of self-interest. Even though monopolistic control over many sectors of the economy has now displaced competition, it is still held that the giant corporations had better not be curbed severely. Only their expansion can keep the economy booming.

Today's massive facts concerning hunger, poverty and ecological limits have discredited the myth that powerful private interests dedicated to growth automatically serve the public good… Suddenly Christians find themselves thrown back upon a much earlier assumption, one that permeates the entire biblical story: justice requires sharing, particularly with the alien, the fatherless, the widow, the innocent, the needy, the afflicted.[25] And the attempt to act on that assumption today means the construction of an economic system, domestically and globally, in which equitable distribution is both achievable and sustainable.

A just and sustainable future for the entire world requires a new norm, the norm of *sufficiency*. Sufficiency must become the controlling consideration for lifestyles, for systems, and for synchronizing lifestyle changes with systemic changes. This norm is required for the just distribution of resources and material goods that are actually or potentially in short supply. The aim of sufficiency is that everyone shall have enough of the things that are needed for a reasonably secure and fulfilling life.

It cannot be our task here to offer an extensive analysis of what sufficiency includes. We are concerned first about basic needs: pure water, food and nutrition, clothing, shelter, health care, literacy and some kind of meaningful work to do. Beyond the absolute necessities, sufficiency is an elastic concept; no definition will hold for all times and places. Sufficiency is bound to be relative to what is available and to a variety of cultural and social considerations and psychological traits that enter into people's assessments of what is sufficient. Individuals do not have identical requirements and likings in order to be happy. But what any one person may include in the idea of what is sufficient for himself or herself is necessarily limited by the ideas of others about their sufficiency and the recognition that some *minimal sufficiency for everyone takes precedence*—whenever a choice is necessary—*over anyone's right to enjoy a surplus.*

There is a vast amount of insufficiency (or misery!) that can be recognized at once, just as there is a vast amount of luxury and waste that obviously goes far beyond the bounds of any reasonable sufficiency. Between the extremes is a large area where people may disagree about sufficiency, where further reflection is required, where judgments change with circumstances and where people must make decisions on the basis of their particular understandings and values. Despite the impreciseness of the concept, there is no doubt that *a generally accepted norm of sufficiency would radically change the lifestyle of most Americans.*

For the poor (those whose poverty is misery), the achievement of sufficiency would mean having more. The present lifestyle of the poor is a compulsory misery from which they cannot escape, except through adequately paid employment or, if they are not able to work, a social security system that provides for an income at a level of simplicity that is higher than mere misery. There are, to be sure, individuals who by dint of effort may rise out of poverty; but that does not alter that fact that the existing system does not even promise full employment, except through a rate of economic growth that has never been achieved (except in wartime) and cannot be sustained. The norm of sufficiency requires, not an acquiescence in residual poverty, but the alteration of the present system.

The poverty classification blends into another classification that might be called near-poverty. If we broaden this a little, it includes a great many hard-working "middle Americans" who feel that they are just barely making ends meet and who would bitterly resent any suggestion that they had more than enough. We may exercise restraint in judging their lifestyle and yet hope that they will share in the redefinition of the consumption levels that can be considered desirable in the present circumstances of the world. The unhappiness often felt by persons of limited incomes is their sense that they have failed to meet the standards of success held by society and by themselves. They are not affluent but wish they were. They want far more of the abundance displayed in the television commercials. They are saddled with debt because they have succumbed too frequently to the lure of the ads. For them the norm of sufficiency would mean less emulation of the rich, together with a new political maturity directed toward limiting the wealth and power of those who have too much.

Even though we cannot draw the line precisely at the point where sufficiency ends and excess consumption starts, a standard appropriate to the present world situation would insist that the majority of Americans consume far too much. The prevailing lifestyle represents an addiction to consumerism—a wasteful appropriation of material goods beyond any legitimate need. The overconsumers need a downward redefinition of their lifestyle in the direction of sufficiency. Such a redefinition is absolutely essential to any serious strategy for enabling the poor to redefine their lifestyles upward in the direction of sufficiency.

It is not just a matter of restricting the superrich. The danger is that most people will conclude too quickly that their lifestyle does not exceed sufficiency... Faithfulness for middle-class people must now entail a thorough and even perhaps a wrenching reassessment of the things they can justify as *needs*. More often than not, this will mean a reduction of their *material* standard of living.

Any lifestyle appropriate to Christian faithfulness entails a voluntary restraint upon consumption. Under such restraint consumption ceases to be simply a matter of what can be afforded. The person with $85,000 per year has no more license to buy material goods beyond the standard of sufficiency than if she or he made only half as much.

But this is not to suggest that people should just hang on to their money. We should seek to use our money in ways that have a benign impact on the environment and do not diminish the resources that cannot be renewed. Money not spent on gasoline or new appliances or grain-fed beef can be used for many sorts of recreational, cultural and educational activities. And it can be given away—to hunger relief, the self-development projects of the poor, citizens' advocacy organizations, political campaigns or simply to some struggling friends whose burden one wants to share.

On the whole, however, the cutbacks in consumption by individuals and families will do little to enable the poor to attain sufficiency unless they are *synchronized with political activities directed toward redistribution*. We cannot expect redistribution ever to be achieved simply through voluntary lifestyle changes.

What the norm of sufficiency may mean for Christians is surely more radical than what it can be expected to mean as an emerging norm for a pluralistic society. Nevertheless, some general movement toward acceptance of a reduced material consumption as sufficient is essential to a strategy for justice. This will not come without a new level of popular understanding of the realities of the world situation, together with a new vision of the just and sustainable future. Understanding and vision by themselves, however, will not establish the norm. Also necessary are *pressures*: the pressures of events and of hard economic realities that are certain to come, but also the pressures of political organization and activity mobilized in behalf of distributive justice. The needed downward redefinition of the lifestyle of the rich and the merely comfortable or wasteful will be a compulsory redefinition, achieved by the political power of the poor, the near-poor and all those who care about the just and sustainable future enough to act with those who lack sufficiency rather than with those who cling to an unjustifiable material abundance.

We are not insisting that everybody proceed by doing the most obvious political things—informing oneself about issues and candidates, voting, communicating opinion to public officials, participating in the organizational and campaign work of political parties, running for office and so on. Not everyone feels called to respond in these ways to the need for social change. Some believe that the propensity of the present political system to perpetuate the existing imbalance of economic power is so irreversible that the only honest political statement they can make at this time includes their nonparticipation in, and thereby their testimony against, the "regular" political process. Even with a limited participation in it, some feel that there is more political significance in the aspects of their lifestyle that express their solidarity with the poor, including their adoption of voluntary poverty. Moreover, a person whose involvement in the political process is extensive should not overlook the political significance of his or her total lifestyle. To opt out of consumerism, especially as this may tie in increasingly with other people's efforts to do the same, subverts a system that depends upon a mass addiction to excessive consumption.

We must acknowledge, also, the ambiguity of many of the specific political goals that may be worthy of support. Will the policies we advocate really change things for the better or only provide palliatives to dampen the discontent of those who are exploited, while leaving unjust power arrangements intact?

Men and women of faith often disagree on their responses to such dilemmas. The political component of a faithful lifestyle, however, cannot be eliminated. To try to do nothing politically is to acquiesce in the status quo. Faithfulness requires us to seek appropriate forms of resistance to injustice, as well as to take advantage of the opportunities we are able to perceive for making social arrangements serve human needs. Paul Tillich reminds us that the resources of religious faith enable people "to give themselves with an absolute seriousness and a complete devotion to an aim that in itself is fragmentary and ambiguous"—to work "with unrestricted devotion to the good and the true," empowered by a realism that is not pessimism and a hope that is not utopian.[26]

The norm of sufficiency pushes us to deal with the question of whether faithfulness requires us simply to help the poor or actually to become poor. Surely it is hypocritical for privileged people to speak of solidarity with the poor and not move in the direction of poverty, by sharing resources with them and giving resources to them or to projects that will help them. Still, the intent of love, the ultimate standard, is that the poor shall be less poor, that they shall have enough.

For some, the best expression of self-giving love may lie more in working for systemic change than in face-to-face alleviation of misery. This may be the most demanding kind of service, requiring study, discipline, planning, organization and the courage to persist in spite of ambiguity. Simply to give away one's goods and become poor may leave the established order not only intact but unthreatened. Seriously to persist in the struggle for justice, however, may arouse the wrath of those who have a vested interest in inequity and who may inflict poverty and defeat on those who try to mobilize against them. Faithfulness thus means a response in love to the need of the poor, but that response may take a variety of forms. Because the poor must have enough, there is an early limit to the extent to which anyone can hold on to more than enough. And whether or not one decides to become poor, in fact, the *risk* of poverty is surely present.

In the context of a world in which poverty is more massive in absolute numbers than ever before and in which the earth's limits must finally be respected, there can be no *minimum* levels of sufficiency unless we find ways to set *maximums* upon incomes and wealth. There is urgent need at this juncture for clarification of the policy goals that can bring minimums and maximums into operation.

The overriding concern of policy must be for the basic needs of all to be met—in a way that is ecologically sustainable. Everything that we say about sufficiency of consumption has immediate implications for production, distribution and recycling.[27] These must be geared to need, that is, toward making enough available to all. The urgent question for economists, business people, workers, political scientists and politicians is how to make need—and the solidarity of human beings in their need—the driving force of economic activity. Growth and profit are not to be ends in themselves, but instruments for the continuing provision of useful and enjoyable goods and services to all. A policy of full employment must be one of putting people to work at meaningful jobs that need to be done. Centralized planning and equitable policies of taxation, social security and resource allocation have to be combined with the encouragement of a great deal of regionalization—local initiatives, democratic organization of small-scale industry and the development of more appropriate technologies that are resource-conservative, respectful of the natural environment and designed to extend and enhance the labor of people rather than to replace it with machines.

We can do no more now than offer those brief suggestions regarding the policies that concerned citizens may be called to clarify, advocate and implement. Despite all the difficulties and ambiguities, the politics of achieving a just and sustainable future belongs to a faithful lifestyle. If the policies that emerge from such a politics should really begin to threaten the present distribution of power, the opposition to them would be fierce and determined, making the price of a faithful lifestyle very high indeed.

Abundance as Community

"I came," said Jesus, "that they may have life, and have it abundantly." [28]

So far the main features of lifestyle change propounded in this paper may appear either negative or heroic. On the one hand, we have insisted that serious attention to the reduction of consumption is mandated by justice. On the other hand, we have noted that this will do little good unless synchronized with political advocacy and action that will be both difficult and costly.

If there were nothing more to say, it perhaps would have been futile to say this much. The pressures and the imperatives, however, are rather marvelously reinforced by the prospect and the promise of a more abundant life. To be sure, for the most mature men and women of faith, even deprivation and suffering can be subsumed under the joy of faithfulness. But all is not grim and hard, and most of us do not have to take ourselves so seriously as to imagine a hero's role just yet.

The shift away from the patterns of consumerism, if that were all, would leave no substitute way of meeting our psychological and spiritual needs for self-esteem and approval. But the overconsumptive style of life is a phony way to meet such needs. Material success and the abundance of possessions do not really measure our worth as human beings. The status that we think we get from conformity to the established patterns of affluence is a poor substitute indeed for the affirmation of ourselves that would come in authentic relationships with our fellow human creatures.

Consumerism itself is the substitute, a most unsatisfactory, though addictive, substitute for that which makes human life meaningful and fulfilling—loving, caring relationships with one another, in which we accept and affirm our dependence on one another, and all the ways in which we may free each other for everything true and good and creative that each of us has in himself or herself to be or to become. In short, consumerism is a substitute for *community*.

The abundance to which Jesus pointed was explicitly not the abundance of possessions.[29] It was the abundance of the restored relationship, the God-relationship. It was the freedom to enjoy the community—the giving-and-receiving relationship with one another—for which we were created.

Because consumerism is a phony substitute for, and therefore a barrier to, community, a reaffirmation of community helps to free us from consumerism, just as a reduction of consumption helps to free us for community. Here then is the third salient feature of lifestyle as faithfulness. In addition to a consumption level that tends toward sufficiency and a political involvement for the sake of a more just distribution of the goods that people need, *a faithful lifestyle entails the affirmation of community and the adoption of patterns of living whereby community may be nurtured and enjoyed*.

For persons seeking seriously to live in a style appropriate to Christian faith and true human selfhood, the all-important step is to enter into a community of support. This may be a small group of people who are consciously seeking to be a support community and to work together regularly on the questions of lifestyle change. In any case, one needs to be related to caring persons; persons with whom he or she can enjoy being and doing things; persons who share a concern to see, accept and enjoy the changes of lifestyle appropriate to their faith and to their world.

The members of the support community, then, can help each other break their long-established, culturally-ingrained habits of consumption: to move beyond talk to really not turning in the old car after the accustomed amount of use, really not redecorating the living room just because it would be nice and can be afforded, really giving up the long-distance luxury vacation for something more modest and closer to home.[30] They can work together on the criteria of responsible spending. They can reinforce each other's efforts to practice a conservation ethic: demanding durable products, repairing appliances instead of replacing them, using car pools and public transportation, recycling everything they can and growing their own food by organic methods.

The members of the community can help each other with decisions on the making and using of money. They may find that they can enjoy a whole new order of magnitude in giving to persons and causes that need support.

Considerations about using money may open up serious personal questions about making money. How appropriate is a person's work to the emergence of a just and sustainable future for the world? Does it perpetuate the problems of poverty, inequality and ecological peril or contribute to their solution? Is it geared to meeting genuine human needs, perhaps even to making systems operate equitably; or are such considerations overwhelmed by the drive for private gain?

The members of the community can explore the possibilities for sharing in their own life together. They may find that they have various kinds of equipment that they can share—lawn mowers, power tools, ladders, rototillers. They may be able to share skills as well—organizational, technical, mechanical, culinary. And they may work together on matters of political advocacy, seeking to translate to the larger society the values of cooperation and solidarity that they have found in their small community, engaging together in the critical thinking that must enter into policy positions and suffering together the attacks of those whose vested interests they may threaten.

We have touched on six distinguishable but related activities in which the community engages, or at least thinks through, together: *consuming, conserving, giving, working, sharing and advocating.* And there is another: *playing*—doing some things just for sheer enjoyment, just because people are and want to be a community, just because their life together is worth celebrating.

The community, seeking a faithful and responsive lifestyle for each member and the whole, is sensitive to the peril of wealth. It moves in the direction of a simpler life. Coming gradually to terms with the meaning of sufficiency for themselves, the members dare to take some risks for the sake of sufficiency for all the members of the one global community. In a world full of greed, apathy and pain, they can still celebrate the love of God and the gift of life. Most of what they do is neither dramatic nor momentous: just the enjoyment of life in relationships of openness and caring and small new steps taken as though the just and sustainable future that they envision had begun. By anticipating that future, they hasten it.

Does such a community exist? We suspect it does. We are sure it could, in many places simultaneously. That, we believe, would make a difference.

From "The Lifestyle of Christian Faithfulness," parts 5 and 6, by William E. Gibson in *Beyond Survival: Bread and Justice in Christian Perspective*, edited by Dieter T. Hessel. Copyright 1977 by Friendship Press. Used with permission.

Simplicity Is Nothing New: A Brief Historical Overview

As a myth of national purpose and as a program for individual conduct, the simple life...has, in a sense, served as the nation's conscience, reminding Americans of what the founders had hoped they would be and thereby providing a vivifying counterpoint to the excesses of materialist individualism.

—*David Shi*

One remarkable feature of the devotional masters is the incredible sense of uniform witness in the midst of such diverse personalities...and the necessity of Christian simplicity is one of their most consistent themes.

—*Richard Foster*

Introduction to The Politics of Simplicity

by Jerome Segal

Dr. Segal is a research scholar at the University of Maryland's Institute for Philosophy and Public Policy. Segal's ideas are more fully developed in his new book, *Graceful Simplicity: Towards a Philosophy and Politics of Simple Living*, published by Henry Holt.

The following essay, excerpted from a longer article, provides a brief historical overview pointing out that simple living has always been part of American cultural history: from the Quakers, through the transcendentalists, to its current popularity. Dr. Segal summarizes some of the primary themes appearing in Dr. David Shi's *The Simple Life*, a well-written, detailed book on the history of simplicity in American culture.

∞

The idea of simple living has always been part of the American psyche—sometimes central, sometimes peripheral. Today it once again resonates strongly throughout our popular culture. Newspapers carry full-page features on personal downsizing, and books on how to live well with less sell hundreds of thousands of copies. A Nexus search for articles on simple living reveals more than 50 entries in just the last two months. Moreover, the interest comes from all parts of society, not just among people on the counter-cultural fringes. For instance, *Working Woman*, an upscale magazine for the career-minded, with a circulation of close to a million, devoted [an entire] issue to how to create a simpler life. There's a Simple Living Network on the Internet, several newsletters, and a host of itinerant lecturers, taped courses, and workshops

...Simple living is not some 1990s fad. Nor is it the product of "foreign" ideologies. David Shi's book *The Simple Life: Plain Thinking and High Living in American Culture* (Oxford, 1985), is must reading for those seeking historical grounding. From the earliest days of the American experience, advocates of simple living have challenged consumerism and materialism, although simple living, or "plain living," as it was sometimes called, has meant different things to different groups.

Puritan simplicity focused on religious devotion, a lack of ostentation, and plenty of hard work. It was not a leisure expansion movement. Nor was simple living a matter of individual choice for Puritans; sumptuary laws restricted consumption display, and economic life was regulated to limit the role of greed in human affairs.

In the worldview of the Quakers, simple living was modified somewhat. The sumptuary laws, which to some extent were designed to prevent those in the lower classes from affecting the manners of those above them, came to apply to all members of the community, and John Woolman, a leading Quaker in the mid-1700s, decried excessively lengthy workdays, and cautioned employers not to work others too hard. Indeed, Woolman made a powerful analytic connection in arguing that the institution of slavery emerged from a wrongheaded pursuit of a life of ease and luxury. Here, perhaps, we find the origins of a radical politics of plain living—the belief that if people adopted the simple life, all of society would be transformed.

In the mid-1700s, republican simplicity emerged. Its ideal was not the simple life of Jesus, an image that inspired many Christian advocates of plain living, but the classical writers Cicero, Tacitus, and Plutarch. Central figures of the revolutionary period, in particular Samuel Adams, were deeply concerned about the relationship between our political health and the individual pursuit of luxury. The rebirth of democracy in the world brought with it an interest in the Greek and Roman experiments, and why they disappeared. There was a concern (as there is today) with the virtue of office-holders. Genuine democracy seemed incompatible with too great a preoccupation with getting rich. There was great fear of the corrupting influences of unbridled commercialism. When the colonists boycotted British goods, it was not just a tactic of the independence movement; they viewed Britain as The Great Satan, exporting the corruptions of capitalism.

John Adams and Thomas Jefferson corresponded about what were the bounds of the possible with respect to building a non-materialist society. Jefferson emphasized civic virtue and looked to public policy, in particular state-supported schools and values education. Adams viewed this as unrealistically "undertaking to build a new universe." He himself feared economic growth, and argued for preventing both extreme poverty and extravagant riches.

In the mid-1800s, the transcendentalist writers such as Emerson and Thoreau envisioned a new form of simple living. While the Puritans saw the virtues in opposition to the passions, the transcendentalists had a different vision. On one end of the spectrum, this period prefigured the 1960s, with communes, vegetarianism, nudism, and concern for animal rights. The advocates of transcendental simplicity reversed the Puritan emphasis on work. For Thoreau, one of the chief reasons for lowering consumption levels was that it allowed for greater leisure to do the better things in life—not religious or civic engagement, but the life of the mind, of art, literature, poetry, philosophy, and an almost reverential engagement with nature. In the main, the project of transforming society was put aside in favor of the experiential and experimental communities seeking the simple life for themselves.

Interest in simple living was harder to find in the post-Civil War period, but it re-emerged strong toward the turn of the century. There was a reaction against materialism, individualism, and the hectic pace of urban life. In those days, it was the *Ladies Home Journal* that led the charge against the dominant materialist ethos. Under a crusading editor, Edward Bok, the magazine served as a guide for those in the middle class seeking simplicity; by 1910, it had a circulation of close to 2 million, making it the largest selling magazine in the world. In this period there emerged a movement of aesthetic simplicity, centered around designers William Morris and Gustav Stickley, and giving rise to so-called "mission" furniture, much sought by antique dealers today.

One dimension of the renewed interest in simple living was a country life movement concerned with using modem technology to improve life for the small farmer and to keep young people on the farm. Later, in 1933, the Department of the Interior created a Division of Subsistence Homesteads to resettle the urban and rural poor in planned communities based on "handicrafts, community activities, closer relationships, and cooperative enterprises." About 100 such communities were established, most of them failing in their grand design to replace individualism with "mutualism."

After World War II, as after the First, the Civil War, and the Revolution, there was a surge in consumption, and simple living receded into the background. But again, in the 1960s, there was a critique of the affluent lifestyle and a renewed interest in plain living. In the 1970s, with the energy crisis, the focus on plain living merged with a growing concern with the environment. The notion of "voluntary simplicity" emerged; the *Whole Earth Catalogue*, a how-to guide to a simpler, environmentally conscious life, sold briskly, and President Jimmy Carter invited E.F. Schumacher, author of *Small is Beautiful*, to the White House.

In his now-infamous 'malaise' speech, Carter criticized the country, decrying that "we worship self-indulgence and consumption. Human identity is no longer defined by what one does but by what one owns." He called for a new cohesive, spiritually rich Commonwealth. The speech, viewed by most Americans as overly moralistic and pessimistic, caused Carter's popularity to plummet. Then came the Reagan and Bush years, during which acquisitiveness and material success, rather than simplicity, were the ideal...

Reprinted From *Tikkun Magazine*, a bi-monthly Jewish critique of politics, culture, and society. Information and subscriptions are available from Tikkun, 26 Fell Street, San Francisco, California 94102. Excerpted from Volume 11, no. 4.

Epilogue from The Simple Life
by David Shi

Born in Atlanta, Georgia, David Shi graduated magna cum laude
from Furman University where he was also named to the All-
South Carolina Football Team. He subsequently earned a masters
and doctorate from the University of Virginia; Dr. Shi currently
serves as President of Furman University in South Carolina. In
addition to *The Simple Life*, his published work includes the book
In Search of the Simple Life: American Voices, Past and Present (1986).
Shi has two children and lives in South Carolina with his wife.
They attend First Baptist Church in Greenville, South Carolina.

Shi's book *The Simple Life* provides a wonderfully-written and
detailed history of simplicity in American culture. Its epilogue
brings a historical perspective to this collection of essays and raises
a number of important questions: Will the simple life remain a
minority concern? Can current ecological and social crises serve as
sufficient motivation to move us toward a more simple, compassionate lifestyle? Dr. Shi also includes a thoughtful discussion of
the ethic's historical strengths and weaknesses.

∞

The quick transition from Jimmy Carter's litany of limits to Ronald Reagan's
promise of boundlessness provides a striking demonstration that Americans remain
ambivalent about the meaning of the good life, as they have since the seventeenth
century. From colonial days, the image of America as a spiritual commonwealth
and a republic of virtue has survived alongside the more tantalizing vision of
America as a cornucopia of economic opportunities and consumer delights. Yet the
simple life as an enduring societal norm has never been realized. Espoused initially
as a communal ethic, for all to embrace, it has in fact garnered only a relatively
few serious adherents over the years. "Simplicity," observed the Quaker reformer
Richard Gregg in 1936, "seems to be a foible of saints and occasional geniuses, but
not something for the rest of us." [31]

Again and again, Americans have espoused the merits of simple living, only
to become enmeshed in its opposite. People have found it devilishly hard to limit
their desires to their needs so as to devote most of their attention to "higher" activities. This should not surprise us. Socrates pointed out centuries ago that "many
people will not be satisfied with the simpler way of life. They will be for adding
sofas, and tables, and other furniture; also dainties, and perfumes, and incense, and
courtesans and cakes." He knew that all notions of moral excellence and spiritual

commitment are by their very nature elitist, since few can live up to their dictates for long. Thoreau likewise noted that simplicity was for the few rather than for the many. He recognized at the beginning of *Walden* that the simple life he described would have little appeal to "those who find their encouragement and inspiration in precisely the present condition of things, and cherish it with the fondness and enthusiasm of lovers." Many Americans have not wanted to lead simple lives, and not wanting to is the best reason for not doing so.[32]

Though a failure as a societal ethic, simplicity has nevertheless exercised a powerful influence on the complex patterns of American culture. As a myth of national purpose and as a program for individual conduct, the simple life has been a perennial dream and a rhetorical challenge, displaying an indestructible vitality even in the face of repeated defeats. It has, in a sense, served as the nation's conscience, reminding Americans of what the founders had hoped they would be and thereby providing a vivifying counterpoint to the excesses of materialist individualism. During periods of martial, economic, or cultural crisis, it has been successfully invoked by statesmen, ministers, and reformers to help revitalize public virtue and stay the contagion of greed and indifference. The genuine sacrifices on the part of citizens during the two world wars and the oil embargo demonstrated the way in which simplicity has provided an emergency reservoir of moral purpose during times of crisis.

Likewise, the diverse exemplars of simple living—Woolman, Emerson, Thoreau, Burroughs, Muir, Bok, the Borsodis and the Nearings, as well as many others—proved that simplicity could be more than a hollow sentiment or a temporary expedient; it could be a living creed. Aspiring, despairing, yet persistently striving to elevate the nation's priorities, they dignified the ideal and invested it with relevance by practicing its tenets and by displaying an enlivening sense of wonder and an ennobling sense of purpose. As Emerson wrote in referring to the Transcendentalists, they served as "collectors of the heavenly spark, with power to convey the electricity to others." The historical prophets of simple living similarly provided through their lives and their dreams a wellspring of inspiration, a living legacy of an heroic conception of life that continues to move us. That they have represented a distinct minority does not detract from their significance. "It is not important," Thoreau recognized in *Civil Disobedience*, "that many be as good as you, as that there should be some absolute goodness somewhere." [33]

Today, thanks in large measure to models of simple goodness such as John Woolman and John Burroughs, most varieties of simple living persevere. The ideal may not move the millions, but it still seizes and nourishes ethically sensitive imaginations. Across the country, Amish, Mennonite, and Hutterite communities sustain a pietistic rural simplicity reminiscent of the early colonial settlements. Quakers and Christians of all denominations continue to bear witness to the power of Jesus's example by combining simplicity and service into a spiritual ethic of conscience. At the same time, thousands practice the homesteading ideal popularized by the

Nearings, and poetic farmers such as Wendell Berry and Donald Hall revitalize the romantic naturalism and rural simplicity of Thoreau and Burroughs. At the other end of the spectrum, prominent conservative spokesman George Will professes an eighteenth-century philosophy of living based upon the patrician simplicity and civic humanism of a John Adams. And, in cities and suburbs, citizens of various political persuasions participate in cooperatives, encourage conscientious consumption, promote the conservation of natural resources, and seek greater self-reliance through mutual aid and home production. That the simple life has survived in such various forms testifies to the continuing attraction of its basic premise. It *can* be a good life. And it is this factor above all that explains its durability.

What does the future hold? As a rule historians should bypass the enticing briar-patch of cultural prophecy, but in this case, past experience does provide a reliable indicator of future behavior. Undoubtedly, the simple life will persist both as an enduring myth and as an actual way of living. There will always be Americans who prefer the pristine pursuit of goodness over the mere pursuit of goods. For simplicity to experience continued vitality, however, its advocates must learn from the ethic's historical strengths and weaknesses.

The weaknesses seem clear. Proponents of the simple life have frequently been overly nostalgic about the quality of life in olden times, narrowly antiurban in outlook, and too disdainful of the benefits of prosperity and technology. "We have heard nothing but despair and seen nothing but progress," said the nineteenth-century English historian Thomas Macaulay, and his sentiment applies equally well to much of the cultural criticism in the United States. Because Americans have been so burdened by a peculiar sense of providentially assigned obligation, the despair felt by moralists in the face of the nation's material progress has been even more pronounced than that of their English and European counterparts. Perhaps it has been more warranted, as well, but too often the critics of American materialism have failed to give adequate recognition to the benefits of modern civilization and economic well-being.

After all, most of the "high thinking" of this century has been facilitated by prosperity. The expansion of universities, libraries, and research centers, the proliferation of learned publications, the democratization of the fine arts, and the ever-widening impact of philanthropic organizations—all of these developments have been supported by the rising pool of national wealth. This is no mean achievement. "A creative economy," Emerson once wrote, can be "the fuel of magnificence." The radical critics of capitalism and promoters of spartan rusticity among the advocates of the simple life would be well advised to acknowledge that material progress and urban life can frequently be compatible with spiritual, moral, or intellectual concerns. As Lewis Mumford, one of the sanest of all the simplifiers, stressed in *The Conduct of Life*: "It is not enough to say, as Rousseau once did, that one has only to reverse all the current practices to be right... If our new philosophy is well-grounded we shall not merely react against the 'air-conditioned nightmare' of our present culture; we shall also carry into the future many elements of quality that this culture actually embraces." [34]

That the practices and prejudices of those advocating the simple life have occasionally been a sorry parody of their principles has also served to diminish the appeal of the simple life. Small can be both silly and bizarre. The lethal fanaticism of the Jonestown settlers and other apocalyptic survivalist groups that have fled the cities and taken up primitive communal living in the countryside reveals the way in which simplicity can be taken to destructive extremes. Moreover, too many advocates have pursued simplicity as a faddish impulse rather than as a sincere discipline. Stylish rusticity has always been quite fashionable among many affluent Americans, but only rarely has it been accompanied by a simplicity in the soul.

Cynics, however, are too often eager to dismiss the significance of simplicity because of the perversities and hypocrisies of some of its proponents. This is unfortunate, for in doing so they ignore the ethic's deep-seated spiritual appeal and the numerous examples of simple living constructively applied in the American experience. The simple life has shared the beauty of every other soaring ideal: the beauty of elevating human aspirations beyond the material and mundane and establishing a standard of conduct worthy of our effort. When the skeptics have had their say, the fact remains that there have been many who have demonstrated that enlightened self-restraint can provide a sensible approach to living that can be fruitfully applied in any era.

If this study has a moral, then, it is that the simple life, though destined to be a minority ethic, can nevertheless be more than an anachronism or an eccentricity. Although it has been most evident during times of national emergency, it requires neither an energy crisis nor a national calamity to make it appealing. What meaningful simple living does require is a person willing it for himself. Attempts to impose simple living have been notoriously ephemeral in their effects. For simplicity to be both fulfilling and sustaining, one must choose it, or, as the Puritans might have said, one must be chosen for it. "Tis a gift to be simple," sang the Shakers, and the lyric still rings true.

If the decision to live a simple life is fundamentally a personal matter, then so, too, is the nature and degree of simplification. There is no cosmic guidebook to follow. Although some prominent enthusiasts have verged on asceticism or primitivism, they have been the exception rather than the rule. Simplicity in its essence demands neither a vow of poverty nor a life of rural homesteading. As an ethic of self-conscious material moderation, it can be practiced in cities and suburbs, townhouses and condominiums. It requires neither a log cabin nor a hairshirt but a deliberate ordering of priorities so as to distinguish between the necessary and superfluous, useful and wasteful, beautiful and vulgar.

Still, it is impossible to specify that this or that possession or activity is universally expendable. Simplicity is more aesthetic than ascetic in its approach to good living. Money or possessions or activities themselves do not corrupt simplicity, but the love of money, the craving for possessions, and the prison of activities do. Knowing the difference between personal trappings and personal traps, therefore, is the key to mastering the fine art of simple living. One of Gandhi's American friends once confessed to the Indian leader that it was easy and liberating for him to discard most of the superfluous clutter in his life and his household, but he could not part with his large collection of books. "Then don't give them up," Gandhi replied. "As long as you derive inner help and comfort from anything, you should keep it. If you were to give it up in a mood of self-sacrifice or out of a sense of duty, you would continue to want it back, and that unsatisfied want would make trouble for you." This means that simplicity is indeed more a state of mind than a particular standard of living. The good life, as Aldo Leopold pointed out, "boils down to a question of degree." [35]

Indeed it does. Determining and maintaining the correct degree of simplicity is not a simple endeavor. Human nature and the imperatives of the consumer culture constantly war against enlightened restraint. Nevertheless, simplicity remains an animating vision of vital moral purpose, for it is our dreams that energize us more than our abilities. In the quest for the good life the possible is as valid as the probable. And for those with the will to believe in the possibility of the simple life and act accordingly, the rewards can be great. Practitioners can gradually wrest control of their own lives from the manipulative demands of the marketplace and workplace. Then they can begin to cultivate a renewed sense of republican virtue, spiritual meaning, and social concern. Properly interpreted, such a modern simple life informed by its historical tradition can be both socially constructive and personally gratifying. This was the message that John Burroughs gave to the school-children of New York City in 1911 when he wrote a letter at the request of the superintendent, explaining to the youngsters why he was so hale and happy at age seventy-four. "With me," he remarked, "the secret of my youth is the simple life—simple food, sound sleep, the open air, daily work, kind thoughts, love of nature, and joy and contentment in the world in which I live... I have had a happy life... May you all do the same." A sentimental creed, perhaps, but one that has repeatedly proven its worth to the moral health of the nation and the spiritual health of its practitioners.[36]

Simplicity Among the Saints

by Richard J. Foster

Richard Foster served for nearly seventeen years as pastor for churches throughout California and Oregon. He has also held professorships (in Bible and Theology) at George Fox College in Oregon and at Friends University at Wichita, Kansas. Foster currently serves as Chair of Renovare as well as Professor of Spiritual Formation at Azusa Pacific University in California. Foster is a prolific writer, renowned for his spiritual insight. His book *Celebration of Discipline* has been translated into nearly twenty languages, including Chinese, Romanian and Ethiopian. *Freedom of Simplicity* has also received international attention. Richard has published numerous articles, many for the journal *Quaker Life*. Richard and his wife Carolynn have two sons and currently reside in Franktown, Colorado.

Foster, with this historical overview, reveals how simplicity is not a recent "fad" within our culture and Christianity. Starting with the early church and finishing with present day writings and practices, this essay discusses the variety of ways Christian simplicity has been practiced through the ages.

∞

I recommend to you holy simplicity.

—Francis de Sales

∞

History has a wonderful way of freeing us from the cult of the contemporary. It opens to us rich new vistas of "the communion of saints." We realize more pointedly than ever before that God has spoken in the past, and that we are not the only ones who have sought to live in faithful conformity to his word. It is humbling to be writing on Christian simplicity and to discover a fifteenth-century tome by Girolamo Savonarola entitled, The Simplicity of the Christian Life. Such experiences have a way of destroying all contemporary arrogance.

One remarkable feature of the devotional masters is the incredible sense of uniform witness in the midst of such diverse personalities. In the words of William James, "There is a certain composite photograph of saintliness." [37] People from different cultures and centuries exhibit a mutual verification that is well nigh amazing. And the necessity of Christian simplicity is one of their most consistent themes. People as divergent as Augustine of Hippo and Francis of Assisi, Blaise Pascal and Robert Barclay, Richard Baxter and John Wesley all called for simplicity of life.

We need to give attention to these voices rising out of the past, hear their witness, and follow their lead. We will investigate six different "models" of Christian simplicity. Obviously, they are only representative of the rich witness of Christians throughout the centuries.

There is no perfect model of anything. As long as we are finite human beings we are bound to make mistakes and distort the truth. Movements throughout the history of the Church are no exception. Each group we will investigate evidenced deficiencies in one form or another. But this fact of human existence should in no way hinder our appreciation for their bright witness to a way of walking with God that is "free from outward cumbers." [38] In each case, particular attention will be given to the most prominent contribution to simplicity found in each movement....

Exuberant Caring and Sharing

In the period directly following the Apostolic Age there was an exuberant caring and sharing on the part of Christians that was unique in antiquity. Julian the apostate, an enemy of Christianity, admitted that "the godless Galileans fed not only their (poor) but ours also." [39] Tertullian wrote that the Christians' deeds of love were so noble that the pagan world confessed in astonishment, "See how they love one another." [40] Exactly what is it that these Christians did which elicited such a response from their enemies?

There was, first of all, an exceptional freedom to care for the needs of one another in the believing community. The *Didache* admonished Christians: "Thou shalt not turn away from him that is in want, but thou shalt share all things with thy brother, and shalt not say that they are thine own." [41] By A.D. 250 Christians in Rome were caring for some fifteen hundred needy people. In fact, their generosity was so profuse that Ignatius could say that they were "leading in love," and Bishop Dionysius of Corinth could note that they were sending "supplies to many churches in every city."...[42]

We gain a helpful glimpse into the caring Christian community from I Clement, "Let everyone be subject to his neighbor...Let the rich man provide for the wants of the poor; and let the poor man bless God, because He hath given him one by whom his needs may be supplied." [43] Tertullian catalogued a long list of groups that were cared for by the Christian believers. They supported and buried the poor, supplied the needs of the boys and girls destitute of means, cared for the elderly that were confined to the house, provided for those who had suffered shipwreck, and gave to those who had been banished to islands or mines for their fidelity to Christ's cause....

Christians also provided for those who lost their jobs because of their faith in Christ. It was assumed, for example, that an actor who became a Christian, and had to give up his profession because of its involvement in pagan mythology, would be cared for by the Church....

But their joyful sharing was not confined to Christians... Bishop John Chrysostom witnessed, "Every day the Church here feeds 3,000 people. Besides this, the church daily helps provide food and clothes for prisoners, the hospitalized, pilgrims, cripples, churchmen, and others.[44] When epidemics broke out in Carthage and Alexandria, Christians rushed to aid all in need..."

These repeated and sustained sacrificial acts of charity cannot be explained in terms of ecclesiastical or secular politics. They grew out of a deep commitment to Christ and his call to care for the needy. These Christians genuinely believed that God was the owner and giver of all good gifts. Their generosity was an imitation of God's generosity. They were free from anxiety because they knew that tomorrow was in God's hands. They lived in simplicity.

Perhaps no one has captured the exuberant spirit of simple caring and sharing better than the Christian philosopher Aristides, whose words (written in A.D. 125) are so moving that they are best quoted in full:

> They walk in all humility and kindness, and falsehood is not found among them, and they love one another. They despise not the widow, and grieve not the orphan. He that hath distributeth liberally to him that hath not. If they see a stranger, they bring him under their roof, and rejoice over him as if he were their own brother: for they call themselves brethren, not after the flesh, but after the Spirit of God; but when one of their poor passes away from the world, and any of them see him, then he provides for his burial according to his ability; and if they hear that any of their number is imprisoned or oppressed for the name of their Messiah, all of them provide for his needs, and if it is possible that he may be delivered, they deliver him. And if there is among them a man that is poor and needy, and they have not an abundance of necessaries, they fast two or three days that they may supply the needy with their necessary food.[45]

This model of simplicity speaks to our condition. How desperately we need today to discover new creative ways of caring and sharing with any in need.

The Power of Renunciation

The power of renunciation as seen in the Desert Fathers is a second model of Christian simplicity.

As the persecution of the early Christians began to die out, it was no longer possible to witness for Christ by martyrdom. But the world had not changed its antipathy to the Gospel message, only its tactics. Persecution was replaced by assimilation.

For the Desert Fathers, the flight to the desert was a way of escaping conformity to the world. The world, including the Church, had become so dominated by secular materialism that, for them, the only way to witness against it was to withdraw from it. Thomas Merton writes in the introduction to his *Wisdom of the Desert*, "Society...was regarded by the Desert Fathers as a shipwreck from which each single individual man had to swim for his life." [46]

...Their experience has particular relevance, because modern society is uncomfortably like the world that they attacked so vigorously. Their world asked "How can I get more?" The Desert Fathers asked, "What can I do without?" Their world asked, "How can I find myself?" The Desert Fathers asked, "How can I lose myself?" Their world asked, "How can I win friends and influence people?" The Desert Fathers asked, "How can I love God?"...

The Desert Fathers renounced things in order to know what it meant to have the single eye of simplicity toward God. They...sought to strip away all hindrances. There is no question that there were excesses in the monasticism of the Desert Fathers, but no more so than the excesses evidenced in the Church of today in the opposite direction.

The renunciation of the Desert Fathers had great transforming power. They renounced possessions in order to learn detachment. These men and women of the desert gained a great freedom when they surrendered the need to possess. Among the sayings of the Fathers is the story of an important dignitary who gave a basket of gold pieces to a priest in the desert, asking him to disperse it among the brethren. "They have no need of it," replied the priest. The wealthy benefactor insisted and set the basket of coins at the doorway of the Church, asking the priest to tell the brethren, "Who so hath need, let him take it." No one touched it, or even cared enough to look at it. Edified, and no doubt astonished, the man left with his basket of gold. [47]

Detachment frees us from the control of others. No longer can we be manipulated by people who hold our livelihoods in their hands. Things do not entice our imaginations, people do not dominate our destinies.

The Desert Fathers renounced speech in order to learn compassion... When Arsenius, the Roman educator who gave up his status and wealth for the solitude of the desert, prayed, "Lord, lead me into the way of salvation," he heard a voice saying, "Be silent." [48]

Silence frees us from the need to control others....We are accustomed to relying upon words to manage and control others....We want so desperately for them to agree with us, to see things our way. We evaluate people, judge people, condemn people. We devour people with our words. Silence is one of the deepest Disciplines of the Spirit simply because it puts the stopper on that.

When we become quiet enough to let go of people, we learn compassion for them. We can be with people in their hurt and need. We can speak a word out of our inner silence that will set them free. (Father) Anthony (251-356) knew that the true test of spirituality was in the freedom to live among people compassionately: "With our neighbor there is life and death: for if we do good to our brother, we shall do good to God: but if we scandalize our brother, we sin against Christ." [49]

The Desert Fathers renounced activity in order to learn prayer. Prayer was at the heart of the desert experience. These athletes of God sought to strip away all superfluous things... Prayer was the great work of their lives. Abbot Agatho declared, "There is no labor so great as praying to God..." [50]

Prayer frees us to be controlled by God. To pray is to change. There is no greater liberating force in the Christian life than prayer. To enter the gaze of the Holy is never to be the same. To bathe in the Light in quiet wonder and glad surrender is to be slowly, permanently transformed. There is a richer inward orientation, a deeper hunger for communion... Few if any of us will be led to the forms of renunciation that characterize the Desert Fathers. But all of us need to seek God for "wineskins" that will build into our lives the simplicity of detachment, compassion, and prayer.

The Joy of Simplicity

The poor little monk of Assisi, St. Francis, and his jubilant band comprise yet another model of Christian simplicity. They tramped the earth inebriated with the love of God, and filled with ecstasy. Buoyant joy was the hallmark of their simplicity.

Francis (A.D. 1182-1226) is one of the most winsome figures in the history of the Christian faith. Born in the ancient Italian town of Assisi of wealthy parents, his adolescent years were spent as a charming and carefree playboy. A leader among the local young aristocracy, he often initiated their fun-loving revelries.

Illness and a military disappointment were among the influences that began to lead the sensitive Francis through a lengthy series of intense struggles of the spirit. The climax came in 1206 when his enraged father brought him before the bishop, to disinherit him. Francis stripped himself naked and walked away determined to follow the Lord's bidding into apostolic poverty.

Moved by his joyousness under oppression and his espousal of Lady Poverty, many flocked to the young Francis. Three years after the decisive call had come to Francis, a young girl of sixteen, Clara, sought to join the movement. Thus a woman's branch of the Franciscans, the Poor Ladies or Poor Clares, came into being. In time, this jubilant group of men and women became one of the largest and most influential orders in the Catholic faith.

The early Franciscan movement had an unusual combination of mystical contemplation and evangelistic fervor....Enthusiastically, (Francis) traversed much of

154 ◆ Simpler Living, Compassionate Life

Italy, preached to the Sultan in Egypt, and sought to engage in ministry among the Moslems in Spain. He was a captivating speaker, and his deep conviction and radiant love aroused an almost delirious enthusiasm on the part of the people.[51]

He sent out his Brothers Minor—Little Brothers—all over Europe and to Morocco. He referred to his humble band as "God's jugglers," whose task was to "revive the hearts of men and lead them into spiritual joy." [52]

The Friars Minor not only preached, but also sang. Exuberant and joyful, they were often caught up in ecstacy as they worshiped. With the soul of a poet, Francis would improvise their hymns. Best known is his *Canticle of the Sun*, with its celebration of Brother Sun and Sister Moon, Brother Wind and Sister Water. It is a joyous adoration of God as the Creator of all good things.

A love for the creation certainly marked these simple Friars. They lived close to the earth and took special joy in it. On one occasion Francis and Brother Masseo went begging bread in a small village. Returning with a few dried crusts, they searched until they found a spring for drinking and a flat rock for a table. As they ate their meager lunch Francis exclaimed several times, "Oh Brother Masseo, we do not deserve such a great treasure as this!" Finally, Brother Masseo protested that such poverty could hardly be called a treasure. They had no cloth, no knife, no dish, no bowl, no house, no table. Elated Francis replied, "That is what I consider a great treasure—where nothing has been prepared by human labor. But everything here has been supplied by Divine Providence, as is evidenced in the baked bread, fine stone table, and the clear spring."...[53]

Francis knew joy, but it was the joy rooted in the Cross, not in escape from it. The delightful story is told about how Francis taught Brother Leo the meaning of perfect joy. As the two walked together in the rain and bitter cold, Francis reminded Leo of all the things that people believed would bring joy, adding each time, "Perfect joy is not in that." Finally, in exasperation Brother Leo asked, "I beg you in God's name to tell me where perfect joy is." Whereupon, Francis began enumerating the most humiliating, self-abasing things he could imagine, adding each time, "Oh, Brother Leo, write that perfect joy is there." To explain and conclude the matter he told him, "Above all the graces and gifts of the Holy Spirit which Christ gives to His friends is that of conquering oneself and willingly enduring sufferings, insults, humiliations, and hardships for the love of Christ." [54]

The life of St. Francis gives us a healthy model of celibacy. (Examples of unhealthy celibacy abound in the history of the Church.) This matter of the single life should not be taken lightly. To be quite blunt about it, celibacy is necessary for some forms of simplicity. Francis could not have done what he did if he had not been single. Nor could Jesus.

Celibacy is not essential to simplicity, but it is essential to some expressions of simplicity. If we want to live like Francis, we had better not be married. If we want to be married, we had better not try to live like Francis. The failure to understand this simple fact has caused a great deal of misery in human society.

Francis and his Friars Minor knew the joy of the Lord. They were stamped by simple love and joyous trust. They led a cheerful, happy revolt against the spirit of materialism and double-mindedness. Nothing is more needed today than a simplicity distinguished by triumphant joy.

Theology in the Cause of Simplicity

…Martin Luther dealt with the matter of simplicity in the most profoundly practical way in his book *The Freedom of a Christian*. What he saw in such sharp focus was that the liberty of the Gospel sets us free to serve our neighbor with singleness of purpose. If our salvation is by grace alone we no longer need to keep juggling a myriad of religious duties to get right with God. We are free from constantly taking our own spiritual temperature.

Our freedom from sin allows us to serve others. Before, all our serving was for our benefit, a means to somehow get right with God. Only because the grace of God has been showered upon us are we enabled to give that same grace to others. Luther expresses this thesis in his famous paradox: "A Christian is a perfectly free lord of all, subject to none. A Christian is a perfectly dutiful servant of all, subject to all." [55] Through the grace of God alone, and not by any work of righteousness on our part, we come into the glorious liberty of the Gospel. We are all lords and kings and priests, as Luther put it. We are set free from the law of sin and death….

A moment's reflection on our part confirms the truth of Luther's insight. If we are still in bondage to sin, our serving will flow out of that center. We will not have the single eye that gives light to all we do. Pride and fear and manipulation will control our actions. We will not be free to serve our neighbor in simplicity. If we are still in bondage to others, our serving will flow out of that center. We will be controlled by a desire to impress them, or receive their help. Without Gospel liberty, we will forever measure who we are by the yardstick of others. We will not be free to serve our neighbor in simplicity.

But once the grace of God has broken into our lives, we are free. When we are free from the control of our neighbor, we are able to obey God. And as we obey God with a single heart, we are given a new power and desire to serve our neighbor, from whom we are now free. We have become "servants of our neighbors, and yet lords of all." [56] We know simplicity of life. Luther concludes, "A Christian lives not in himself, but in Christ and his neighbor. Otherwise he is not a Christian." [57]

John Calvin developed a theology of the state that was the source of tremendous social power… He viewed Christians as the instruments of God in the transformation of the entire society.

This approach took seriously the role of Christian political activism. Christians must concern themselves with matters of justice and service. A social order that caters to the privileged elite, while masses of its people are deprived of necessities, cannot be tolerated. Christians have a responsibility to bring social justice into realization. These are concerns close to the heart of Christian simplicity. Concerning government authorities, Calvin could say, "They are not to rule for their own interest, but for the public good; nor are they endued with unbridled power, but what is restricted to the well-being of their subjects." [58] In other words, the state has a God-given task to provide justice for all people alike, and Christians have a responsibility to see that it fulfills this function....

Luther and Calvin help us to understand the importance of both liberty and justice in our search for Christian simplicity. We need to join with Luther in seeking the freedom of the Gospel which allows us to serve our neighbor in love. We need to join with Calvin in seeking social justice in all of society, which allows human beings to live in peace.

Hearing and Obeying

Holy obedience to the living voice of Christ brought birth to a vigorous form of simplicity among seventeenth-century Quakers. Offense at the gluttonous excess of his day led young George Fox (A.D. 1624-1691) to seek after God, a seeking that reached an important turning point when he heard a voice which said, "There is one, even Christ Jesus, that can speak to thy condition." [59] And so from the very outset Quakerism centered in the conviction that the voice of Christ could be heard and his will obeyed. This listening to Jesus Christ is what led the early Quakers to a radical simplicity testimony.

If the early Quaker preaching were to be brought into one sentence, it would be, "Christ has come to teach his people himself." These people were convinced that Christ was the fulfillment of the "prophet like unto Moses" who had been prophesied (Deut.18:15-18, KJV). As prophet, Christ is able to teach us the righteousness of God. We can hear his voice if we will listen....

Not only does Christ our Prophet teach us, but he gives us the power to obey. George Fox declares that "God doth draw people from their unrighteousness and unholiness to Christ the righteous and holy one, the great prophet whom Moses said God would raise up whom people should hear in all things," and he urges all Christians to consider "whether you do believe that God raised up this prophet Christ Jesus? And if so, whether you do hear him?" [60]

A simplicity that took exception to many of the customs of the day resulted from this hearing and obeying the word of Christ. The early Quakers witnessed to simplicity in their attire: they rejected the gaudy superficial fashions that abounded in that day, and instead adopted the plain clothing of the working class. They refused to remove their hats in deference to the nobility, because they were convinced that all people deserved equal honor.

They witnessed to simplicity in their speech, in which honesty and integrity were the distinguishing characteristics. It was said that a Quaker's word was as good as his bond....

They witnessed to simplicity by vigorously opposing injustice and oppression. They condemned the "price fixing" of the day, which discriminated against the poor and needy, and insisted instead on a one-price system for all. Their writings were shot through with outraged cries against the conspicuous consumption of the wealthy because of its connection with the poverty that was rampant in the land. In *No Cross, No Crown*, William Penn scathingly denounced the practice of 95 percent of agriculture going to feed "the inordinate lusts and delicious appetites" of 5 percent of the population.[61] When the wealthy rationalized their extravagance under the excuse that it provided employment for the poor, George Fox rebutted, "If you say how shall the poor live if you do not wear that; give them all that money which you bestow upon all that gorgeous attire, and needless things, to nourish them, that they may live without making vanities." [62]

These early "Publishers of Truth," as they called themselves, took with utter seriousness the task of hearing the voice of Christ and obeying his word. They would ask, "What does it mean to live faithful lives in our day?" And they fully expected to receive an answer…They also waited to receive the power to obey that word.…

We who live in a world of half-truths and rationalizations and intellectual gymnastics that keep us from hearing and obeying the word of Christ need to hear their witness. Because we live in a different culture, we must once again ask what it means to live faithful lives in our day. But we must ask fully expecting to receive an answer and fully expecting to be given the power to obey the call.

Simplicity in Action

Examples abound of Christian simplicity in the task of evangelism, in the service of the poor, and in the cause of social justice. The vigorous evangelistic efforts of John Wesley and the early Methodists are well known. The simplicity of their lifestyle gave integrity to the Gospel they preached. Wesley is reported to have told his sister, "Money never stays with me. It would burn me if it did. I throw it out of my hands as soon as possible, lest it should find its way within my heart." He told everyone that, if at his death he had more than ten pounds (about $23) in his possession, people had the privilege of calling him a robber.[63] Near the end of his life he wrote in his journal very simply, "I left no money to anyone in my will, because I had none."…[64]

Christians have also raised the standard of simplicity in the service of the poor. At the early age of twenty, Antoine Frederic Ozanam persuaded some of his fellow students to help him in serving the destitute and underprivileged of France. It was the beginning of the St. Vincent de Paul Society. Begun in 1833, it quickly spread to many countries.

William Booth established the Salvation Army out of a burning desire to help the dregs of the industrial urban civilization. Ministering among the worst slums of London, Booth first sought to bring these broken and dispossessed people into the churches. Unwilling to receive them, the churches rejected Booth and his followers. Booth turned to unconventional open air meetings on the streets, complete with drums, tambourines, and trumpets. His book, *In Darkest England and the Way-*

Out, is a scathing expose of the economic, social, and moral conditions in the slums, and in it Booth made daring proposals to overcome these conditions. Along with other things he called for a poor man's bank, rescue homes for prostitutes, and model suburban villages.... [65]

In the twentieth century, one thinks immediately of Albert Schweitzer. Extremely versatile, Schweitzer was a New Testament scholar, a distinguished organist and authority on Bach, and an accomplished philosopher and theologian. He chose, however, to give the bulk of his adult career to serving the people of French Equatorial Africa as a medical missionary.

Simplicity also has been a vigorous force in the cause of social justice. David Livingstone is well known for missionary exploits and especially for his determined efforts to abolish what he called "the open sore of the world," the African slave trade. Living in great simplicity, both in inward spirit and in outward lifestyle, he persistently pleaded the cause of the helpless of Africa. The horrors of the slave trade, said Livingstone, were beyond exaggeration. "To overdraw its evils is a simple impossibility." [66] Among the last words which he was to write in his journal were these: "I will forget all my cold, hunger, suffering and trials, if I can be the means of putting a stop to this cursed traffic." [67]

Clarence Jordan has made an important imprint upon twentieth-century America by his courageous life of simplicity in the cause of social justice. The founder of Koinonia Farm and author of the Cotton Patch version of the New Testament, he has sometimes been called a theologian in overalls. He withstood harassment, economic boycott, and gunfire from nightriders in order to make a bold social witness for peace, community, and racial equality....[68]

And today many groups have arisen which have battled for justice out of Christian conviction. Among some of the better known of these groups are the Berkeley Christian Coalition in Berkeley, California, which publishes *Radix*; Voice of Calvary in Mendenhall, Mississippi, which publishes *The Quiet Revolution*; Jubilee Fellowship in Philadelphia, Pennsylvania, which publishes *The Other Side*; the Catholic Worker Movement in many American urban centers, which publishes *The Catholic Worker*; and The People's Christian Coalition in Washington, D. C., which publishes *Sojourners*. Whatever may be the shortcomings of these many movements, certainly one of their greatest assets has been their understanding of how intrinsic Christian simplicity is in the cause of justice....

In a small way, we have entered the "communion of saints" in this chapter. We have heard the witness of men and women throughout the centuries who have sought to walk with God faithfully and simply. Their message is clear, and is perhaps best summed up in the words of Francis de Sales, "In everything, love simplicity." [69]

EDITOR'S NOTE: Foster concludes his article with a brief historical perusal of Christian writings related to simplicity. Below find a summary listing of those works:

Clement's *The Rich Man's Salvation* and Cyprian's *On Good Works and Alms Giving*, and *Letters of St. Jerome*; the works of Eckhard, Tauler, and Suso; Savonarola's *The Simplicity of the Christian Life*, and John Woolman's *The Journal* and *A Plea for the Poor*; the writings of the Radical Reformation and the *Epistles of George Fox* and William Penn's *No Cross, No Crown*. And, of course, many modern writers have addressed this subject with new vigor, including: Francis Florand's *Stages of Simplicity*, Arthur Gish's *Beyond the Rat Race*, Ronald Sider's *Rich Christians in an Age of Hunger* and Soren Kierkegaard's *Purity of Heart is to Will One Thing*.

Theology in Support of Simplicity and Eco-Justice

What we need…is a thoroughgoing reformation of our
public theology of growthism.

—*Timothy Weiskel*

It is no accident that those who care about the
socially marginalized and the environment are
usually people who have spent time experiencing and developing positive relations with
oppressed peoples or with the natural
world. Intrinsic value cannot be simply
asserted; it has to be discovered, and it
can be discovered only through such
positive experience of others.

—*Carol Johnston*

Some Notes From Belshaz'zar's Feast

by Timothy C. Weiskel

Dr. Timothy Weiskel is Director of the Environmental Ethics and
Public Policy Program, the Director of the Harvard Seminar on
Environmental Values and a member of Harvard's Committee on
the Environment. He is an anthropologist and an historian of culture change. His doctorate is from Oxford University where he
studied as a Rhodes Scholar. African history, historical ecology,
and ecological anthropology are among the courses he has taught
at Williams College, Yale and Harvard. Dr. Weiskel has field experience in Syria, Lebanon and throughout West Africa. Over the
last several years he has worked on the ethical implications of
environmental policy and is the principal author of *Environmental
Decline and Public Policy: Pattern, Trend and Prospect.*

Weiskel's essay provides a very thoughtful and concise overview of
human cultural ecological impacts through the ages. He reviews
extinctions, human population fluctuations, and increased urbanization. He says, "as humans we are an evolutionary outcome of
natural processes, but our theology determines the character of our
engagement with these processes, and it will thereby condition the
outcome of the story itself." Thus, after his overview, he states his
belief that the only "real chance we have of surviving as a species
is through a radical theological revolution." That revolution needs
to address the most pervasive religion of our day: "growthism."
And our theology needs a firm grounding in the recognition of
limits and must speak to the misery many experience—must speak
to those left behind by growthism.

∞

*King Belshaz'zar made a great feast for a thousand of his lords, and
drank wine in front of the thousand. They drank wine, and praised the
gods of gold and silver, bronze, iron, wood, and stone.*

*Immediately the fingers of a man's hand appeared and wrote on the
plaster of the wall of the king's palace, opposite the lampstand; and the
king saw the hand as it wrote. Then the king's color changed, and his
thoughts alarmed him; his limbs gave way and his knees knocked
together. The king cried aloud to bring in the enchanters...and the*

astrologers…Then all the king's wise men came in, but they could not read the writing or make known to the king the interpretation.

Then Daniel answered before the king: …you have praised the gods of silver and gold, of bronze, iron, wood, and stone, which do not see or hear or know, but the God in whose hand is your breath, and whose are all your ways, you have not honored.

"Then from his presence the hand was sent, and this writing was inscribed. And this is the writing that was inscribed: MENE, MENE, TEKEL, and PARSIN. This is the interpretation of the matter: MENE, God has numbered the days of your kingdom and brought it to an end; TEKEL, you have been weighed in the balances and found wanting; PERES, your kingdom is divided and given to the Medes and Persians."

—Daniel 5:1, 4, 5-6, 8, 17, 23-28

∞

Throughout his writings Father Tom Berry, whose seminal theological reflections have given us new ways to think about God, has reminded us of two central themes: First, as human beings we are part of natural history, a larger evolutionary story, a geological story—indeed a cosmic story. Secondly, in that larger narrative we now find ourselves at a critical juncture—a key turning point in that entire narrative, the outcome of which will be determined in part by the beliefs we affirm through our daily behavior. Given his geological training and orientation Berry phrases this turning point in geological terms. We live, Berry says, in what can be described as the "terminal Cenozoic era." Before us we face the choice between the "technozoic" or the "ecozoic." In short, as humans we are an evolutionary outcome of natural processes, but our theology determines the character of our engagement with these processes, and it will thereby condition the outcome of the story itself.

One of the reasons some people find Berry's insights so disturbing is that it is uncomfortable to be reminded that we live simultaneously in multiple nested realities. When people point this out to us in everyday experience and we come to realize that they are right, we frequently feel we have been stupid, naive, duped, or misguided. The net result is that we feel sheepish about our previously bold assertions and a little humiliated by the whole experience.

The insights of geologists force this recognition upon our culture as a whole because geologists have a different sense of time than those of us preoccupied with day-to-day events. Their professional perspective spans millions or billions of years. The evolution and extinction of entire species form but a small part of their purview. They are aware that the earth's history is nested within a larger narrative of cosmic evolution…. While much of this process has involved gradual, cumulative patterns of change, geologists are aware that there have been numerous abrupt discontinuities in the earth's history, marked by massive extinctions of numerous species.

In the face of the accelerating rate of ecological decline in our own experience, these large-scale scientific insights about the origins and cosmic context of human activity can prove to be disconcerting. Looking at the larger picture, for example, biologists reassure us that the invertebrates and microbial species are likely to survive our current epoch relatively unscathed. Yet, if you are anything like me, this message provides small comfort when one begins to realize that the larger point is that *life as we know it* is undergoing massive extinction. More precisely, geologists, evolutionary biologists, and paleontologists are now reporting evidence in their professional journals that we are currently in the midst of a global "extinction event" which equals or exceeds in scale those catastrophic episodes in the geological record that marked the extinction of the dinosaurs and numerous other species.

At least two important differences exist between this extinction episode and those previously documented in the geological record. First, in previous events of similar magnitude the question of agency and the sequence of species extinctions have remained largely a mystery. In the current extinction event, however, we now know with a high degree of certainty what the effective agent of system-wide collapse is, and we have a fairly good notion of the specific dynamics and sequence of species extinctions. Second, previous events of this nature seem to have involved extraterrestrial phenomena, like episodic meteor collisions....

In contrast to these extraterrestrial or celestial phenomena that served as the forcing functions behind previous mass extinctions, the current extinction event results from an internally generated dynamic. The relatively stable exchanges between various biotic communities have shifted in a short period of time into an unstable phase of runaway, exponential growth for a small sub-set of the species mix—namely, human beings, their biological symbionts, and their associates.

The seemingly unrestrained growth of these populations has unleashed a pattern of accentuated parasitism and predation of these growing populations upon a selected number of proximate species that were deemed by them to be useful. This accentuated parasitism led to the creation of anthropogenic biological environments which, in turn, drove hundreds of other species directly into extinction—sometimes within periods of only a few centuries or decades. More significantly, however, this pattern of unrestrained growth and subsequent collapse has repeated itself again and again, engendering in each instance a syndrome of generalized habitat destruction and over time precipitating the cumulative extinction of thousands of species as one civilization after another has devastated its environment and dispersed its remnant populations far afield in search of new resources of plunder and squander.

For a variety of reasons—some of them apparently related to their religious beliefs—humans remain fundamentally ignorant of or collectively indifferent toward the fate of their fellow species, insisting instead that measurements of human welfare should be the only criteria for governing human behavior. Apparently, the "right to life" is effectively defined as the "right to *human* life."... Scientists and techno-boomers alike promise us that technological miracles will save us from our rapidly deteriorating ecological circumstance and that no substantial sacrifice will be required of us. After all, "thanks to science" we have miracle crops, miracle drugs and miracle whip! What more can we hope for?

Well, the fact is we need a great deal more to survive as a society and as a species. In reality, we are just beginning to recognize the true immensity of the problem.

Consider, for example, the truly dramatic dimensions of our recent growth as a species. By recent here, I mean in evolutionary terms and in terms of the relatively long time scales required to engineer stable social adjustment to changing circumstance. In evolutionary terms, it took since the dawn of humanity to roughly 1945 for the human species to reach the total figure of about 2 billion people. That figure has more than doubled—indeed, nearly tripled—just since 1945. During the rest of our lifetime experts say that figure could well reach a total of 9 billion people if left to grow at projected rates.

Consider, as well, the overall ecological footprint of human expansion over the millennia, particularly as we have come to congregate in cities. Depending upon how one wishes to segment us from our biological relatives, humans have been around for roughly a million years or so. It is only in the last 1.2% of that history— roughly the last 12,000 years—that we have come to depend upon agriculture, and only the last 6,000 years or so that we have begun to transform our settlement patterns into urban concentrations. We are still in the midst of what might be called the "urban transition" in the human evolutionary experiment. It is not clear that the transition will be successfully achieved or that the human bio-evolutionary experiment will endure very much longer in evolutionary terms. Nevertheless, there is enough evidence available about the urban transition in human history to begin generating some general statements.

The new evidence of environmental archaeologists is especially sobering in this context. The history of cities has been associated with the history of repeated ecological disaster. The growth of cities has engendered rapid regional deforestation, the depletion of groundwater aquifers, accelerated soil erosion, plant genetic simplification, periodic epizootics among pest species and animal domesticates, large-scale human malnutrition, and the development and spread of epidemic disease. In many cases the individual elements of ecological decline have been linked in positive feedback processes, which reinforced one another and led to precipitous collapse of particular cities.

To overcome the limitations imposed by these patterns of localized ecological collapse, cities have historically sought to dominate rural regions in their immediate vicinity and extend links of trade and alliance to similarly constituted cities further afield. As arable land and strategic water supplies became more scarce and more highly valued, violent conflict between individual city-states emerged, leading in short succession to the development of leagues of allied cities and subsequently to the formation of kingdoms and empires with organized armies for conquest and permanent defense.

Even with the limitations of preindustrial technology, the results of these conflicts could be devastating indeed to local or regional ecosystems, particularly when victorious groups sought to destroy the ecological viability of defeated groups with such policies as scorched-earth punishment and the sowing of salt over the arable land in defeated territory. The ecological impact of warfare and the preparation for warfare has been devastating in all ages. C.S. Lewis's observation has proved sadly correct that "the so-called struggle of man against nature is really a struggle of man against man with nature as an instrument."

Demographic historians have added further details to the picture of repeated ecological disaster painted by environmental archaeologists. Human populations have demonstrated again and again the long-term regional tendency to expand and collapse. These undulating patterns are referred to by demographers as the "millennial long waves" (MLW), and they appear to be manifest in both the old world and the new...[70]

Two patterns are discernible across all cases despite the considerable differences between each region. First, the human population is both highly unstable and highly resilient. That is to say, there is considerable variation in the amplitude of the population waves and therefore human populations cannot be considered stable in regional terms. Moreover, the population is resilient in the sense that it "bounces" back from demographic catastrophe with an even stronger surge in reproductive performance. The second phenomena of the MLW on the regional level is that the frequency between their occurrences is successively shortened. Thus, populations seem to be collapsing and rebounding at higher and higher levels more and more frequently as we approach the present.

When we move beyond the regional evidence to a global scale, another important pattern emerges. On this level of analysis it seems that human populations seem to expand in spurts, corresponding to the quantities of energy they are able to harness with their available technology. This may emerge as a new way of stating the Malthusian theory of population limit. Thomas Malthus focused on the relation of populations to their food supply and pointed out that while populations tend to grow exponentially the food supply tends to grow only arithmetically. As a result, populations are ultimately limited, according to Malthus, as their reproductive performance outstrips the food supply needed to keep them alive, and there are periodic widespread famines.

Since Malthus we have come to realize that "food" itself is really "energy"—a form of captured solar energy (i.e., kilocalories) that humans can assimilate to maintain themselves and do work. If we build upon this observation to reformulate Malthus's observation in terms of energy instead of food itself, we are probably close to a broad-level truth about the human species. Simply put, the Malthusian law can be restated in these terms: human populations tend to expand to the levels supported by the supplies of energy that they can mobilize with available technology.

The industrial era in world history marks an unprecedented period in human evolution history from this perspective. Never before have global populations experienced such high rates of growth for such sustained duration, reaching a worldwide climax with an average annual population increase of 2% during the decade from 1965 to 1975. The demographic historian Paul Demeny has described this extraordinary period quite succinctly:

> It took countless millennia to reach a global 1700 population of somewhat under 700 million. The next 150 years, a tiny fraction of humankind's total history, roughly matched this performance. By 1950 global human numbers doubled again to surpass 2.5 billion. The average annual rate of population growth was 0.34% in the eighteenth century; it climbed to 0.54% in the nineteenth century, and to 0.84% in the first half of the twentieth. In absolute terms, the first five decades following 1700 added 90 million to global numbers. Between 1900 and 1950, not withstanding two world wars, an influenza pandemic, and a protracted global economic crisis, the net addition to population size amounted to nearly ten times that much.[71]

As Dr. Demeny summarized the situation:

> Clearly, viewed in an evolutionary perspective, the 250 years between 1700 and 1950 have witnessed extraordinary success of the human species in terms of expanding numbers, a success that invokes the image of swarming [emphasis added].[72]

For demographic historians, then, it would seem that humans in the modern era are behaving much like a plague of locusts.

What is even more striking is that the pattern of distribution of this burgeoning population is one of rapid relocation into massive urban agglomerations. In 1700 less than 10% of the total world population of 700 million lived in cities. By 1950 a full 30% of the global population lived in cities. In North America the urban proportion of the population had reached 64% by that time, while in Europe it was 56%.

In 1700 only 5 cities in the world had populations of 500,000 people. By the turn of this century that number had risen to 43 cities in the world with populations of 500,000 or more. Of those, only 16 cities had populations over 1,000,000. By now, however—that is to say, in a span of under 100 years—there are nearly 400 cities that exceed 1,000,000.... The numbers of mega-cities—those in excess of 10,000,000 people—will reach 21 by the turn of the century, with 13 of these in the Asia-Pacific region. By the year 2020 the report estimates that 1.5 billion more people will be living in Asian cities than live there today. This is the equivalent of creating a brand-new city of 140,000 people every day for the next thirty years.[73]

The localized and global ecological costs of this seemingly unstoppable rush toward urban life are difficult even to imagine. While some techno-boomers and inveterate optimists suggest that newly planned cities might prove to be more energy and resource efficient, this kind of rapid urbanization has historically been accompanied by accelerated resource depletion, increased pollution and a decline of public health and welfare. In this large-scale process the "good life" for some has generally been purchased by the increased immiseration of many more and the nearly complete foreclosure on possibilities for a sustainable and stable livelihood of future generations....

So much, then, for the environment and the transformations of it that we have wrought as a species. What about the "good life"? The obvious comment to be made in this context is that in our culture a desire to pursue "the good life" aggravates our momentous ecological crisis. Consumption patterns of the "Northern" countries and the "Western" countries are obscene by global standards, yet there is no apparent end in sight to the gluttony. Indeed, as citizens of the United States we have the right to "the pursuit of happiness" written into our constitution, and in culture the prevailing message is that happiness itself is inextricably linked to an ever greater consumption of material goods and energy.

In some cases, of course, individuals, households, and even entire communities have made great strides in efforts to reduce, reuse, and recycle. Nevertheless, the underlying economic logic of an economy based on unlimited growth remains largely unchallenged in public discourse. Not a single national political leader has been elected on a plank of steady-state economics. Indeed, I know of no candidate that would attempt to seek public office on a no-growth or a slow-growth platform.

Even if an exceptional candidate could be found to articulate this kind of appeal, such an effort would be laughed off the public stage. The reasons for this have as much to do with arguments about social justice as they do with shameless consumerism. After all, growth has become the only means that late capitalism has devised to cope with the increasingly evident problem of inequity. The promise of more tomorrow is at least partially successful in silencing those who object to the current distribution of goods and privileges. Political and social liberals are particularly easy to divert with this appeal. In general, they are well enough off in material terms not to question the fundamental system from which they benefit. When they go further and express concern for the welfare of those who have been left out of the system, they seem to be easily persuaded by the promise that more tomorrow will eventually do everyone good. After all, the system worked for them, why shouldn't it be thought to work for all others? In short, there is no significant debate between conservatives and liberals on the question of growth. Squabbles over relative rates or targeted sectors may occur, but they serve only to underscore the broadly shared consensus that growth itself is an unquestioned virtue and the only legitimate goal of all public policy.

This is why both national political leaders and Wall Street alike are driven with religious zeal to preach one or another variant of the gospel of growth. Ironically, those most victimized and marginalized by this organized system of accumulation are frequently persuaded by the proselytizers of growth that generalized expansion is their best available strategy for self improvement. Thus it is that the poor become both the strongest justification of and supporters of the pro-growthevangelists.

Without any exaggeration, therefore, it is fair to say that in practical terms the most pervasive form of this religiously held belief in our day is that of *growthism* founded upon a doctrine of *techno-scientific salvation*. For the most part, the recent surge of "environmentalism" has not challenged this form of public religion. The fundamental belief is still that the earth and all it contains is constituted simultaneously as a treasure trove of raw materials and a repository for our wastes. When the absolute supply of resources is diminished, scientific discoveries and technical inventions, so it is believed, will save us from the constraints of absolute scarcity as new and more efficient production processes and waste treatment technologies are developed. Recycling itself is touted as a "growth industry" and a promising investment prospect on Wall Street. The sacred creed remains both pure and simple: *more is better; growth is good*. Anyone who expresses misgivings about this credo is soon taught through public rebuke and personal ridicule that it is blasphemy to question this golden rule of growthism.

We are confronted, therefore, in every respect with a growing problem. Given the pervasive character of the public faith in growth, it is impossible for the dominant forms of public religion to offer us a way out of our environmental crisis. From the vantage point of a systems ecologist or a "geologian," like Tom Berry, growth is the problem, not the solution. Yet the principle of continuous growth has achieved godlike status in the pantheon of modern religious icons.

When the high priests of public religion are asked, Can we survive?, their answer is emphatic: *Of course we can!* All we need is adequate investment incentives, a sense of determination, good ol' American inventiveness, and political will to make the "tough" decisions. One can hear the strains of "Onward Christian Soldiers" playing in the background as if we were "marching into war." The trouble with this is that the problems we are up against will no longer be solved simply with a new dose of messianic triumphalism.

In a narrow sense and in the short run we may succeed in "saving ourselves" from immediate manifestations of disaster, but it is essentially beside the point. The far more compelling question on a large scale and in the long run is, *will* we—as a species—survive? Not just theoretically, *can* we, but in a very practical sense, *will* we? This can only be answered by looking carefully at what we mean by "we" and what we mean by "survive." Growth evangelists and techno-scientific salvationists—like other fundamentalists—are regrettably silent and often sadly ignorant of the social dimensions of the changes required to answer this larger set of questions. Indeed, I would argue they are helpless in the face of such questions. Techno-boomers can do no more than offer us more of what got us into our sad circumstance in the first place.

It follows, therefore, that the only real chance we have of surviving as a species is through a radical theological revolution—that is, a thorough-going re-examination of those cultural beliefs we hold to most religiously. From the point of view of ecological sustainability, we have been weighed in the balance and found wanting. At current rates of growth and consumption our days have been numbered and the culture of growthism will be brought to an end whether we like it or not.

In some quarters this theological reformation is already underway. One can point to the most recent of a whole host of writers, from James Nash to Sallie McFague or Jay McDaniel to Michael Fox, by way of supporting the point that church people and academic theologians are beginning to rethink concepts like "dominion," "stewardship," and "covenant" in terms that are more consistent with our contemporary ecological circumstance....

Much of this effort is intended explicitly or implicitly to refute the assertion that the Judeo-Christian value system is somehow uniquely responsible for humankind's exploitative relationship with nature. Professor Lynn White, Jr. leveled a stinging indictment at the dominant religious traditions of the West in just these terms in a 1968 article in *Science* magazine, and many of the writings from religious circles over the last twenty-five years have been largely defensive efforts protesting "no, it isn't so."

Other works from avowedly secular sources have served to let the Judeo-Christian tradition off the hook by pointing out that other ancient cultures were also devastating to their environments and seemed to similarly privilege human agency in the cosmic order of things. Thus, works like Donald Hughes's *The Ecology of Ancient Civilizations*, and a whole variety of subsequent ecological histories that it inspired have succeeded in spreading the blame fairly uniformly across all cultural traditions. Perhaps only the Native American tradition has been spared a full-length ecological critique, but even here the burden of the evidence now being collected indicates that pre-Columbian civilizations did not represent the kind of ecological nirvana that some strains of contemporary environmentalism would have us believe.

These religious and cultural critiques are well intentioned and no doubt quite important in their own terms, but we need now to ask more fundamental questions. O.K., let's assume as given the two central points of all this recent scholarship: first, the Judeo-Christian tradition is more complex than one might think at first glance, allowing for, or indeed perhaps even encouraging, a far more ecologically sustainable approach to the environment than heretofore recognized. Secondly, virtually all other cultural traditions have in practice been equally exploitative of their resources. What of value, then, have we learned from all this? Have we learned to live more lightly on the earth? Have we effectively challenged the public theology of growthism in our day?

I think not. I would argue that what we need now is far more profound than proof texting and retranslating our received traditions or launching yet other campaigns of cultural chauvinism in favor of one or another variant of the human achievement. What we need instead is a thoroughgoing reformation of our public theology of growthism.

We are all guests at Belshaz'zar's feast. On a global scale the handwriting is already on the wall for the culture of consumerism and its theology of growthism. Moreover, the meaning of this handwriting has been made plain. We are faced, as Tom Berry has suggested, with a choice between the "ecozoic" or the "technozoic." The question remains: will we behave like the king's "wise men"—the "enchanters" and the "astrologers"—and remain profoundly confused, or will we have the prophetic insight and the internal fortitude to challenge the public theology of our day?

The fundamental problem is that because of our patterns of growth our ecological impact as a species far outstrips our capacity to construct responsible communities of concern. We are just now beginning to monitor the radiological impact of the Chernobyl incident upon populations in nations far removed from the former Soviet Union. Less obviously but more insidiously, it is now possible to detect PCBs in the body fat of penguins in Antarctica. That is to say, the growing urban agglomerations around the world are already registering their ecological "footprint" in the snows of the last uninhabited continent. The mounting tragedy is that just as our collective behavior is registering a wider and wider ecological impact, our sense of effective community under stress is sharply shrinking.

A sense of moral compulsion cannot be imposed effectively from above, no matter how loudly it is preached from on high. Moral and ethical imperatives emerge spontaneously from a shared sense of community—a feeling that what "I" do or what "we" do matters to others within a community of which I wish to be a part. Our past record as a species is not encouraging in this regard. Historically, those considered to be *outside* the moral community have simply been ignored or—worse yet—legitimately persecuted in the name of the ethical principles of those *within* the boundaries of the recognized moral community. Clearly, our notions of what is *outside* and what is *inside* must change if we are to survive much longer as a human species in a wider biological community.

Environmental ethics, then, can be seen as an aspect of the more fundamental problem of community. In the time we have remaining can we fashion and believe in a collective sense of belonging to a global life process that transcends our home, our family, our class, our nation, and indeed our species? If our contemporary reactions to Somalia, Liberia, East Timor, Haiti, Zaire, and numerous other "hot spots" around the world are any indication of what is to come, the signs are not entirely encouraging. Left to our default behavioral modes our effective sense of community seems to shrink in time of crises.

The discouraging fact is that throughout history religious identities and concepts of God have all too frequently been implicated in this pattern of inward-looking retreat from responsibility. In historical terms humans have not shown an ability to create and control stable ecological communities for very long, and many societies have accelerated their decline through an unreflective affirmation of outmoded religious beliefs. Unless exceptional leaders—religious and otherwise—can articulate a new vision of community and a compelling theory of human limit, we are likely to accelerate our demise by winning in the competitive struggle for dominance over all other species.

This, then, is what is meant by the need for a new theology. A theology is in essence a theory of human limit. Each culture and each age has had its own functional theology as the experience of human limit has varied through space and time. In our place and our time a forceful theory of human limit needs yet to be proclaimed with all the clarity of the prophetic pronouncements of old. The essential elements of such a theology are apparent: we live in a world we did not create and cannot control. This awareness inspires in whole people a feeling of humility, an enduring sense of wonder, and an abiding reverence for life itself. These sensibilities generate a profound sense of gratitude and motivate and orient our pursuit of truth, our struggles for justice, and our efforts to realize our potential as human beings. The outcome of our enterprise is *not* entirely in our hands, but the little that we do know about the world and our place within it allows us, nevertheless, to affirm meaning in the face of mystery.

This is where, in a modest way, I would say my own outlook departs most markedly from that of Tom Berry. The new narrative of cosmic "creation theology" that Tom Berry has inspired goes a long way to resituate the human species and its evolution in its proper natural history context; but there is a subtle danger in recounting this story, and it is simply this: we humans inevitably assign ourselves too large a role in the cosmic trajectory, as if our species were the goal or crowning achievement of evolution itself and perhaps of all cosmic process. In some formulations this perspective assigns to man a co-creative role with God for the unfolding of the future history of creation. This cannot be proved, but as with all fundamental beliefs it can be affirmed, declared, and proclaimed. In an effort to emphasize the important character of our responsibility as a species, it is tempting to emphasize the extraordinary power of the human species.

My own hunch is that such affirmations are a bit too grandiose.... In some of its formulations the new narrative of creation theology can serve to engender and support an anthropocentrism which I feel is no longer credible and is potentially quite dangerous in sustaining the illusion that the future of the natural world is in *our* hands.

It is of course important to understand the beneficial ways in which we can interact with the environment, but it is equally important to understand the limits of human achievement in this regard and specifically what it is that we are not capable of doing. Announcing that we are co-creators with God in some process of cosmic self-realization is a bit like the rooster asserting that by crowing he makes the sun rise. If we are to be honest with ourselves and acknowledge what we have come to learn from science, we will need to start recognizing some real and palpable limits to the human prospect.

We are unlikely, for example, to be able to know enough to predict or perhaps even survive global climate change, so we had better build into our societies buffers and margins of collective safety that are much larger than any we have developed to date. We are unlikely to be able to win the co-evolutionary race with new and resurgent diseases, so we had better anticipate broad new public health strategies which are not predicated upon the "conquest" of disease.

We cannot regulate the earth's water cycle at will, particularly in the face of a potentially changing climate, so we should expect that limits on the availability and distribution of fresh water will pose limits on human expansion and industrial activity. Despite all our bio-technological wizardry in altering or modifying genetic material, humans have not "created" a single species. Instead we have only manipulated existing species for our perceived short-term benefit. Quite apart from the moral questions involved in the genetic manipulation of other species for human ends, it is unlikely that we will ever develop a predictive ecology that will be sophisticated enough to foresee the ultimate impact of introducing genetically altered species into the earth's complex ecosystem. We are not currently able to accomplish this kind of prediction for the thousands of new synthetic chemicals we introduce to the environment each year, and predicting the synergisms between these chemicals and life forms will probably prove to be beyond our reach.

Meanwhile, valuable genetic material in indigenous crop species and medicinal plants is being driven into extinction at rates that far exceed our capacity to catalogue the tragedy, let alone introduce new cultigens to take their place. We are unlikely to increase markedly the photosynthetic efficiency of the green leaf, so we had better begin to acknowledge that there are practical limits to the expansion of human numbers imposed by some photosynthetic process. Already it is calculated that roughly 40% of terrestrial photosynthesis is devoured by human beings, their animals or their industries. Even if we achieve the impossible and capture 100% of terrestrial photosynthate, the world's population cannot continue to double at its current rate without running into catastrophes of biblical proportions.

A sober assessment of our collective human limits suggests that even at our best we are perhaps not so co-creative as some new creation narratives would have us believe. This is not because we have merely been sloppy or asleep at the wheel. The problem goes deeper than this.

Human limits in the ecosystem stem from the basic fact that human societies and ecosystems operate most of the time on fundamentally different principles. As the noted ecologist Eugene Odum has phrased it, humans maximize for net production while ecosystems maximize for gross production. Ever since the advent of agriculture, human societies have driven inexorably toward the logic of *more is better; growth is good*. Natural ecosystems operate on the contrasting principle: *enough is enough; balance is best*. The tension between these two principles is the ecological root of all evil. Humankind's repeated insistence upon trying to manipulate the larger ecosystem on the basis of its species-specific logic is the ecological equivalent of "original sin." The "sin" is original in the sense that it is built into our condition as humans. We can do no other. This aspect of the human condition cannot be overcome by pious good intentions to "do better" or earnest attempts to improve the efficiency of our maximizing strategies. It is these strategies themselves that are the source of the problem.

The only salvation from this condition is to step outside the strategy itself—to decenter ourselves and recenter our awareness around the logic of the larger system of which we are a part. This effort to recognize ourselves as part of a larger logic has been at the heart of both religious experience and scientific inquiry. Indeed, as William James pointed out nearly a century ago, the two endeavors are intimately linked:[74]

> ...All the magnificent achievements of mathematical and physical science—our doctrines of evolution, of uniformity of law, and the rest—proceed from our indomitable desire to cast the world into a more rational shape in our minds than the crude order of our experience. The principle of causality, for example—what is it but a postulate, an empty name covering simply a demand that the sequence of events shall some day manifest a deeper kind of belonging of one thing with another than the mere arbitrary juxtaposition which now phenomenally appears? It is as much an altar to an unknown god as the one that Saint Paul found at Athens. All our scientific and philosophic ideals are altars to unknown gods.

If the story of Belshaz'zar's feast tells us anything, however, it is surely that we should be wary of altars to unknown gods. It is as if we have been warned that in our quest for what James calls "a deeper kind of belonging" we should accept no substitutes.

Most disturbing of all, however, is the implication that even if we finally get our theology right—as Belshaz'zar appears to have done—this fact is not redemptive. There is no opportunity for confession, contrition, and absolution—no assurance of forgiveness nor possibility of salvation. Consider the story's outcome. In spite of the fact Belshaz'zar has come to understand the writing on the wall and appears to be genuinely chastised, duly fearful, and appropriately grateful to Daniel, he is not spared. The narrative records that after the feast he died that very night.

For those of us who have been steeped in Christo-centric theology, this is disconcerting. We would prefer a more comforting closure. The message is that even if we get around to reading the handwriting on the wall and earnestly desire to change our ways, it is probably too late for those of us who are already at Bel-shaz'zar's feast. If the story can be repeated often enough and widely enough, perhaps others will benefit, but we will not be spared.

It is perhaps precisely for this reason that notes on Belshaz'zar's feast may well speak more directly to our culture's condition than the comfortable stories of one-ness with nature or the new narratives of belonging to a cosmic creation. The mes-sage from researchers like Dennis Meadows and others, including demographers, agronomists, atmospheric scientists, and even some economists, is quite simply that the ecosystem will not support or tolerate a global repetition of the development patterns characteristic of the West and the North. In particular if the countries in Asia seek to replicate historical patterns of Western resource use and energy exploitation and, in effect, praise as we have "the gods of gold and silver, bronze, iron, wood, and stone," the fate of our species as a whole does not look hopeful....

Where is God in all of this? Are we prepared to believe in a God that seems poised to wreak such destruction, confusion and such massive suffering on the already poor and destitute? Whether or not academic theologians get their narra-tives reworked and their texts re-translated in time, I suspect that the effective theologies of the modern world are in for a radical and brutal transformation in the decades ahead. While from a comfortable distance we are on the verge of announcing that God's handiwork as manifest in the natural environment is a glorious harmonious whole, the mass of the world's humanity is about to endure a very different experience of human limit and divine presence. Metaphors of wan-ton destruction, vindictive revenge, and suffering innocence will probably be more consistent with their experience, and the concept of redemption may not take the form of worldly survival.

In short, while considering "God, the environment, and the good life" in the comfortable surrounding of New England, I suspect we should all be wary of overly domesticating...God and re-creating him/her too much in our image. It is under-standable that we all yearn for a new sense of belonging, a new sense of reconcilia-tion with an alienated nature, but in our earnest and devout efforts to achieve this reconciliation we should be prepared to understand as well that for the mass of humanity other, more terrible concepts of God are likely to predominate for the foreseeable future. Unless we understand this and can learn to speak to this condition, we will have learned nothing from the notes we have taken at Belshaz'zar's feast.

Timothy Weiskel, "Some Notes from Belshaz'zar's Feast" from *Greening of Faith*, edited by John Carroll, © 1997 by the Trustees of the University of New Hampshire, by permission of University Press of New England.

Creation's Care and Keeping

by Calvin DeWitt

Since his first turtle at the age of three, Dr. Calvin DeWitt has cared for and protected animals and their habitats. He currently serves as Professor of Environmental Studies at the University of Wisconsin-Madison where he especially delights in advising students dedicated to environmental stewardship. Dr. DeWitt and his wife live on an island in the Waubesa Marsh which serves as a field study site for a number of his classes. Dr. DeWitt also directs The Au Sable Institute which has served eighty church-related institutions of higher learning. The goal of the Institute is to find the connections between environmental science, ethics and practice. Au Sable recently opened a new campus in Washington state on Puget Sound's Whidbey Island.

Dr. DeWitt's commitment to his principles is actively demonstrated in his private as well as professional life. He became Chair of his hometown, Dunn, Wisconsin, and developed a model land stewardship plan which received the Renew America Award in 1995. Dr. DeWitt and his wife are members of the Geneva Campus Church.

Throughout his written work, Dr. DeWitt has emphasized the importance of respect for God's creation. Central to his faith is the belief that our goal "should be to live rightly on Earth (as in Heaven) and to image God's love for the world in our thinking and doing." In this piece, Dr. DeWitt highlights Scriptural "principles" revealing his belief that the Bible can be an "ecological handbook." It provides a helpful balance to the predominant view that Christianity has little to say about care for the earth. We include it here to emphasize the strong connections between faith, simplicity and ecological concerns.

...We know that over the centuries the Bible has been critically important to people who seek to live in love and obedience to God. The Bible's importance continues today, not only for church and home, but (and this surprises many Christians and non-Christians alike) also for the environment... In fact, the Bible provides such powerful environmental teachings that it can be thought of as a kind of ecological handbook on how to rightly live on earth!

Among its many teachings, the Bible helps us understand our privilege and our responsibility for environmental stewardship. It also helps us to address thoughtfully who we are, what we are prone to do, and the problems we create in creation.

The Bible's serious treatment of environmental matters should not surprise us. Since God created and sustains all of creation, we should expect the Bible to call us to bring honor to God. We should expect the Scriptures to support creation's proper care and keeping and to encourage us to maintain the integrity of the creation that, in the first chapter of Genesis, God repeatedly calls "good." Moreover, since the Bible professes Jesus Christ as the one through whom *all things* are reconciled, we certainly should expect the Bible to decry creation's destruction, to call for creation's restoration, and to look forward to the whole creation being made right again. And so it does!

Keeping in mind the abuses we have committed against creation and the need for restoration, it is helpful to read the Scriptures afresh, searching for their ecological insights on how we can rightly live on this planet. As we look into God's word, I will identify [a number of principles] that help disclose the Bible's profound environmental message. No doubt you will be able to find many more.

Principle 1
As the Lord keeps and sustains us, so must we keep and sustain our Lord's creation.

Genesis 2:15 conveys a marvelous teaching. Here, God expects Adam to *serve* the garden and to *keep* it.

The Hebrew word for serve (*abad*) is translated as *till, dress,* or *work* in most recent translations of the Bible. Adam and his descendants are expected to meet the needs of the garden so that it will persist and flourish. But how on earth can we serve creation? Shouldn't creation serve us instead?

When I discovered this translation of the word *abad*, I called the library at Calvin College and Seminary to ask the reference librarian, Conrad Bult, if he could find any Bibles that translated this word as *serve*. Bult discovered, in *Young's Literal Translation of the Bible: A Revised Edition* (Grand Rapids, MI: Baker Book House, 1953), Genesis 2:15 translated in this way: "And Jehovah God taketh the man and causeth him to rest in the garden of Eden, to serve it and to keep it." What this means I will leave to you my dear reader, as a puzzle that you can discuss with your friends.

God also expects us as Adam's descendants to *keep* the garden. This word keep is sometimes translated *tend, take care of, guard* and *look after*. The Hebrew word upon which these translations of keep are based is the word shamar. And shamar indicates a loving, caring, sustaining type of keeping.

In our worship services, we often conclude with the Aaronic blessing from Numbers 6:24: "The Lord bless you and keep you." The word keep here is the same Hebrew word used in Genesis 2:15: *shamar*. When we invoke God's blessing to keep us, we are not asking that God keep us in a kind of preserved, inactive, uninteresting state. Instead we are calling on God to keep us in all of our vitality, with all of our energy and beauty. The keeping we expect of God when we invoke the Aaronic blessing is one that nurtures all of our life-sustaining and life-fulfilling relationships with our family members, with our neighbors and our friends, with the land, air, and water, and with our God. We ask God to love us, to care for us, and to sustain us in relationship to our natural and human environment.

So too with our keeping of God's creation. When we fulfill God's mandate that Adam and Eve *keep* the creation, we make sure that the creatures under our care and keeping are maintained in their proper, natural contexts. They must remain connected to members of the same species, to the many other species with which they interact, and to the soil, air, and water upon which they depend. The rich and full keeping that we invoke with the Aaronic blessing is the kind of rich and full keeping that we should bring to God's garden, to God's creatures, and to all of creation.

Principle 2

We must be disciples of Jesus Christ, the Creator, Sustainer, and Reconciler of all things.

No question about it—the Bible calls us to be disciples, or followers after someone. But we are not to be disciples of the first Adam who neglected to serve (*abad*) and to keep (*shamar*) the creation. He failed in his task of caring service and diligent keeping...

Instead, the Bible tells us, we must be disciples of the last Adam, Jesus Christ (1 Cor. 15:45)... Those who follow the last Adam, Jesus Christ, follow the example of the one who makes all things new, the one who makes all things right again. Colossians 1:19-20 puts it this way: "For God was pleased to have all his fullness dwell in him, and through him to reconcile to himself *all things.*"

Who is this Christ we are to follow? He is the One *by whom* all things were created (John 1). He is the One *for whom* all things were made (Col. 1). And he is the one *through whom* God redeems his people (Heb. 1)...

Principle 3

We must provide for creation's Sabbath rests.

In Exodus 20 and Deuteronomy 5, the Bible requires that one day in seven be set aside as a day of rest for people and animals. This Sabbath day is given to help us all get "off the treadmill" to protect us all from continuous work, to help us pull our lives together again. It is a time to enjoy the fruits of creation, a time of rest and restoration. In Exodus 23 God commands, "Six days do your work, but on the seventh day do not work, so that your ox and your donkey may rest and the slave born in your household, and the alien as well, may be refreshed" (v. 12).

That same passage tells us that the land also needs a time of rest. "For six years you are to sow your fields and harvest the crops, but during the seventh year let the land lie unplowed and unused. Then the poor among your people may get food from it, and the wild animals may eat what they leave" (vv. 10-11).

Was this command problematic for God's Old Testament people? Listen to this discussion from Leviticus 25:20-21: "You may ask, 'What will we eat in the seventh year if we do not plant or harvest our crops?' I will send you such a blessing in the sixth year that the land will yield enough for three years." God was instructing the people not to worry, but to practice his law so that the land would be *fruitful*. "If you follow my decrees and are careful to obey my commands, I will send you rain in its season, and the ground will yield its crops and the trees of the field their fruit." (Lev. 26:3-4).

In the New Testament, Christ clearly defines the place of the Sabbath in our lives: The Sabbath is made for we who are served by it, not the other way around. The Sabbath is made for the land, for the people, and for God's other creatures. Thus, the Sabbath year is given to protect the land from relentless exploitation, to help the land rejuvenate, to help it pull itself together again.

This Sabbath is not merely a legalistic requirement; rather, it is a profound principle. That's why in some farming communities the Sabbath principle is practiced by letting the land rest every *second* year, because "that is what the land needs." The Sabbath is made for the land, and not the land for the Sabbath. The Sabbath rule is not therefore restricted to agriculture but applies to all creation. It affects our use of water and air. It has implications for where we discharge our exhaust, smoke, sewage, and other things that we "throw away."...

Principle 4
We should enjoy, but must not destroy, creation's fruitfulness.

God's blessing of fruitfulness is for the fish of the sea and the birds of the air as well as for people. In Genesis 1 God declares, "Let the water teem with living creatures, and let birds fly above the earth across the expanse of the sky" (v. 20). And then God blesses these creatures with fruitfulness: "Be fruitful and increase in number and fill the water in the seas, and let the birds increase on the earth" (v. 22).

God's evident hand in creation reflects a commitment to providing for the land and life on earth. Psalm 104 depicts God's care for the world:

> *He makes springs pour water into the ravines; it flows between the mountains. They give water to all the beasts of the field: the wild donkeys quench their thirst. The birds of the air nest by the waters; they sing among the branches. He waters the mountains from his upper chambers; the earth is satisfied by the fruit of his work.*
>
> —vv. 10-13

And Psalm 23 describes how our providing God "... makes me lie down in green pastures...leads me beside quiet waters... restores my soul."

As God's work brings fruit to creation, so should ours. As God provides for the creatures, so should we people who were created to reflect God whose image we bear. Imaging God, we too should provide for the creatures. And, as Noah spared no time, expense, or reputation when God's creatures were threatened with extinction, neither should we. In Noah's time a deluge of water covered the land. In our time a deluge of people sprawls over the land, displacing God's creatures, limiting their potential to obey God's command to "be fruitful and increase in number." To those who would allow a human flood to roll across the land at the expense of all other creatures, the prophet Isaiah warns: "Woe to you who add house to house and join field to field till no space is left and you live alone in the land" (Isa. 5:8).

Thus, while we are expected to enjoy creation, and while we are expected to partake of creation's fruit, we may not destroy the fruitfulness upon which creation's fullness depends. We must, with Noah, save the species whose interactions with each other, and with land and water, form the fabric of the biosphere. We must let the profound admonition of Ezekiel 34:18 reverberate and echo in our minds: "Is it not enough for you to feed on the good pasture? Must you also trample the rest of your pasture with your feet? Is it not enough for you to drink clear water? Must you also muddy the rest with your feet?"...

Principle 5
We must seek true contentment.

Genesis 1 through 11 and our own experience tell us that, even from the time of Adam and Eve, humanity has not been satisfied with the fruitfulness and grace of the Garden—the productive and beautiful creation that God has provided for us. Since the beginning of time people have chosen to go their own way, grasping more and ever more from the creation for selfish advancement. In our modern age we feel the effects of this relentless urge to press land and life to produce more, ever more, without limit...this drive is seriously degrading the earth's environment today. Our prayer should be that of Psalm 119:36: "Turn my heart toward your statutes and not toward selfish gain."

If searching for contentment through accumulating the goods of creation is harmful, then where do we find true happiness? By doing the work that God would have us do in his world. 1 Timothy 6:6 says, "godliness with contentment is great gain." True contentment means aiming to have the things that will sustain us, but not going beyond that. An Amish saying based on this passage goes like this: "To desire to be rich is to desire to have more than what we need to be content."...

Being content also helps us preserve creation's integrity. All the things we use, all the things we make, everything we manipulate, everything we accumulate, derives from the creation itself. If we learn to seek godly contentment as our great gain, we will take and shape less of God's earth. We will demand less from the land. We will leave room for the other creatures. We will responsibly exercise dominion over the earth and will preserve it. We will thus allow creation to heal itself and to perpetuate its fruitfulness, to the praise of its Creator.

Principle 6
We must practice what we believe.

Finally, the Scriptures admonish us to act on what we know is right. Merely knowing God's requirements for stewardship is not enough... Unless we act on our belief and put God's requirements to use, they do absolutely no good.

The inactivity of God's people is well-documented and questioned in the pages of Scripture:

> *My people come to you, as they usually do, and sit before you to listen to your words, but they do not put them into practice. With their mouths they express devotion, but their hearts are greedy for unjust gain. Indeed, to them you are nothing more than one who sings love songs with a beautiful voice and plays an instrument well, for they hear your words but do not put them into practice.*
>
> —Ezekiel 33:31-32

> *Why do you call me "Lord, Lord," and do not do what I say?*
>
> —Luke 6:46

Christian environmental stewardship does not end with the last chapter of a book we are reading on the subject... Instead, studying the Bible to learn God's requirements for stewardship of creation marks a beginning point. It brings us directly to the life-and-death question, "Now what must we *do?*" ...Our devotion to God and to the Word requires us to care for others—to share our food with the hungry, to loosen the chains of injustice, to let the oppressed go free. The challenge of environmental stewardship is to move forth and put what we know and believe into practice.

The Discipline of Simplicity

by Richard J. Foster

Richard Foster introduces the theme of this essay when he writes, "the Christian discipline of simplicity is an inward reality that results in an outward lifestyle." After laying the foundation for a biblical perspective on economic issues, he suggests that the majority of Christians have not seriously considered the resulting "call" of simplicity because it "directly challenges...an affluent lifestyle." Foster acknowledges that the practice of simplicity can lead to legalism and then dares to suggest ten principles for the "outward expression of simplicity"—a difficult, but important, venture.

Foster is one of the more prominent Christian voices for simplicity. See what you think of his ideas.

∞

When we are truly in this interior simplicity our whole appearance is franker, more natural. This true simplicity…makes us conscious of a certain openness, gentleness, innocence, gaiety, and serenity, which is charming when we see it near to and continually, with pure eyes. O, how amiable this simplicity is! Who will give it to me? I leave all for this. It is the Pearl of the Gospel.

—Francois Fenelon

∞

Simplicity is freedom. Duplicity is bondage. Simplicity brings joy and balance. Duplicity brings anxiety and fear. The preacher of Ecclesiastes observes that "God made man simple; man's complex problems are of his own devising" (Eccles. 7:30, JB). Because many of us are experiencing the liberation God brings through simplicity we are once again singing an old Shaker hymn:

'Tis the gift to be simple,
'Tis the gift to be free,
'Tis the gift to come down where you ought to be,
And when we find ourselves in the place just right,
'Twill be in the valley of love and delight.
When true simplicity is gained,
To bow and to bend we shan't be ashamed.
To turn, turn will be our delight
'Till by turning, turning we come round right.

The Christian Discipline of simplicity is an *inward* reality that results in an *outward* lifestyle. Both the inward and the outward aspects of simplicity are essential. We deceive ourselves if we believe we can possess the inward reality without its having a profound effect on how we live. To attempt to arrange an outward lifestyle of simplicity without the inward reality leads to deadly legalism.

Simplicity begins in inward focus and unity… Experiencing the inward reality liberates us outwardly. Speech becomes truthful and honest. The lust for status and position is gone because we no longer need status and position. We cease from showy extravagance not on the grounds of being unable to afford it, but on the grounds of principle. Our goods become available to others. We join the experience that Richard E. Byrd, after months alone in the barren Arctic, recorded in his journal, "I am learning… that a man can live profoundly without masses of things." [75]

Contemporary culture lacks both the inward reality and the outward life-style of simplicity. We must live in the modern world, and we are affected by its fractured and fragmented state. We are trapped in a maze of competing attachments. One moment we make decisions on the basis of sound reason and the next moment out of fear of what others will think of us. We have no unity or focus around which our lives are oriented.

Because we lack a divine Center our need for security has led us into an insane attachment to things. We really must understand that the lust for affluence in contemporary society is psychotic. It is psychotic because it has completely lost touch with reality. We crave things we neither need nor enjoy. "We buy things we do not want to impress people we do not like." [77] Where planned obsolescence leaves off, psychological obsolescence takes over. We are made to feel ashamed to wear clothes or drive cars until they are worn out. The mass media have convinced us that to be out of step with fashion is to be out of step with reality. It is time we awaken to the fact that conformity to a sick society is to be sick. Until we see how unbalanced our culture has become at this point, we will not be able to deal with the mammon spirit within ourselves nor will we desire Christian simplicity.

This psychosis permeates even our mythology. The modern hero is [one] who purposefully becomes rich rather than [one] who voluntarily becomes poor... Covetousness we call ambition. Hoarding we call prudence. Greed we call industry...

Courageously, we need to articulate new, more human ways to live. We should take exception to the modern psychosis that defines people by how much they can produce or what they earn. We should experiment with bold new alternatives to the present death-giving system. The Spiritual Discipline of simplicity is not a lost dream, but a recurrent vision throughout history. It can be recaptured today. It must be.

The Bible and Simplicity

Before attempting to forge a Christian view of simplicity it is necessary to destroy the prevailing notion that the Bible is ambiguous about economic issues. Often it is felt that our response to wealth is an individual matter. The Bible's teaching in this area is said to be strictly a matter of private interpretation. We try to believe that Jesus did not address himself to practical economic questions.

No serious reading of Scripture can substantiate such a view. The biblical injunctions against the exploitation of the poor and the accumulation of wealth are clear and straightforward. The Bible challenges nearly every economic value of contemporary society. For example, the Old Testament takes exception to the popular notion of an absolute right to private property. The earth belongs to God, says Scripture, and therefore cannot be held perpetually (Lev. 25:23). The Old Testament legislation of the year of Jubilee stipulated that all land was to revert back to its original owner. In fact, the Bible declares that wealth itself belongs to God, and one purpose of the year of Jubilee was to provide a regular redistribution of wealth. Such a radical view of economics flies in the face of nearly all contemporary belief and practice. Had Israel faithfully observed the Jubilee it would have dealt a death blow to the perennial problem of the rich becoming richer and the poor becoming poorer.

Constantly the Bible deals decisively with the inner spirit of slavery that an idolatrous attachment to wealth brings. "If riches increase, set not your heart on them," counsels the Psalmist (Ps. 62:10). The tenth commandment is against covetousness, the inner lust to have, which leads to stealing and oppression....

Jesus declared war on the materialism of his day. (And I would suggest that he declares war on the materialism of our day as well.) The Aramaic term for wealth is "mammon" and Jesus condemns it as a rival God: "No servant can serve two masters; for either he will hate the one and love the other, or he will be devoted to the one and despise the other. You cannot serve God and mammon" (Luke 16:13). He speaks frequently and unambiguously to economic issues. He says, "Blessed are you poor, for yours is the kingdom of God" and "Woe to you that are rich, for you have received your consolation" (Luke 6:20, 24)....He saw the grip that wealth can have on a person. He knew that "where your treasure is, there will your heart be also," which is precisely why he commanded his followers: "Do not lay up for yourselves treasures on earth" (Matt. 6:21, 19). He is not saying that the heart should or should not be where the treasure is. He is stating the plain fact that wherever you find the treasure, you *will* find the heart.

He exhorted the rich young ruler not just to have an inner attitude of detachment from his possessions, but literally to get rid of his possessions if he wanted the kingdom of God (Matt. 19:16-22). He says "Take heed, and beware of all covetousness; for a man's life does not consist in the abundance of his possessions" (Luke 12:15). He counseled people who came seeking God, "Sell your possessions, and give alms; provide yourselves with purses that do not grow old, with a treasure in the heavens that does not fail..." (Luke 12:33). He told the parable of the rich farmer whose life centered in hoarding—we would call him prudent; Jesus called him a fool (Luke 12:16-21). He states that if we really want the kingdom of God we must, like a merchant in search of fine pearls, be willing to sell everything we have to get it (Matt. 13:45, 46). He calls all who would follow him to a joyful life of carefree unconcern for possessions: "Give to every one who begs from you; and of him who takes away your goods do not ask them again" (Luke 6:30).

Jesus speaks to the question of economics more than any other single social issue. If, in a comparatively simple society, our Lord lays such strong emphasis upon the spiritual dangers of wealth, how much more should we who live in a highly affluent culture take seriously the economic question.

The Epistles reflect the same concern. Paul says, "Those who desire to be rich fall into temptation, into a snare, into many senseless and hurtful desires that plunge men into ruin and destruction" (1 Tim. 6:9)...A deacon is not to be "greedy for gain" (1 Tim. 3:8). The writer to the Hebrews counsels, "Keep your life free from love of money, and be content with what you have; for he has said, 'I will never fail you nor forsake you'" (Heb. 13:5)...Paul calls covetousness idolatry and

commands stern discipline against anyone guilty of greed (Eph. 5:5; 1 Cor. 5:11)...
He counsels the wealthy not to trust in their wealth, but in God, and to share generously with others (1 Tim. 6:17-19).

Having said all this, I must hasten to add that God intends that we should have adequate material provision. There is misery today from a simple lack of provision just as there is misery when people try to make a life out of provision. Forced poverty is evil and should be renounced. Nor does the Bible condone an extreme asceticism. Scripture declares consistently and forcefully that the creation is good and to be enjoyed. Asceticism makes an unbiblical division between a good spiritual world and an evil material world and so finds salvation in paying as little attention as possible to the physical realm of existence.

Asceticism and simplicity are mutually incompatible. Occasional superficial similarities in practice must never obscure the radical difference between the two. Asceticism renounces possessions. Simplicity sets possessions in proper perspective. Asceticism finds no place for a "land flowing with milk and honey." Simplicity rejoices in this gracious provision from the hand of God. Asceticism finds contentment only when it is abased. Simplicity knows contentment in both abasement and abounding (Phil. 4:12).

Simplicity is the only thing that sufficiently reorients our lives so that possessions can be genuinely enjoyed without destroying us. Without simplicity we will either capitulate to the "mammon" spirit of this present evil age, or we will fall into an un-Christian legalistic asceticism. Both lead to idolatry. Both are spiritually lethal.

Descriptions of the abundant material provision God gives his people abound in Scripture. "For the Lord your God is bringing you into a good land... a land... in which you will lack nothing" (Deut. 8:7-9). Warnings about the danger of provisions that are not kept in proper perspective also abound. "Beware lest you say in your heart, 'My power and the might of my hand have gotten me this wealth'" (Deut. 8:17).

The Spiritual Discipline of simplicity provides the needed perspective. Simplicity sets us free to receive the provision of God as a gift that is not ours to keep and can be freely shared with others. Once we recognize that the Bible denounces the materialist and the ascetic with equal vigor, we are prepared to turn our attention to the framing of a Christian understanding of simplicity.

A Place to Stand

Archimedes once declared, "Give me a place to stand and I will move the earth." Such a focal point is important in every Discipline but is acutely so with simplicity. Of all the Disciplines simplicity is the most visible and therefore the most open to corruption. The majority of Christians have never seriously wrestled with the problem of simplicity, conveniently ignoring Jesus' many words on the subject. The reason is simple: this Discipline directly challenges our vested interests in an affluent lifestyle. But those who take the biblical teaching on simplicity seriously are faced with severe temptations toward legalism. In the earnest attempt to give concrete expression to Jesus' economic teaching, it is easy to mistake our particular expression of the teaching for the teaching itself. We wear this attire or buy that kind of house and canonize our choices as the simple life. This danger gives special importance to finding and clearly articulating an Archimedian focal point for simplicity.

We have such a focal point in the words of Jesus: "Therefore I tell you, do not be anxious about your life, what you shall eat or what you shall drink, nor about your body, what you shall put on. Is not life more than food, and the body more than clothing? Look at the birds of the air: they neither sow nor reap nor gather into barns, and yet your heavenly Father feeds them. Are you not of more value than they? And which of you by being anxious can add one cubit to his span of life? And why are you anxious about clothing? Consider the lilies of the field, how they grow; they neither toil nor spin; yet I tell you, even Solomon in all his glory was not arrayed like one of these. But if God so clothes the grass of the field, which today is alive and tomorrow is thrown into the oven, will he not much more clothe you, O men of little faith? Therefore do not be anxious, saying, 'What shall we eat?' or 'What shall we drink?' or 'What shall we wear?' For the Gentiles seek all these things; and your heavenly Father knows that you need them all. *But seek first his kingdom and his righteousness, and all these things shall be yours as well*" (Matt. 6:25-33 [italics added]).

The central point for the Discipline of simplicity is to seek the kingdom of God and the righteousness of his kingdom *first* and then everything necessary will come in its proper order....Nothing must come before the kingdom of God, including the desire for a simple life-style.

Simplicity itself becomes idolatry when it takes precedence over seeking the kingdom. In a particularly penetrating comment on this passage of Scripture, Soren Kierkegaard considers what sort of effort could be made to pursue the kingdom of God. Should a person get a suitable job in order to exert a virtuous influence? His answer: no, we must *first* seek God's kingdom. Then should we give away all our money to feed the poor? Again the answer: no, we must *first* seek God's kingdom. Well, then perhaps we are to go out and preach this truth to the world that people are to seek first *God's* kingdom? Once again the answer is a resounding: no, we are *first* to seek the kingdom of God. Kierkegaard concludes, "Then in a certain sense it is nothing I shall do. Yes, certainly, in a certain sense it is nothing, become nothing before God, learn to keep silent; in this silence is the beginning, which is, *first* to seek God's Kingdom." [77]

Focus upon the kingdom produces the inward reality, and without the inward reality we will degenerate into legalistic trivia. Nothing else can be central. The desire to get out of the rat race cannot be central, the redistribution of the world's wealth cannot be central, the concern for ecology cannot be central. Seeking *first* God's kingdom and the righteousness, both personal and social, of that kingdom is the only thing that can be central in the Spiritual Discipline of simplicity.

The person who does not seek the kingdom first does not seek it at all. Worthy as all other concerns may be, the moment *they* become the focus of our efforts they become idolatry. To center on them will inevitably draw us into declaring that our particular activity *is* Christian simplicity. And, in fact, when the kingdom of God is genuinely placed first, ecological concerns, the poor, the equitable distribution of wealth, and many other things will be given their proper attention.

As Jesus made clear in our central passage, freedom from anxiety is one of the inward evidences of seeking first the kingdom of God. The inward reality of simplicity involves a life of joyful unconcern for possessions. Neither the greedy nor the miserly know this liberty. It has nothing to do with abundance of possessions or their lack. It is an inward spirit of trust....

Freedom from anxiety is characterized by three inner attitudes. If what we have we receive as a gift, and if what we have is to be cared for by God, and if what we have is available to others, then we will possess freedom from anxiety. *This is the inward reality of simplicity.* However, if what we have we believe we have gotten, and if what we have we believe we must hold onto, and if what we have is not available to others, then we will live in anxiety. Such persons will never know simplicity regardless of the outward contortions they may put themselves through in order to live "the simple life."

To receive what we have as a gift from God is the first inner attitude of simplicity. We work but we know that it is not our work that gives us what we have....We are dependent upon God for the simplest elements of life: air, water, sun....When we are tempted to think that what we own is the result of our personal efforts, it takes only a little drought or a small accident to show us once again how utterly dependent we are for everything.

To know that it is God's business, and not ours, to care for what we have is the second inner attitude of simplicity. God is able to protect what we possess. We can trust him.... It is only common sense to take normal precautions, but if we believe that precaution itself protects us and our goods, we will be riddled with anxiety. There simply is no such thing as "burglar proof" precaution. Obviously, these matters are not restricted to possessions but include such things as our reputation and our employment. Simplicity means the freedom to trust God for these (and all) things.

To have our goods available to others marks the third inner attitude of simplicity. If our goods are not available to the community when it is clearly right and good, then they are stolen goods. The reason we find such an idea so difficult is our fear of the future. We cling to our possessions rather than sharing them because we are anxious about tomorrow. But if we truly believe that God is who Jesus says he is, then we do not need to be afraid.... If someone is in need, we are free to help them. Again, ordinary common sense will define the parameters of our sharing and save us from foolishness.

When we are seeking first the kingdom of God, these three attitudes will characterize our lives. Taken together they define what Jesus means by "do not be anxious." They comprise the inner reality of Christian simplicity. And we can be certain that when we live this way the "all these things" that are necessary to carry on human life adequately will be ours as well.

The Outward Expression of Simplicity

To describe simplicity only as an inner reality is to say something false. The inner reality is not a reality until there is an outward expression. To experience the liberating spirit of simplicity *will* affect how we live. As I have warned earlier, every attempt to give specific application to simplicity runs the risk of a deterioration into legalism. It is a risk, however, that we must take, for to refuse to discuss specifics would banish the Discipline to the theoretical.... [So, I] suggest ten controlling principles for the outward expression of simplicity. They should never be viewed as laws but as only one attempt to flesh out the meaning of simplicity for today.

First, buy things for their usefulness rather than their status. Cars should be bought for their utility, not their prestige. Consider riding a bicycle. When you are considering an apartment, a condominium, or a house, thought should be given to livability rather than how much it will impress others....

Consider your clothes. Most people...buy clothes because they want to keep up with the fashions. Hang the fashions! Buy what you need.... If it is practical in your situation, learn the joy of making clothes.... John Wesley writes, "As... for apparel, I buy the most lasting and, in general, the plainest I can. I buy no furniture but what is necessary and cheap." [79]

Second, reject anything that is producing an addiction in you. Learn to distinguish between a real psychological need, like cheerful surroundings, and an addiction.... If you have become addicted to television, by all means sell your set or give it away. Any of the media that you find you cannot do without, get rid of: radios, stereos, magazines, videos, newspapers, books. If money has a grip on your heart, give some away and feel the inner release. Simplicity is freedom, not slavery. Refuse to be a slave to anything but God.

Remember, an addiction, by its very nature, is something that is beyond your control. Resolves of the will alone are useless in defeating a true addiction. You cannot just decide to be free of it. But you can decide to open this corner of your life to the forgiving grace and healing power of God. You can decide to allow loving friends who know the ways of prayer to stand with you....

Third, develop a habit of giving things away. If you find that you are becoming attached to some possession, consider giving it to someone who needs it. I still remember the Christmas I decided that rather than buying or even making an item, I would give away something that meant a lot to me. My motive was selfish: I wanted to know the liberation that comes from even this simple act of voluntary poverty. The gift was a ten-speed bike. As I went to the person's home to deliver the present, I remember singing with new meaning the worship chorus, "Freely,

freely you have received; freely, freely give." When my son Nathan was six years old he heard of a classmate who needed a lunch pail and asked me if he could give him his own lunch pail. Hallelujah!...

Fourth, refuse to be propagandized by the custodians of modern gadgetry. Time-saving devices almost never save time.... Most gadgets are built to break down and wear out and so complicate our lives rather than enhance them. This problem is a plague in the toy industry.... Often children find more joy in playing with old pots and pans than with the latest space set. Look for toys that are educational and durable. Make some yourself.

Usually gadgets are an unnecessary drain on the energy resources of the world. The United States has less than six percent of the world's population, but consumes about thirty-three percent of the world's energy....[79] Environmental responsibility alone should keep us from buying the majority of the gadgets produced today....

Fifth, learn to enjoy things without owning them. Owning things is an obsession in our culture. If we own it, we feel we can control it; and if we can control it, we feel it will give us more pleasure. The idea is an illusion. Many things in life can be enjoyed without possessing or controlling them. Share things. Enjoy the beach without feeling you have to buy a piece of it. Enjoy public parks and libraries.

Sixth, develop a deeper appreciation for the creation. Get close to the earth. Walk whenever you can. Listen to the birds. Enjoy the texture of grass and leaves. Smell the flowers. Marvel in the rich colors everywhere. Simplicity means to discover once again that "the earth is the Lord's and the fullness thereof" (Ps. 24:1).

Seventh, look with a healthy skepticism at all "buy now, pay later" schemes. They are a trap and only deepen your bondage. Both Old and New Testaments condemn usury for good reasons. ("Usury" in the Bible is not used in the modern sense of exorbitant interest; it referred to any kind of interest at all.) Charging interest was viewed as an unbrotherly exploitation of another's misfortune, hence a denial of community. Jesus denounced usury as a sign of the old life and admonished his disciples to "lend, expecting nothing in return" (Luke 6:35).

These words of Scripture should not be elevated into some kind of universal law obligatory upon all cultures at all times. But neither should they be thought of as totally irrelevant to modern society.... Certainly prudence, as well as simplicity, demands that we use extreme caution before incurring debt.

Eighth, obey Jesus' instructions about plain, honest speech. "Let what you say be simply 'Yes' or 'No'; anything more than this comes from evil" (Matt. 5:37). If you consent to do a task, do it. Avoid flattery and half-truths. Make honesty and integrity the distinguishing characteristics of your speech. Reject jargon and abstract speculation whose purpose is to obscure and impress rather than to illuminate and inform.

Plain speech is difficult because we so seldom live out of the divine Center.... But if our speech comes out of obedience to the divine Center, we will find no reason to turn our "yes" into "no" and our "no" into "yes." We will be living in simplicity of speech because our words will have only one Source. Soren Kierke-gaard writes: "If thou art absolutely obedient to God, then there is no ambiguity in thee and… thou art mere simplicity before God… One thing there is which all Satan's cunning and all the snares of temptation cannot take by surprise, and that is simplicity." [80]

Ninth, reject anything that breeds the oppression of others. Perhaps no person has more fully embodied this principle than the eighteenth-century Quaker tailor John Woolman. His famous *Journal is* redundant with tender references to his desire to live so as not to oppress others. "Here I was led into a close and laborious inquiry whether I…kept clear from all things which tended to stir up or were con-nected with wars;…my heart was deeply concerned that in [the] future I might in all things keep steadily to the pure truth, and live and walk in the plainness and simplicity of a sincere follower of Christ…And here luxury and covetousness, with the numerous oppressions and other evils attending them, appeared very afflicting to me…" [81] This is one of the most difficult and sensitive issues for us to face, but face it we must. Do we sip our coffee and eat our bananas at the expense of exploit-ing Latin American peasants? In a world of limited resources, does our lust for wealth mean the poverty of others? Should we buy products that are made by forc-ing people into dull assembly-line jobs? Do we enjoy hierarchical relationships in the company or factory that keep others under us? Do we oppress our children or spouse because we feel certain tasks are beneath us?

Often our oppression is tinged with racism, sexism, and nationalism. The color of the skin still affects one's position in the company. The sex of a job applicant still affects the salary. The national origin of a person still affects the way he or she is perceived. May God give us prophets today who, like John Woolman, will call us "from the desire of wealth" so that we may be able to "break the yoke of oppression." [82]

Tenth, shun anything that distracts you from seeking first the kingdom of God. It is so easy to lose focus in the pursuit of legitimate, even good things. Job, position, status, family, friends, security—these and many more can all too quickly become the center of attention. George Fox warns, "…there is the danger and the tempta-tion to you, of drawing your minds into your business, and clogging them with it; so that ye can hardly do anything to the service of God…and your minds will go into the things, and not over the things…And then, if the Lord God cross you, and stop you by sea and land, and take (your) goods and customs from you, that your minds should not be cumbered, then that mind that is cumbered, will fret, being out of the power of God." [83]

May God give you—and me—the courage, the wisdom, the strength always to hold the kingdom of God as the number one priority of our lives. To do so is to live in simplicity.

Worldviews: The Lens through Which We See

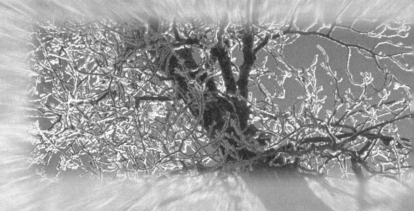

While the effects of our crisis are most evident in the
(ecological) sphere, the crisis itself is not first of all
an ecological crisis. It is a crisis concerning the
way we think. We are treating our planet in an
inhuman and God-forsaken manner because we
see things in an inhuman, God-forsaken way.

—*Philip Sherrard*

The only real chance we have of surviving as
a species is through a radical theological
revolution—a thoroughgoing re-examination of those cultural beliefs we hold to
most religiously.

—*Timothy Weiskel*

Worldview as Inheritance

by Michael Schut

Sometimes it hits us squarely between the eyes—maybe visiting another culture or simply visiting with someone as close as our own spouse or a good friend: our worldview, the glasses through which we see the world, is not the only way to perceive reality. And yet the assumptions embedded within that particular world-view often go un-examined, leading us to live a life largely defined by the larger, dominant culture. In light of current ecological and social issues, it is crucial to examine these assumptions: do they still serve us well?; do they help us live life abundantly?

Both my mother and father are one of six children; both were raised in small, Midwestern, Dutch communities. Their parents farmed, and raised their families in the Dutch Reformed Church. That culture and its beliefs and values are a significant part of who I am. And though some of my beliefs have changed, that way of seeing the world (my worldview) will always reflect those roots.

∞

The interesting thing about the ways we perceive the world, is how generally unaware we are of them. Charlene Spretnak points out that the modern worldview "is to us as water to a fish." It is all around us, defining all that we do and see.

Webster defines "worldview" as "a comprehensive, personal philosophy of the world and of human life." It is our particular "picture of reality." Worldviews essentially provide us with a way of understanding and organizing our lives and making sense of the larger world.

The sociologists Berger and Luckmann suggest that our worldviews are constructed for us by the particular family, religious institution, and culture in which we live (see *The Social Construction of Reality*). In other words, our worldviews are inherited. In spite of this, they point out, we do not experience our reality as relative; we assume that our particular way of perceiving the world around us is somehow *the* way. (Accepting Berger and Luckmann's premise can be threatening. If our "reality," including some of the foundational beliefs and tenets crucial to our perception and understanding, is relative, then what can we rely on, what can we trust? Are there absolutes? It is important to point out, therefore, that Berger and Luckmann do not claim there are no absolutes. They are not interested in proving or disproving the possible presence of absolutes beyond the particular reality which society bequeaths us. What they do suggest, however, is that a person's or church's claim to truth has a historical and cultural past, and is thus not necessarily *the* truth.)

No matter how we grow up or who is most responsible for our socialization, we are exposed to a certain "construction of reality" which becomes part of our story. Mine happens to include midwest, Dutch, farming culture and a certain strain of Protestantism. Berger and Luckmann describe this accumulated and passed-on reality, this story, as a "social stock of knowledge" *which places certain assumptions and beliefs in the foreground of our awareness and leaves others in the background.*

When imparting a worldview and its accumulated stock of knowledge, then, a society is essentially defining that which is important and deserves attention. For individuals within that society, the inherited worldview also defines our sense of self, the way in which we experience ourselves.

As I see it, most Christian churches impart to their members a worldview which sees humanity as separate from (and often superior to) the rest of creation; love for and relationship with the rest of the natural world is simply not legitimized. Nor are churches likely to teach a worldview which sees the connections between social and ecological justice—between caring for people and caring for the earth. In my own church experience, I thankfully recall a strong concern for issues of social justice, but rarely, if ever, did I hear a prayer for God's bleeding creation or a sermon on God's love for all S/he had made. Finally, the "sense of self" imparted to me by my church (as well as the larger culture) was very individualistic—it did not recognize my inherent connections with the natural world.

In the face of today's social and environmental problems, it is crucial that we begin to expand our sense of self to include our connections with each other and with the natural world. (And the Church, as a uniquely powerful "worldview-definer," can play a significant role in this process.) If I do not somehow perceive you as intrinsically connected to me, it is much easier not to care for you. Similarly, if I do not perceive the natural world as somehow deeply connected to me, it is easier to neglect or destroy that world. Consider Jay McDaniel's words as a picture of this expanded sense of self:

> *If we consider a woman—as a self—we see that her identity includes, rather than excludes, her relationships with other human beings. Her children and husband are part of who and what she is, as are her friends, her neighbors... In addition, those whom she has known in the past are part of her identity... This principle of inclusion applies to non-human nature as well. Through the food she eats, the land on which her house resides, the flora and fauna that inhabit that land... the natural world is part of her identity... Her self is an en-peopled self, an embodied self, and an en-natured self.*
>
> —McDaniel, p. 207

McDaniel expands the implications of this principle of self-inclusion. First, he states that "solidarity with," rather than "disengagement from," the world is a more appropriate attitude toward life. Second, he emphasizes that it is the *world* that "merits an attitude of solidarity...rather than simply a human community, the nation, or the church." Third, he sees that God is not a "disengaged observer whose primary preoccupation is with reward and punishment. Instead, God is a nurturing self..." (McDaniel, 207-208).

McDaniel's principle of "self-inclusion" resonates with a native American sense of self as described in Jamake Highwater's book, *The Primal Mind*. Highwater states that "the existence of the individual presupposes the existence of the community" (p. 172). People briefly reside on the planet, enriching their community, and then pass on, but the community remains. According to Highwater, Native Americans comprehend themselves (their "self") through relationships—not limited to happenings within their own skin or even to those within their human community, but expanding outward to include "all things of the world."

Both McDaniel's principle of self-inclusion and Highwater's description of the native American mind-set recognize connections and relationship. Such a recognition of interconnectedness, when combined with empathy and justice, can lead toward a compassionate way of life. When Jesus commanded us to "love our neighbors as ourselves," was he not recognizing interconnectedness and calling us to a compassionate way of life?

So far, this essay has generally considered the inherited nature of our worldviews and specifically the Church's impact on our sense of self. Our worldviews (including our image of God) also significantly influence our attitudes toward simplicity and the connotations the word brings to mind. For example, those attending a church emphasizing wealth (and often conspicuous consumption) as a "sign of God's blessing" might look at simplicity as, at best, a curious phenomenon if not a threatening absurdity. For those attending a church emphasizing God's justice and love and Christ's life of service on behalf of the poor, a move toward simplicity might seem an act of solidarity and an expression of compassion. Others may perceive simplicity as forced asceticism, a necessary path required by a demanding, punishing God. Finally, some may perceive simplicity as a move toward greater freedom and a grateful response to the beauty and mystery of God-given life.

No matter the view, to the extent that the church has been co-opted by the "American dream of success," a move toward simplicity will require not only swimming against the materialism of our society, but also against the implicit, if not explicit, message of many of our churches.

EDITOR'S NOTE: Swimming against such strong cultural currents is difficult if not impossible on your own. We encourage you to check out the group learning experience at the back of this book. It is designed to help create a community of support.

McDaniel, Jay. "Christianity and the Need for New Vision." In *Religion and Environmental Crisis*, Eugene Hargrove, Editor. University of Georgia Press, Athens, Georgia, 1986, pp. 188-212.

Highwater, Jamake. *The Primal Mind*. Harper and Row, New York, NY, 1981.

Traditional Western View of Reality

by Duane Elgin

Duane Elgin is a former senior social scientist at the California think tank SRI International. He lives in Mill Valley, California, where he directs the nonprofit organization Choosing Our Future. Best known for his classic book on ecological lifestyles, *Voluntary Simplicity*, Elgin also wrote *Awakening Earth* and along with Joseph Campbell and others co-authored *Changing Images of Man*.

In this pithy excerpt from his important work *Voluntary Simplicity*, Elgin briefly uncovers some of the primary assumptions underlying the Western culture's worldview. While acknowledging some of its very real contributions, he proceeds to discuss some of its limitations which significantly influence our current ecological and social problems. (In this excerpt, Elgin lumps together Greek philosophical and Judeo-Christian traditions. While the marriage between these two traditions has deeply affected Western culture, it is important to point out that the Judeo-Christian tradition does not inherently share all of the following characteristics. For example, the dualism of Greek philosophy is not also inherently Christian. The next article by Bhagat briefly addresses this topic.)

∞

By "Western" view of reality I am referring to a perspective that historically has developed in Western European nations and is exemplified by the Greek philosophical traditions and the Judeo-Christian religious traditions. There are several key features of this view that serve to distinguish it from its Eastern counterpart.

First, the Western scientific view of the universe is profoundly materialistic. The fundamental stuff of the universe is conceived to be elementary particles of matter that interact with one another in a predictable fashion. Not surprisingly, this has sometimes been described as a "billiard ball" model of the universe.

Second, the Western view of reality is profoundly dualistic. The Judeo-Christian religious tradition sets "God" apart from this reality. God is viewed as the force that created this complex machine-universe; having created it and set it into motion, God could then be viewed as apart from "his" creation.

Third, the West tends to view the universe as being largely lifeless. Since the stuff of the universe is seen as consisting of elementary particles of matter, the foundations of the universe are viewed as essentially nonliving. The universe is seen as an inanimate machine wherein humankind occupies a unique and elevated position among the sparse life-forms that do exist. Assuming a relatively barren universe, it seemed only rational that humankind exploit the lifeless material universe (and the lesser life-forms of nature) on behalf of the most intensely living—humankind itself.

Fourth, the Western view places the intellect and rationality at the pinnacle of human faculties. The faculty of the intellect is viewed as the primary instrument of worldly-mastery. With rational thought and the power of reason, it was felt that humankind could discover the natural laws governing the vast machine-universe and thereby acquire growing mastery over nature.

Fifth, the Western view affirms the potential for material change and progress. The material world is viewed as an arena or field of action where the interplay between God and humankind could manifest as an unfolding drama. The ancient Jewish tradition, in particular, injects this sense of spiritual involvement in the course of worldly evolution. The result is that the material world is viewed as "going somewhere." There is a sense of real potential for social and material progress.

Sixth, in a materialistic and largely lifeless universe, who "we" are has been defined by the perimeter of the physical body. In other words, our individuality has been viewed as synonymous with our physical existence. The individual, then, is both unique and alone—apart from others and apart from the Divine. The know-ing faculty, or consciousness, is viewed as little more than the product of biochemi-cal activity in the brain. Thus, consciousness is not viewed as a bridge beyond physical separateness.

The foregoing greatly simplifies the Western view of reality and by no means exhausts the pattern of thought and assumption that characterize the Western world view. Yet, it is sufficient to allow us to note important contributions and limitations of this view.

The Western view of reality has been enormously successful in realizing its own overriding goal: that of material and social development. This includes not only more goods and services, but also the development of highly efficient modes of organization—economic, legal, political—designed to promote and support the material development of society. In realizing this goal, Western cultures have also cultivated the development of autonomous individuals capable of relatively high levels of self-regulating behavior. Although personal material gain has often been the motivating force for self-regulation, the Western setting has pushed the indi-vidual to learn to take charge of his or her own life, particularly with regard to material and social concerns. Thus, the principal contributions of the Western world view are, I think, twofold: sociomaterial growth and psychological maturation.

Yet, the unparalleled achievements in these two areas have not been without their costs. Material growth without a larger sense of purpose makes living little more than "only not dying." Institutional development without the simultaneous growth of life-serving social purposes results in those institutions being run on behalf of the narrow concerns of special interest groups. Psychological maturation without balanced integration of the spiritual or consciousness dimensions of life yields autonomous individuals who tend to be alienated from self, society, and the cosmos.

The overriding limitation of the traditional Western scientific view of reality is, I think, that it tends to encourage a socially and materially oriented existence that lacks depth of meaning, connection, and purpose. To acknowledge the superficiality of the Western view of reality—to say that it touches only a very thin veneer of life—does not mean that the learning of the West should be discarded. Rather, it points to the importance of recognizing the partiality and incompleteness of the Western view of reality. In sensing the very real limitations of the Western view of things, we are naturally invited to explore other perspectives that may fill out dimensions of life we have overlooked in our rush toward material development.

Healing Ourselves and the Earth

by Shantilal Bhagat

Shantilal P. Bhagat is a consultant for global missions in the Church of the Brethren for whom he formerly directed eco-justice ministries. For over two decades he has been actively involved with the environmental and economic justice concerns of the National Council of Churches of Christ in the USA. He has participated in many UN conferences including the Earth Summit in Rio de Janeiro (1992) and the Climate Change convention in Berlin (1995). He holds academic degrees in agriculture and agronomy and is known throughout ecumenical Christian circles as a dynamic promoter of justice for the poor and the disadvantaged. In addition to three books, he has authored and edited study/action resources for congregations on the care of creation, world hunger, US homelessness, and racism.

In the previous article, Duane Elgin delineated certain salient characteristics of our Western worldview. In so doing he at times lumps together the Judeo-Christian tradition with that worldview. For example, Elgin states that "the Western view of reality is pro-

foundly dualistic. The Judeo-Christian religious tradition sets
God apart from...creation," concluding that it is therefore dualistic. While this is true of many expressions of Western Christianity,
by no means is it inherently dualistic. Bhagat makes this point in
the following brief essay, and proceeds to discuss, from a Christian
perspective, three other common beliefs that need "rethinking."
He shows that while certain oppressive ways of thinking and acting are common to Christianity, they are not reflective of a more
accurate understanding of Scripture and the broader Christian
tradition.

∞

Beliefs That Need Rethinking

We will not heal the Earth until we have healed ourselves of certain beliefs that
are destroying us and our planet: concepts of reality, human nature, God, and death
which are still widely accepted but no longer valid (if they ever were). We will
examine four common beliefs that we need to work on.

Our dualistic view. First of all, we have a dualistic view of reality. The Bible has
been made to appear to Western Christians to be much more anti-nature than it is.
This comes about through a particular line of interpretation, shaped in nineteenth-
century western European Protestantism. It espouses a sharp dualism between history and nature. History was seen as the true realm of the human, ascendant over
"nature," and, for that reason, the authentic sphere of the presence of the true
"God" of the Bible. "Nature" was understood as subhuman, as the sphere of necessity, as the realm to be negated in order to ascend into humanness and freedom.
Divinities revealed in and through nature were, by definition, false Gods.

More recent explorations of the Bible, undertaken out of ecological concern,
have shown that the Hebraic understanding of the God of Israel did not set history
against nature, but rather experienced God as Lord of heaven and earth, whose
power filled all aspects of their lives. The same steadfast love of God is present
when God "spread out the earth on the waters...made the great lights," and when
God "brought Israel out from among them with a strong hand and an outstretched
arm...divided the Red Sea in two and made Israel pass through the midst of it but
overthrew Pharaoh and his army in the Red Sea" (Ps. 136:6-15). This is one lived
reality in time and place that is not differentiated into separate spheres of "creation" and "redemption."

With our dualistic understanding and approach, we draw straight lines to divide
light and darkness, good and evil, black and white, women and men, soul and
body, Earth and Heaven, and on and on. We see these opposites locked in cosmic
struggle. For example: good must overcome evil; light must overcome darkness.
Our dualistic view allows us to designate some group as our enemy justifying espi-
onage, economic pressures, and sometimes war against them.

The hierarchical understanding of creation. Second, and closely related to our dualistic view of reality, is our unthinking acceptance of hierarchical models as the natural order of nearly everything. In other words, our culture teaches us to conceptualize reality in terms of a ladder, be it corporate, academic, political, athletic, ecclesiastic or metaphysical. Our western classical worldview, for example, has a hierarchical understanding of creation. It represents a three-tiered structure with God, whose nature is pure spirit, at the top, and the Earth, whose nature is material, at the bottom. So we have a polarity between the spiritual and the material, the divine and the bodily. Ranged in between are the other "orders" of creation: humans) men, women, children, enemies and slaves (in that order. Still lower are animals in various gradations, followed by plants, and then, at the bottom of the ladder, the Earth itself. The closer you get to God, the higher is the moral worth attributed to that order of creation. Thus the Earth itself is far from God and of little worth.

Our fragmented view that there are gradations of worth among people concentrates wealth and power in the hands of a few and has impoverished and oppressed many. But even human equality doesn't go far enough, for as we now know, the Earth is not the bottom of the heap. It is a delicately balanced ecosystem in which all things are interdependent. We need to internalize our interdependence with the whole planet.

Anthropocentrism. This is the third area of concern. The word means human domination of the other members of creation. We have assumed an attitude of superiority and divine right over the other species whose home is also this planet. Our disregard for them has resulted in terrible suffering, cruel death, and endangered and extinct species.

What should be our relationship to other members of creation? *God blessed them* (humans), *and God said to them, "Be fruitful and multiply, and fill the earth and subdue it; and have dominion over the fish of the sea and over the birds of the air and over every living thing that moves upon the earth."* Dominion, to some, means domination. The phrase "subdue the earth" has also been misunderstood. The account of Noah clarifies this troubling point found in Genesis 1:28, an injunction given to sinless humanity before the fall. Different injunctions to till and keep the earth are given in Genesis 2:15. But after the fall and after the flood, when God in effect starts over with Noah and his family, God again repeats the command of Genesis 1:28 "Be fruitful and increase, and fill the earth" omitting the injunction to "subdue it" (Gen. 9:1). The story of Noah decisively eliminates any notion that God intends for a *fallen humanity* to have oppressive dominion over the earth. For a *sinless humanity*, dominion means stewardship and caring. For a *fallen humanity*, dominion means oppressive rule.

Otherworldly orientation. Promoted by some religious groups, this is the fourth factor affecting the future of the Earth. Apocalyptic Christianity, for example, emphasizes God as "our heavenly Father." Our real life is not here on Earth, but begins after we die and go to heaven. If we endure all the troubles and trials of the world patiently, great will be our reward in heaven. As long as the center of our lives is in heaven, what happens to the Earth does not matter.

Some Christians find it easy to believe that God will save individuals, but they find it more difficult to believe that God's intention is to save and restore the whole creation. Christians who ignore the desecration of the Earth, believing it will be destroyed anyway or that God only saves people's souls, are denying the truth of the Bible.

Adapted from *Your Health and the Environment: A Christian Perspective* by Shantilal Bhagat. Published by the Eco-Justice Working Group, National Council of Churches of Christ. 800-762-0968; Order No. EJ-9780.

(Bhagat adapted this article from Elizabeth Watson's booklet *Healing Ourselves and Our Earth* published by Friends Committee on Unity with Nature.)

Sacred Cosmology and the Ecological Crisis

by Dr. Philip Sherrard

The late Dr. Philip Sherrard (1922-1995) was an Orthodox theologian, biblical scholar and translator, and poet. His books include *Human Image: World Image—The Death and Resurrection of Sacred Cosmology; The Rape of Man and Nature;* and *The Sacred in Life and Art.*

In the introduction to this book, under the idol of anthropocentrism, I suggested that perhaps it is not that we are too human-centered, but too me-centered. In a me-centered universe, other humans, species and places lose (to a greater or lesser extent) their importance. Sherrard goes further, saying we lose our sense of the sacredness of "the other." He writes provocatively of the profound importance of re-claiming and re-inhabiting a sacred universe. Doing so would fundamentally alter the ways in which we relate with and treat the natural world and each other.

∞

One thing we no longer need to be told is that we are in the throes of an appalling crisis. We tend to call this crisis the ecological crisis, and this is a fair description insofar as its effects manifest above all in the ecological sphere. For here the message is quite clear: our entire way of life is humanly and environmentally suicidal. Unless we change it radically, there is no way in which we can avoid catastrophe. Without such change, the whole adventure of civilization will come to an end during the lifetime of many now living.

Unhappily we do not yet appear to have realized the urgency of the need for such change. In spite of everything, we continue to blunder along in a kind of blindfold nightmare, enacted with all the inevitability of a Greek tragedy, extending our empire of sterilized artificiality and specialist methodology ever further, advancing into the computerized or electronic wilderness, devising bigger banking systems, manipulating the reproductive processes of plants, animals and human beings, saturating our soils and crops with high-powered chemicals and poisons, and behaving generally in a manner which, even if we had deliberately programmed it, could not be more propitious to our own annihilation and to that of the world about us. It is as if we are in the grip of some monstrous collective psychosis, as if a huge death-wish hangs over the so-called civilized world.

In the ecological sphere, the message is clear, however much we may try to ignore it. While the effects of our crisis are most evident in this sphere, the crisis itself is not first of all an ecological crisis. It is a crisis concerning the way we think.

We are treating our planet in an inhuman and god-forsaken manner because we see things in an inhuman, god-forsaken way. And we see things in this way because that is basically how we see ourselves.

This is the first thing about which we have to be absolutely clear if we are to find a way out of the hells of self mutilation to which we have condemned ourselves. How we see the world depends upon how we see ourselves.

Our model of the universe, our world-image, is based upon the model we have of ourselves, upon our own self image. When we look at the world, what we see is a reflection of our own mind. Our perception of a tree, a mountain, a face, or a bird is a reflection of our idea of who we think we are.

This means that before we can deal effectively with the ecological problem, we have to change our world image. This in turn means that we have to change our self image. Unless our evaluation of ourselves changes, the way we treat the world will not change either. And unless that happens, conservation theory and practice, however well-intentioned, will not touch the heart of the problem. They will at best represent an effort to deal with what in the end are symptoms, not causes.

I do not want in the least to belittle ecological efforts, which are often heroic, lonely and against all odds. One of the terrible temptations we face is that of thinking that the problem is so big that nothing we can do can possibly have any effect: we must leave it to the experts.

That is a fatal attitude. Every single gesture, however pathetic it may seem, counts, and may have incalculable consequences. Thought not accompanied by corresponding practice soon becomes sterile. Yet practice springing from incorrectly based thought easily becomes counter-productive because practice deals with symptoms. Causes are rooted in the way we think, and it is because of this that our crisis is first a question of our self image and world-view.

This is the crux of our situation. The industrial and technological inferno we have produced has not come about accidentally. It is the consequence of allowing ourselves to be dominated by a certain paradigm of thought—by embracing a certain human image and world image—to such a degree that it determines virtually all our mental attitudes and actions.

It is a paradigm of thought that impels us to look upon ourselves as little more than two-legged animals whose destiny and needs can best be fulfilled through the pursuit of social, political and economic self interest. To correspond with this self image, we have invented a world view in which nature is seen as an impersonal commodity, a soulless source of food, raw materials, wealth, and so on, which we think we are entitled to exploit and abuse by any technique we can devise in order to satisfy this self interest.

Having in our own minds desanctified ourselves, we have desanctified nature too, in our own minds. We have removed it from the suzerainty of the divine and have assumed that we are its overlords. Under the aegis of this self image and world view, we have succeeded in converting ourselves into the most depraved and depraving of all creatures upon the earth.

This self image and world view have their origin in a loss of memory, in a forgetfulness of who we are, and in a fall to a level of ignorance and stupidity that threatens the survival of our race. So long as we persist in this course, we are doomed to advance blindly toward total loss of identity and eventually to self destruction. Nothing can stop this process except a reversal of direction, a complete change in the way we look at ourselves and in the way we look at the world about us. Without this change, we will simply add fuel to our own funeral pyre.

Can we make this reversal, this complete change? The answer is that no one can stop us except ourselves. The question—the only question—is what self-image and worldview are we to put in place of the bankrupt stereotypes, the unensouled fictions, which have taken us over?

Here a certain act of recollection is needed. In the great cultures of the world, human beings do not regard themselves as two-legged animals, whose needs and satisfactions can be achieved through social, political and economic self-interest. They think of themselves first as descended from God, or from the gods, and as heirs to eternity. Their destiny goes far beyond politics, society and economics, or anything that can be fulfilled in material terms. They think of themselves as sacred beings, not in their own right, but as creations in the divine image, in the image of God. They come from a divine Source, and the divine world is their birthright, their true home.

In the same way, they do not look upon the natural world as a chance association of atoms or as something impersonal, soulless, inanimate, which they are entitled to manipulate, exploit and generally to tamper and mess around with in order to gratify their greeds and power-lusts. They look upon nature as a divine creation, as full of hidden wisdom as they themselves are. They sense that every part of the earth is sacred. Every leaf, every grain of sand or soil, every bird, animal and star, the air and every insect is holy. They may trade in the gifts creation offers—in precious stones and spices, in corn and cattle. They may in ignorance be excessive in their demands on them, in grazing their flocks or in felling too many trees. But they do not deliberately "trade in nature itself."

Yet such an understanding, and the sense of the sacredness of both man and nature, as well as the awe and reverence that they inspire, are often characterized as primitive, or regarded as belonging to the pre-scientific age and as something promoted only by those who have failed to move into the twentieth century.

And this in spite of the fact that—to limit ourselves to the European tradition alone—there is no major philosopher, from Plato to Berdyaev, and no major poet, from Homer to Yeats, who has not explicitly or implicitly affirmed the kind of cosmology that we now tend to repudiate or ignore.

In this connection there is one particular fallacy from which we must free ourselves, and this is the idea that contemporary scientific theories, and the descriptions that go with them, are neutral or value-free, and do not presuppose the submission of the human mind to a set of assumptions in the way that is said to be demanded by adherence to a religious faith. This idea is propagated and even believed by many modern scientists themselves. On it is based the claim that scientific descriptions...are objective descriptions. It is not that these scientists deny that there are values. It is that insofar as they are scientists they claim to operate independently of value judgements, and to be engaged in what they like to call disinterested scientific research.

This is one of the most insidious fallacies of which we tend to be victims. Even people who maintain that they are fighting for a new philosophy of ecological values repeat it as though it were beyond dispute. In fact, far from being beyond dispute, it represents a total lie. Every thought, every observation, every judgement, every description, whether of the modern scientist or anyone else, is soaked in "a priori," preconceived, value judgements, assumptions and dogmas at least as rigid, if not more rigid (because they are often unconsciously embraced), than those of any explicitly religious system. The very nature of human thought is such that it cannot operate independently of value-judgements and assumptions.

Alongside this fallacy is another of which we still tend to be the victims. This is the notion that modern science is valid in relation to that limited aspect of things which is material or phenomenal that it sets out to study. This notion involves the claim that there are two levels of reality; that each level can be studied apart from, and without reference to, the other; and that the knowledge gained as a result of studying the one level is just as valid as the knowledge gained as a result of studying the other level.

This way of envisaging things is a fallacy because the primary determinant of the knowledge that we form of things is not the level of reality to which this knowledge is said to apply. There are not two sciences, one concerned with the material and the other with the spiritual dimension. There is only one science. But there are two dominant modes of consciousness in man: his ego-consciousness, which is his lowest mode of consciousness, and his spiritual consciousness, which is his higher mode of consciousness. Of course, there are endless permutations between these modes, depending upon whether the consciousness gravitates more to the one or the other.

If we could perceive and experience with the full clarity of our higher or spiritual consciousness, we would be able to see that no visible thing possesses existence in its own right. We would understand that, apart from its inner spiritual dimension and identity, it possesses no reality whatsoever, whether physical, material or substantial, and that the notion that it does so is merely a distortion inherent in the viewpoint of the ego-consciousness. In no way is it possible to separate physics from metaphysics, and insofar as we think it is possible, we simply confirm the inanity of our thought.

Insofar as modern science presupposes the notion that we can obtain a knowledge of phenomena apart from a prior knowledge of their inner and spiritual dimension, it is based totally upon ego-consciousness, or—which comes to the same thing—it is still in servitude to a dualism that opposes mind and matter, subject and object, the knower and what is to be known—a dualism which represents a total distortion of reality. This means it is tainted with the inhuman and satanic characteristics in man of which this consciousness is the vehicle. That is why its application is liable to be fraught with consequences that are equally inhuman and satanic, whether with regard to our own being or the natural physical world.

That is why every extension of the influence of our contemporary secular scientific mentality has gone hand in hand with a corresponding and increased erosion in us of the sense of the sacred. In fact, we do not have any respect, let alone reverence, for the world of nature because we do not have any respect, let alone reverence, for ourselves. It is because we cripple and mutilate ourselves that we cripple and mutilate everything else as well. Our contemporary crisis is really our own depravity writ large.

The only real answer to this crisis is to stop depraving ourselves. It is to recover a sense of our true identity and dignity, of our self image as sacred beings, as immortal beings. A false self-view breeds a false world view, and together they breed our nemesis and the nemesis of the world.

Once we repossess a sense of our own holiness, we will recover the sense of the holiness of the world about us. Then we will act toward the world with the awe and humility that we should possess when we enter a sacred shrine, a holy temple in which we worship and adore. Only in this way will we again become aware that our destiny and the destiny of nature are one and the same. Only in this way can we restore a cosmic harmony. If we do not take this way out, then that is that, for there is no other way out. To fail here is to fail irrevocably: there can be no escaping our inhuman genocide.

Without a sense of the holy and without humility toward the whole—towards man, nature and that which is beyond both man and nature, their Transcendent Source and Origin—we will simply proceed headlong along the course to self-destruction to which we are now committed and for which we are entirely responsible.

All this means that if we are to confront our contemporary crisis in a way that goes to its roots, our task is twofold: First we have to get absolutely clear the paradigm of thought that underlies and determines our present self-image and world view. Unless we first do this, we are liable to become victims of a double-think, attacking the symptoms while remaining subject to the causes that produce the symptoms. And it is all the more important for us to do it because we tend to forget what the assumptions and presuppositions that characterize this paradigm are: they are so deeply imbedded beneath the ramparts of our ordinary thought-processes that we are unaware that they underlie and determine these processes.

Second, we have to recover the vision of man and nature—what might be called the anthropocosmic vision—that will make it possible for us to perceive and experience both ourselves and the world we live in as the sacred realities that they are. Unless we recover a sense of their sacredness, based upon a coherent understanding of why they are sacred, our attempts to reaffirm this quality may be debilitated by what in the end is little more than sentimental prejudice.

Our enquiry, therefore, is simultaneously anthropological—concerned with the question of who man is—and cosmological—concerned with the question of the nature of the universe. It is ultimately an attempt to reaffirm sacred images of both man and nature: to affirm a sacred human image and a sacred world image.

Adapted from the "Introduction" to *Human Image: World Image*, available from James Wetmore, RD 2, Box 223 Ghent, NY, 12075. (518) 672-4323.

This essay was originally submitted to the 1989 conference "For the Transfiguration of Creation." An edited version appeared in both *Firmament* and *Green Cross* magazines. Reprinted here with permission from Fred Krueger, formerly of *Green Cross*, and from Sherrard's widow, Denise Sherrard.

Widening Our Circle of Community: Journey to Abundant Life

The abundance to which Jesus pointed was explicitly not the abundance of possessions. It was the abundance of the restored relationship, the God-relationship. It was the freedom to enjoy the community—the giving-and-receiving relationship with one another for which we were created.

—William Gibson

A sense of moral compulsion cannot be imposed effectively from above, no matter how loudly it is preached from on high. Moral and ethical imperatives emerge spontaneously from a shared sense of community—a feeling that what "I" do or what "we" do matters to others within the community of which I wish to be a part...Historically, those considered to be outside the moral community have simply been ignored or...persecuted in the name of the ethical principles of those within the boundaries of the recognized moral community.

—Timothy Weiskel

$\mathcal{B}$uilding Community

by Cecile Andrews

For Cecile Andrews, one "absolute basic requirement" for community is laughter! She says laughter is an indicator "of people accepting each other. You are valued because you are alive, not because of how much money you earn or how big your house is. When we have that sense of being valued...we don't need to prove that we have worth." Although Americans (and Europeans) are by and large affluent beyond the dreams of the rest of the world, many of us have lost something invaluable: belonging to a community. The presence of community is a powerful reminder that authentic wealth does not consist in the size of one's bank account, but in the depth and diversity of relationships within the community: the mechanic who won't overcharge you, the neighbor you can trust your kids with, and the landscape and other creatures so familiar to you that you know you are home. Andrews writes very practically about ways we can rebuild communities—through urban villages, celebrations, town centers and joining with others in service to the larger society.

∞

Like so many others, my husband and I wanted a greater sense of community in our lives. So we joined a book club. We managed to participate regularly for three years, but then we dropped out. We discovered we had begun to dread going. Instead of an informal, supportive, conversational setting, the group created a pseudo-college English class. Each meeting got worse—I began to feel like my grade was on the line, that if I said something others thought was stupid, I would get a C minus. But this wouldn't be just a grade. It would actually mean my friends would reject me. I dreaded sneers and sarcastic remarks. I worried they would think my book selection was stupid, let alone my comments about it. I felt that after three years we should have known each other better; but instead, I felt I knew the people in the club less.

So when my neighbors talked of starting a book club, I said no, no, no. We started a video club instead. On the last Friday night of each month, we gather together and watch a movie on video. Now, sometimes the pressure's on to select a video that everyone likes, but at least our friendship isn't on the line.

What we do in the video group that we had quit doing in the book club is laugh. That's the absolute basic requirement for me in community. If we're not laughing, I'm not going to do it.

Laughing means people are enjoying each other. It brings a state of felicity, of delight. You feel glad to be alive and you think, this is it! You just don't need much more than this—a group of friends enjoying each other.

But laughter is really an indicator of something more basic: of people accepting each other. You are valued because you are alive, not because of how much money you earn or how big your house is. When we have that sense of being valued, of being connected, we don't live lives of consumerism and ambition. We don't need to *prove* that we have worth.

I learned this many years ago when I was looking through my father's things. My father had died in an airplane crash when I was eight and left his trunk from the war years when he had been a pilot in World War II. One day, when I was rummaging through his trunk, I found a quote in a little picture frame: "A friend is not someone who is taken in by sham, a friend is one who knows your faults, and doesn't give a damn."

There it was, it seemed to me, the key to community. We must have a group of people to whom we can express our true selves. We must have a group of caring people who affirm our true selves.

Of course, neighbors are perfect for this. They know things about you that no one will ever know at work. They see your house in its real state. They see you in your ratty clothes. And you can really help each other out. You can help out in little ways, like taking care of someone's dog or buying their kid's school candy. Or you can help in bigger ways, like comforting them when a family member dies.

There will be different kinds of communities. There is potential for community at work, in your church, in your neighborhood, in your professional organizations. But none of these groups will develop into a community unless people learn the skills for building community. We can learn those skills by exploring the ways people are building community.

Urban Villages

There is a lot of new community growth in what I am calling urban villages. This is an area smaller than the public arena, and larger than a neighborhood. It might take in several neighborhoods and be a distinct part of town. In these areas people are organizing food co-ops, community gardens, tool banks, and systems of bartering....

Strong neighborhood centers can bring alive this concept of an urban village. In my neighborhood there is a center that is located in a former elementary school, called the Phinney Neighborhood Association. It brings so much life to the wider neighborhood. This former school has been turned into a gathering place with lots of activities and classes. There's day care in the morning and a coffeehouse with music at night. Any evening you can find yoga in one classroom, salsa dancing in another, a string quartet in another, and simplicity circles in another. To get to the classes you walk through an ever-changing art show. On weekends there are flea markets and plant exchanges and mystery novel swaps. The center organizes work parties to fix up the homes of people with disabilities and to work with a local church to feed and house the homeless. There's a "well home" program with tool rentals and do-it-yourself classes. The center organizes dinner "circles" for people, sponsors a garden club, holds gallery walks, sponsors street cleanups, holds classes on bicycle maintenance, and sponsors community meetings on earthquake safety.

There is a paid staff, but the money to pay them has been generated by neighborhood involvement in the programs. Every urban village needs a physical place to gather and any community could do this.

Neighborhood

All these levels of community are important, but maybe the easiest way we can begin to create community is at the neighborhood level or in our homes. This is something we can do by just walking across the street and inviting a couple of our neighbors over. It's hard, isn't it? You feel like you're interrupting or imposing or coming to beg for someone's company. There seems to be an embarrassment about needing to have friends. Is our individualism so extreme that we are ashamed of a basic human need? Or is it the fear of rejection that makes inviting friends over so hard? You worry that maybe they have something better to do than come to your house.

It's interesting to think about your own experiences of neighborhood. The most community-oriented place I ever lived was graduate-student housing. The apartment complexes were built around courtyards of grass with little playgrounds of slides and swings in the middle. Through the grass ran a curving sidewalk for the older kids to ride bikes while the little ones played in the sand in the center. We each had little fenced patios with picnic tables, and since we were in California, we ate outside a lot. Of course, you could often hear your neighbors through the walls, but that gave it kind of a cozy feeling. The smallness of the units made it even cozier. Since they were *all* small, there was no feeling of inadequacy or inferiority about someone having a bigger house than you. We got to know our neighbors really well.

I realized how much easier it was to develop community there than it was where I had lived growing up, out in the suburbs—big houses set back from the streets, double door garages opened by remote control, big lawns with patios in the back. There you could avoid ever having to meet a neighbor if you didn't want to, and of course if you *did* want to, it would be pretty hard to make contact. If you got lonely during the day and thought about popping into a store for a loaf of bread there was no place you could walk to, and even your car only took you to huge shopping centers where you couldn't get to know anyone anyway.

What were we thinking about? Was this all planned by major retailers? Suburban living practically guaranteed that we would become a nation of shoppers. We had to buy lots of cars, first. Then, the one family-one house idea we aspired to meant we all bought our own appliances. In order to combat the loneliness of the streets, you spent more time at the shopping malls. It's depressing to even think about it.

Today city planners are coming up with some new ideas. For lots of places it's too late, but new developments could benefit. Sometimes old places can adapt a few of the ideas....

Neighborhood Stores

For many years we've lived in a neighborhood that has a little grocery store. It's a part of a larger co-op system, so it has lots of organic foods and bulk items. You know all the checkers by name and sometimes they even help coordinate your shopping. It was not unusual for my husband to stop by the store right after I had been there. The checker would tell him, "Oh, Cecile already got that." Or if I was in the store when Paul came in, they would get on the loudspeaker and announce, "Cecile, Paul's here in the store."

And you can walk to a neighborhood store. When you walk, you not only get exercise, save on pollution and car expenses, you also get to visit with neighbors along the way. Having a neighborhood store certainly improves my social life. I don't think I've ever made a trip to that little store without running into a friend. I can have a great social life on Saturday night just hanging out by the produce.

Town Centers

One of the nicest places for me to walk is a neighborhood shopping district about two miles from my house. It's a place with interesting shops and cafes—there are restaurants, grocery stores, drug stores, used bookstores, a video rental store, and a library where the librarians call me by name. In fact, this area has the only shopping mall I've ever liked. They have taken an old school and put shops on the bottom and middle floors and apartments on the top. It's small enough so that you can get to know the shop owners. The bookstore even rents out books and so I can get new mysteries without having to wait. Close by is a tea shop with lots of tables where people can hang out and read at all hours.

Celebration

We must start bringing back fun things that build community: conversation, singing, dancing, storytelling, games. I have a friend—she's French, so maybe that's why she can get away with it—who has singing parties. First we sing a song in French and then one in English (after having great French food that everyone brings). When I told my other friends about the singing parties, and suggested that we have one too, I mainly got strange looks. They were worried, of course, that they would make fools of themselves. But a bunch of us had one, and everyone loved it.

One Valentine's Day, I had a sock hop. This really scared some of my more reserved friends. But I moved the furniture back and put on old Beatles and Rolling Stones tapes and everybody danced. Well, most people. The reason we could get as many as we did to dance was because everybody danced with their kids.

What are other things that some neighborhoods are doing? I've heard of a cooking co-op where three families take turns cooking each week and delivering food to the others. I've heard of a lot of eating co-ops where several people eat together two or three times a week, rotating houses. I've heard of women getting together not only to share child care, but to clean each other's houses.

But we don't have to just stick to work. You can plan fun things with friends like going camping together or having picnics. Some people start annual events, like a Fourth of July potluck or Christmas caroling. There's something about doing something with the same people year after year that makes it more special.

Personal

One of the biggest changes people seek is in their living patterns. It's not just college kids who share houses anymore. More and more adults of all ages are finding big houses and moving in together. Others are involved in the more formal planning of co-housing, where people buy land together and build several smaller houses around one community center—a community building with facilities for cooking and social events. Seniors are forming cooperatives so that they will have support without having to go to a nursing home. Many single women rent out a room in their home so they have extra money and don't feel so vulnerable.

Some of these things people do to save money. As is usually the case, when people are in economic straits, they often join together.

Service

A lot of people are creating community by joining together in their spare time to contribute to the well-being of the larger society.

Most of us know about people building homes for the poor through programs like Habitat for Humanity. People are even using their vacations to join programs that "make a difference." Every year, Arthur Frommer, the travel guide expert, puts out another edition of *New World of Travel*, a book featuring "alternative vacations that will change your life." New journals such as *Yes! A Journal of Positive Futures* and *Hope, Humanity Making a Difference* are featuring people getting together to make a difference.

Electronic Communities

I still refuse to think of anything on-line as a real community. But the question is, would those shy, introverted techies be forced to go out and talk if they didn't have their computers? Or would they just be more isolated?

You can always generate controversy by discussing community and computers. Some people absolutely love e-mail and say they communicate with their friends and relatives in other parts of the country much more. Others comment that now they don't even talk to the person in the office next door because they communicate on e-mail.

For some, communicating in electronic communities is a safe place to say things that they can't say to friends and families—the anonymity frees them, like talking to a stranger on a train. But don't we get enough anonymous talk as it is? I can't even keep up with my real friends, so why would I want to take time away from them to chat with strangers?

The challenge, it seems to me, is how to get the best of electronic community without having it eat up all of our time so that we have no time for anything else. One school reported that kids were coming to counselors because they were spending too much time on the Internet and it was disrupting the other parts of their lives.

For me, the Internet was mostly irritating and boring, until I got involved with the many social-action web sites on the World Wide Web. Here is the hope for me—electronic democracy. As our institutions get bigger and bigger and corporations take over more and more broadcasting stations, this may be a way to take back people's power. In the activist web sites you can not only get information on social and environmental issues, you can communicate directly to your senators and representatives by e-mail.

Re-Creating Democracy

Ultimately, we won't change things in our world until we change the system of domination, until we re-create democracy. And we won't make a dent on the system of domination until people learn, really learn, how to be equals. And of course, you learn by experiencing. Unless we have that experience of day after day being treated with respect, affection, and dignity, we will accept our culture's idea that some people are better than others. We will accept people degrading us or being rude to us, or not listening to us.

Unless we give people the feeling that their voice is important, that they have the right to speak out, we will not be able to fight the dominance of the corporate system and we will be unable to save either people or the planet.

It is the experience of community that leads to the re-creation of democracy.

Winter Solstice at the Moab Slough

by *Terry Tempest Williams*

Terry Tempest Williams was born in 1955. She grew up within sight of the Great Salt Lake, where her grandmother, Mimi, would take her to the bird refuge. These early experiences instilled in her a profound and lasting awe for the natural world, a rich and recurring theme in all her writing. As she says, "I am a woman whose ideas have been shaped by the Colorado Plateau and the Great Basin…These ideas are then sorted out through the prism of Mormon culture" (in which Williams was raised). Williams states that "every opportunity I find to be in nature is a worship for me… sometimes, just partaking in the glory of nature propels me, and feeds my curiosity."

With degrees in Biology and Environmental Education, Williams worked for ten years as Naturalist-in-Residence at the University of Utah's Museum of Natural History. Williams lives in Salt Lake City with her husband. Her published work includes *Desert Quartet* (1995), *An Unspoken Hunger* (1994) and *Refuge: An Unnatural History of Family and Place* (1991). Terry's forthcoming book is entitled *The Woman Who Stares at Bosch*.

Williams writes, "…How cautious I have become with love. It is a vulnerable enterprise to feel deeply and I may not survive my affections." As Wendell Berry intoned (see "Word and Flesh"), as Jesus commanded when summarizing the law, now Terry Tempest reminds us: in order to embody a compassionate response to the realities of today's world, we must love. Must love our neighbors, those within our community. In this essay, she reminds us that our neighbors include not only humans but other species and even places as well.

∞

It is the shortest day of the year. It is also the darkest. Winter Solstice at the Moab Slough is serene. I am here as an act of faith, believing the sun has completed the southern end of its journey and is now contemplating its return toward light.

A few hundred miles south, the Hopi celebrate Soyalangwul, "the time to establish life anew for all the world."

At dawn, they will take their prayer sticks, pahos, to a shrine on the edge of the mesa and plant them securely in the earth. The pahos, decorated with feathers, will make prayers to the sun, the moon, the fields, and the orchards. These prayer feathers will call forth blessings of health and love and a fullness of life for human beings and animals.

And for four days, the Hopi will return to their shrine and repeat the prayers of their hearts.

My heart finds openings in these wetlands, particularly in winter. It is quiet and cold. The heat of the summer has been absorbed into the core of the redrocks. Most of the 150 species of birds that frequent these marshes have migrated. Snowy egrets and avocets have followed their instincts south. The cattails and bulrushes are brittle and brown. Sheets of ice become windowpanes to another world below. And I find myself being mentored by the land once again, as two great blue herons fly over me. Their wingbeats are slow, so slow they remind me that, all around, energy is being conserved. I too can bring my breath down to dwell in a deeper place where my blood-soul restores to my body what society has drained and dredged away.

Even in winter, these wetlands nourish me.

I recall the last time I stood here near the Solstice—June 1991. The Moab Slough was christened the Scott M. Matheson Wetland Preserve. The Nature Conservancy set aside over eight hundred acres in the name of wildness.

A community gathered beneath blue skies in celebration of this oasis in the desert, this oxbow of diversity alongside the Colorado River. A yellow and white tent was erected for shade as we listened to our elders.

"A place of renewal..." Mrs. Norma Matheson proclaimed as she honored her husband, our governor of Utah, whose death and life will be remembered here, his name a touchstone for a conservation ethic in the American West.

"A geography of hope..." Wallace Stegner echoed. "That these delicate lands have survived the people who exploited this community is a miracle in itself."

We stood strong and resolute as neighbors, friends, and family witnessed the release of a red-tailed hawk. Wounded, now healed, we caught a glimpse of our own wild nature soaring above willows. The hawk flew west with strong, rapid wingbeats, heartbeats, and I squinted in the afternoon sun, following her with my eyes until she disappeared against the sandstone cliffs.

Later, I found a small striated feather lying on the ground and carried it home, a reminder of who we live among.

D. H. Lawrence writes, "In every living thing there is a desire for love, for the relationship of unison with the rest of things."

I think of my own stream of desires, how cautious I have become with love. It is a vulnerable enterprise to feel deeply and I may not survive my affections. Andre Breton says, "Hardly anyone dares to face with open eyes the great delights of love."

If I choose not to become attached to nouns—a person, place, or thing—then when I refuse an intimate's love or hoard my spirit, when a known landscape is bought, sold, and developed, chained or grazed to a stubble, or a hawk is shot and hung by its feet on a barbed wire fence, my heart cannot be broken because I never risked giving it away.

But what kind of impoverishment is this to withhold emotion, to restrain our passionate nature in the face of a generous life just to appease our fears? A man or woman whose mind reins in the heart when the body sings desperately for connection can only expect more isolation and greater ecological disease. Our lack of intimacy with each other is in direct proportion to our lack of intimacy with the land. We have taken our love inside and abandoned the wild.

Audre Lorde tells us, "We have been raised to fear the yes within ourselves...our deepest cravings. And the fear of our deepest cravings keeps them suspect, keeps us docile and loyal and obedient, and leads us to settle for or accept many facets of our own oppression."

The two herons who flew over me have now landed downriver. I do not believe they are fearful of love. I do not believe their decisions are based on a terror of loss. They are not docile, loyal, or obedient. They are engaged in a rich, biological context, completely present. They are feathered Buddhas casting blue shadows on the snow, fishing on the shortest day of the year.

Pahos. Prayer feathers. Darkness, now light. The Winter Solstice turns in us, turns in me. Let me plant my own prayer stick firmly in the mud of this marsh. Eight hundred acres of wetlands. It is nothing. It is everything. We are a tribe of fractured individuals who can now only celebrate remnants of wildness. One red-tailed hawk. Two great blue herons.

Wildlands' and wildlives' oppression lies in our desire to control and our desire to control has robbed us of feeling. Our rib cages have been broken and our hearts cut out. The knives of our priests are bloody. We, the people. Our own hands are bloody.

"Blood knowledge," says D. H. Lawrence. "Oh, what a catastrophe for man when he cut himself off from the rhythm of the year, from his unison with the sun and the earth. Oh, what a catastrophe, what a maiming of love when it was made a personal, merely personal feeling, taken away from the rising and setting of the sun, and cut off from the magical connection of the solstice and equinox. This is what is wrong with us. We are bleeding at the roots..."

The land is love. Love is what we fear. To disengage from the earth is our own oppression. I stand on the edge of these wetlands, a place of renewal, an oasis in the desert, as an act of faith, believing the sun has completed the southern end of its journey and is now contemplating its return toward light.

Epilogue

Love all God's creation, the whole of it and every grain
of sand. Love every leaf, every ray of God's light! Love
the animals, love the plants, love everything. If you
love everything, you will perceive the divine mystery
in things. And once you have perceived it, you will
begin to comprehend it ceaselessly, more and more
every day. And you will at last come to love the
whole world with an abiding, universal love.

—*Fyodor Mikhail Dostoevsky*

pilogue

by James T. Mulligan and Michael Schut

Simpler Living, Compassionate Life guides you through a lot of territory: from time, money, consumption, and economics, to food, history, theology and community. As I reflect on where we've been, two undergirding themes emerge as essential to moving ourselves and our culture toward the abundant life.

First, we need fundamental changes in the way we think, in our worldviews (and theologies). Philip Sherrard's essay introduced one of the crucial characteristics of this change: we must re-inhabit a sacred universe. We must begin to see the sacred in the ordinary.

Second, we need fundamental changes in the way we act, acts characterized by compassion. Embodied compassion is not nebulous or vague. On the contrary, it is concrete, seen specifically in the type of economy we create, in the policies we enact, and in how we spend our time and money. Embodied compassion is love in action. And as Wendell Berry wrote in *Word and Flesh*, "Love is never abstract. It… adheres to the singular sparrows of the street, the lilies of the field, the 'least of these my brethren.'"

We close now with two stories which characterize the fundamental changes mentioned above. The first story, by James Mulligan, poignantly describes bread-making and keeping a worm bin as experiences of "seeing the sacred in the ordinary." The second story recounts a powerful experience which awakened compassion in me and inspired me to action. Both were originally published in Earth Ministry's mini-journal *Earth Letter*.

Seeing the Sacred in the Ordinary *by Jim Mulligan*

My brother, Tim, is a kind of anomaly. He lives in a rural part of Vancouver Island, British Columbia, and maintains a lifestyle of simplicity and self-sufficiency. As a physicist he spends his work days directing research studies and doing detailed mathematical analyses of data. But when at home, he and my sister-in-law spend many hours in their two large gardens. In addition to gardening, they hunt and fish, and thereby provide for a sizeable portion of their total annual food. They engage in all this hard work for many reasons, but among them is a sincere love of nature and a fascination with exploring its mysteries.

As I see it, he periodically takes a religious pilgrimage. About once a year he and one or two colleagues from the research center where he works go on a two-week hunting trip into the vast wilderness of northern British Columbia. On winter evenings he spends considerable time consulting topographic maps. He assesses the working condition of countless bits of gear. He seeks out others who have made forays to these locations before. He listens to their first-hand accounts. He envisions in his mind what the various components of such a venture might require of him and his companions. He maintains a faithful practice of regular aerobic exercise. He reads. Through all this he prepares himself for these excursions with a kind of devoted thoroughness which parallels the spiritual disciplines of pilgrims throughout history. And he, as they, returns from these travels renewed, having deepened his connections with the larger world, connections which nurture body and soul.

He also returns with interesting tales. A few years ago he told me that in camp one night he was thinking about what some "alien" (perhaps an anthropologist by training) might conclude should he secretly land his space craft near their campsite and meticulously observe the behaviors of the hunting party. Tim speculated that the alien would surely notice that every morning before dawn the entire entourage would arise, hurriedly dress, gather in silence in front of their tent, and with lanterns and flashlights process from the clearing of the campsite a hundred and fifty yards or so into the dense forest. There, silently they form a small circle at the base of a large tree. This tree holds aloft three or four pure white containers (suspended by cords some twenty or so feet above the ground). These mysterious containers would be slowly lowered, carefully handed one at a time to each of the attendants, who would wait in the stillness. When all these casks had been lowered and given to their appointed guardian, the group solemnly recesses single-file, retracing their steps, out of the forest back to the campsite. There, the white casks would be opened at intervals (always with great care) and some of their contents used in the activities of the day. However the casks were never left in camp unattended.

Doubtless the alien also could not help but notice that the reverse of the morning ritual occurred every evening, just before the group bedded down for the night. Again, silently processing through the dark, the flickering lanterns lighting the way, the white receptacles occasionally reflecting the dim light. The processional gathering beside the same massive trunk slowly raising the casks on high, then recessing silently once again. This ritual completed, with few words they would take their rest.

Tim surmised that seeing this solemn process enacted in this exact fashion each day, the alien might well conclude that this must be some sort of primitive religious rite, in which these simple hunter-gatherers were attempting to show their gratitude to whatever image of "divine mystery" they might recognize. (Whether or not the alien would also note that this "rite" was an effective way to keep their grub away from the other critters would be hard to say.)

Since then I have thought that this alien might actually have a point. There could be something more sacred here than meets our eye. We do tend to constantly overlook the daily miracle of God's "satisfying the desire of every living thing," "giving them their food in due season." If we have food for the day we see it as a mark of our own foresight, hard work and careful planning. But while we may plant the seed and harvest the produce, we cannot cause germination, orchestrate the sun or the rain, or manufacture the fertility of the soil. We serve as mere attendants to the processes of earth's generativity. In our day we are coming to be painfully aware of how little we even comprehend these central complex miracles which serve as the foundation for all of life as we know it. We are finally reawakening our sensitivity to God's sacramental presence throughout creation.

With this perspective in mind, I have begun to look at some of my own rituals of everyday life, to see what they might reflect about my orientation to this divine mystery in our midst. After all, seeing the "divine hand" at work within the "guise of the ordinary" is a central part of traditional Christian faith, the belief that God takes part in the actual affairs of life. Historically speaking, this "taking part" is sometimes dramatic—"the mighty acts of God"—but more often it is not. It can go almost unnoticed: the stranger on the road to Emmaus, the spirit blowing unseen like the wind, the seed germinating buried in the soil. It can even be seen in the plainly ordinary events of daily life: a farmer sowing seed, a woman baking bread, a man building a house. In my mind I play with this notion of "the sacred rites of everyday contemporary life," carriers of divine truth largely unnoticed, the sacred reflected in mundane activities. I look at my own life's routines to see what they might signal to any unseen alien who observes my particular activities.

Two examples come quickly to mind. They both embody the daily cycles of life, death, and new life. First, I noticed my habitual patterns in making bread. I don't tend to bake bread if my life is feeling rushed, but only on those days when there is time, unhurried time. Usually I am alone in the kitchen. The alien could look at our kitchen counter as a kind of "altar" for this ritual. It must be freshly cleaned and the utensils arranged in orderly fashion. I go to the pantry and bring out the "sacred vessels," some of which are used only for this particular ritual: the heavy crockery bowl, the tin bread-pans, the jar holding the special mixture of oils (which assures easy removal of bread from pan). I gather the elements: whole wheat flour, salt, water, yeast. These are all placed upon this altar, each in its appropriate place. In the corner stands "the book," which I faithfully consult as I proceed. This is not a ritual to be toyed with. I treat the yeast with special care, aware that it is a living colony. Without the life and death of these small beings the resulting bread would be hard, flat, and "lifeless." I measure and mix the elements with deliberateness, careful not to spill, always closely following the exact order of the rite as prescribed by the book.

Next, I wash my hands, roll up my sleeves, and remove my rings. I gather up the damp mass from the central vessel and place it on the cleansed surface. Just as others have done before me from one generation to the next, I begin working the formless mass with my hands. For me this is one of the more contemplative times in this process. Here, I do not consult the book, I only attend to working the mass, rhythmically pressing and folding, noticing the gradual transformation, the building cohesion, the development of elasticity. My mind at some level may know that this pressing and folding is assisting the gluten in the flour to separate and form strands, strands which envelope the starch, water and yeast, thus providing a structure for a "community of yeast life", a sanctuary in which the living yeast will both thrive and be sacrificed for the life of another community. But consciously I am only aware of the rhythm, the feel of the developing dough in my hands, the pressing and folding, the muscular energy of this melding. Like a monk lost in contemplation, I am not consciously attending to any thoughts.

When the dough is kneaded to a proper springiness, I shape it into a ball, and place this miniature globe gently in the crockery bowl. Over this vessel I place a linen cloth, and carry the covered bowl to an undisturbed place. Here the yeast will thrive within its own soft sanctuary. It will taste the bread before any of the rest of us. In the process of its digestion, it will produce the carbon dioxide which will cause the dough to rise from its former lifeless self to become a matrix of life. While these transformations are happening I am "out of the loop," often out of the kitchen, off doing something completely different, usually not the least bit mindful of the miraculous drama taking place within the sacred vessel. Meanwhile, the yeasty "incense" of this rite fills the kitchen with a scent uniquely its own.

The timer having sounded, the next stage goes in similar fashion. I gently lift the dough out, tuck it into shape and ease it into the oiled pan. I cover it again with the linen cloth, and once more abandon it as its process of transformation continues. Again later, when its time has come, the loaf having risen to have just enough springiness, I place the pan in the hot oven. Here the yeast will die and the dough at last become bread. Now the ancient fragrance of fresh bread begins to fill the house. And the "staff of life" will emerge from the oven to fulfill its age-old promises with its customary humbleness.

The second "ritual" the alien might observe takes place in the kitchen again, and the basement as well. Again it centers around food, includes life and death and involves a wonderful entourage of other creatures in the process. The first sign of our house also being the home of these creatures is a white container on the kitchen counter. Our observer might see me (and any others who help prepare food in this place) taking regular "offerings" of the food we eat and placing them in this white cask, before and after a meal.

About once a day, usually at the end of the cleansing rituals in the kitchen, this white cask is lifted from its appointed place and taken down the stairway to the basement. There, in the corner beside the washing machine, sits a large wooden chest. This chest can be seen as a multi-purpose shrine: part altar, part dormitory and mess-hall, part casket. This wooden shrine houses a constant flux of tiny life. Here the waste from our eating becomes the food for a myriad of amazing creatures, visible and invisible: red-wigglers, other invertebrates crawling contentedly around, fungi, molds, you name it. Together this miniature community of life performs a sacred act, transforming this "waste" into incredibly rich fertilizer, a foundation for more life.

This miraculous worm bin has not only brought a part of the outdoors inside (the original worms having come from an old compost pile), it has become a fabulous "window" on the world of invertebrates, and their role in maintaining life as we know it on earth. A quote from the *New York Times* sums up the ecological centrality of worms and other invertebrates rather succinctly:

> *Humans may think they are evolution's finest product, but the creepies, crawlies, and squishies rule the world. Remove people from the face of the earth and the biosphere would perk along just fine, ecologists say. Remove the invertebrates—creatures like insects, spiders, worms, snails and protozoans—and the global ecosystem would collapse, humans and other vertebrates would probably last only a few months, and the planet would belong mostly to algae and bacteria. Invertebrates, it turns out, are the biological foundation of ecosystems and crucial to every one of the ecosystem processes.*

"Bugs Keep Planet Livable Yet Get No Respect," *New York Times*, Dec. 21, 1993, C1.

There is something fascinating about lifting the lid of that worm bin and seeing all that tireless activity. Justin, my grandson, at three and a half, loves to go there with me. "Can I hold some, Grandpa?" he says, extending his cupped hand while looking up at me expectantly. "Can I hold that big one over there?" I carefully lift the four-inch worm out of the bedding and place it on Justin's palm. He watches its gentle wriggles, fascinated. "Can I take him home with me? Please?" "Maybe you'd better ask your Mommy about that, first," I respond with some mild apprehension. Together we bend over the bin in Gulliver-like fashion, absorbed by the teaming busyness, the almost inaudible squishy sound, the field of constant motion, the intriguing mystery of its striking "otherness." Justin does not know that these tiny creatures are "redeeming" our waste, their constant activity renewing the earth's cycles of fertility, as they have been doing since they wriggled their way into evolutionary history. But his wonder is not diminished by what he does not understand; his experience is more direct. We talk a little, but mainly we watch. We cradle an occasional worm in our palms, watching its gentle gyrations. Seeing him hold one so carefully, looking at it so enraptured, it seems to me that he treats it with that kind of deference we grown-ups show in holding newborns, or handling a treasured family heirloom, or performing a role in a sacred rite. Mainly there is silence and wonder, as we kneel on the floor leaning over the worm bin, sharing the fascination. Finally, we place them back in the dark mix, lower the lid, turn out the light, and head back upstairs.

Next spring he may "help" as I spread the vermicompost from the worm bin on the garden. In the summer he will hold the basket as we gather herbs, carrying it ever so carefully, with both hands, back to the kitchen. There, he will climb up on a chair at the sink, and with fixed concentration, will carefully wash each leaf, one leaf at a time. I will trim off the "over-the-hill" spots. When all are finally clean and patted dry, we will put the trimmings in the white pail, beginning the cycle once more.

Extending Our Circle of Compassion *by Michael Schut*

I believe it was the summer of 1993, a hot late-afternoon in Eugene, Oregon. I remember my roommate, Chris, walking dejectedly into our kitchen, asking in disbelief, "Have you heard that the Governor of Alaska is allowing wolves to be herded together with helicopters and then shot?" In order to (temporarily) increase the caribou population, and thus increase the number of hunters (and their money) the state could "entertain," wolves were being gunned down from the sky. My response to this news was complex, and has lived in my memory ever since.

My first reaction was one of denial, of disbelief, which soon gave way to anger. Of all ecological lessons, I reasoned, hadn't we at least learned of the futility of tampering with the balance between predator and prey? How long would we continue to worship at the altar of economic growth, accepting as unfortunate, but accepting nonetheless, the damage to the integrity of creation? When would humility in the face of ecological complexity counterbalance our arrogant assumption that we can predict and understand the relational reverberations of interfering so forcefully in the web of life?

I paced the living room, frustrated and brooding. Eventually I found myself outside and sat down on the edge of our shaded front porch, my toes absent-mindedly curling the grass underfoot and my chin cradled in my hands.

I sat there for some time. Anger gradually gave way to sadness and I was somewhat surprised to find tears pooling in my eyes and wetting my cheeks. As I watched my tears fall to earth, I imagined the dry summer soil welcoming those few drops and the grass' fibrous roots absorbing the scarce moisture. I thought of the sun's relentless summer energy evaporating the water particles, drawing my tear towards itself. I pictured that water vapor being caught up into the atmosphere, eventually blown to Alaska and cooled in the northern air. As it cooled, the vapor coalesced into rain drops, some falling on an Alaskan stream. I imagined a wolf pack padding toward that rushing stream for a cool drink. Was it possible that my tear (brought on by the death of a pack member) might provide life to another pack member as he or she lapped the refreshing water?

My response still surprises me. In retrospect, it might have made more sense to me if a favorite pet or a respected leader had died. But, I somehow felt deeply connected to those wolves. I felt that their death made me less complete. I do not know how or why. Although I grew up in Minnesota (with a large wolf population of its own), wolves are not particularly "special" animals in my life. I have never seen a wolf in the wild.

Perhaps it was the joy of knowing they were safe in their homes that died a little; perhaps my hope that our crowded world might reserve earth's remaining wild places for wild things died a little; perhaps the wild and instinctual part of me died a little; perhaps the dream of someday encountering wolves in the Minnesota or Alaskan wilderness on a moonlit night died a little. Perhaps my hope that we humans might "come to our senses," that our relationships with the natural world might indeed heal, died a little. But all of that seems too analytical and does not convey my sense of their death being partly a kind of death within me: the mystery of my feeling diminished knowing that they were gone.

Now, as I re-tell this story, I sometimes feel a hint of embarrassment, self-consciousness and slight skepticism. In some circles, reporting such deep connections with animals is suspect at best, heretical at worst; did I really feel, do I really believe, some part of me died? How am I possibly diminished by a wolf's death? What difference could the shooting of a few Alaskan wolves possibly make in my life?

If I were listening to someone else tell this story, my modern, rational mind would ask such questions. Yet I tell the story anyway, willing to face the questions from within and without.

Such stories must be told. This is one I tell again and again for it speaks to me of the potential extent of the circle of human compassion, a sign of connection with all of creation. I felt and shared in another's loss, even when the "other" was one with whom I didn't realize I shared an intimate connection. For a moment the perceived walls of my separation came down.

More often than not, however, those walls remain intact. In these days of ecological and social degradation, of such loss to human and non-human communities, I suspect they serve an important function. They are powerful defense mechanisms, shutting out the pain around us. For "…it is a vulnerable enterprise to feel deeply and I may not survive my affections," as Terry Tempest Williams so recently reminded us; but "…what kind of impoverishment is this to withhold emotion, to restrain our passionate nature in the face of a generous life just to appease our fears?"

Keeping those sturdy walls intact, blocking out that pain, is to protect ourselves, but it is also to numb ourselves—keeping the pain at bay, but ultimately also the joy.

For while this story began as a painful one, I also understand it as a joyful one: the joy of realizing my connectedness to "the other," the joy that life unexpectedly may spring on me. As if just underneath the fabric of our everyday lives is a tapestry so rich, complex and beautiful that if we were but able to see, we might realize our constant participation in the dance of creation. A dance revealing that another's joy is our own joy, that another's pain is our own pain.

I also see it as a joyful story because I and many others were inspired to act. At the time, I was in an Environmental Studies graduate program. The news spread quickly amongst us; many chose to write letters to the governor and members of Congress. Eventually enough people around the country acted on their sense of connection to those wolves to force Alaska's governor to rescind his order.

I believe we, all of us, have such stories to tell. We began this book with Frederick Buechner listening to his life "as a whole…for whatever of meaning, of holiness, of God, there may be in it to hear. My assumption is that the story of any one of us is in some measure the story of us all."

As Buechner listens to his own story, through moments ordinary and extraordinary, moments of pain and joy, he discovers that life itself is sacramental. That not only in those moments the Church recognizes as sacramental, but also in our daily lives, the sacredness of life can be revealed to us. Moments when the eternal breaks through time and reveals to us something deep inside time. In my own experience, such moments occur when my sense of separation from others and this earth temporarily disappears and time itself feels transparent, when the barriers between myself and others fall away and I rejoice in our unity. Times like these define the boundaries of our "sense of self" much more widely than the skin-encapsulated egos we so often associate with "self." Times like these grow compassion in us. For compassion requires that we begin to know what it is like to walk in the shoes or pad in the footsteps of another, knowing "there can never really be peace and joy for any until there is peace and joy finally for all." (Buechner)

I see my response to the shocking news of these fly-by shootings as a sign of timeless grace: grace because I did not seek out such an experience, it was all a gift; timeless as only self-forgetfulness and intense relationship can be.

Simpler Living
Compassionate Life

Study Guide

by Michael Schut

How to Use This Material

Welcome to the study guide designed to accompany *Simpler Living, Compassionate Life*. We are very excited to offer this course and glad for your interest in it. We have tried to make this curriculum both flexible and easy to use. Because going through all 12 sessions, the most comprehensive option, is not possible for some church and/or small group situations, we suggest **optional course lengths of 4, 6, or 8 weeks.** (See the section on page 232 titled "If You Have Four, Six or Eight Weeks.") Some groups desiring to explore all 12 sessions may find it appealing to spread the course out over a longer time period—six sessions in the fall and six sessions in the spring, or even four sessions in the fall, four in the spring and the remaining four the next fall. Whatever your group's special needs, this guide can be custom fit!

Before you gather for Meeting One, be sure to read the introductory material and the essays to be discussed at the first meeting. (See top of page 234 under "Read Before Meeting One.")

Course Goals

Your own goals and hopes will surely vary, but below are a number of the goals which guided us in the writing of this course:
- To make connections between faith and simplicity;
- To build a sense of community and support within the group;
- To understand the connections between consumption, global economics and increasing inequity between rich and poor;
- To encourage actions and lifestyles which more deeply reflect your core Christian values and result in more meaningful, joyful living.

Course Organization

Facilitator: The role of Facilitator rotates each week; the course does not require an experienced leader, expert, or teacher. This should contribute a shared sense of ownership, responsibility, and community to the course. The Facilitator for Meeting One will likely be the person who organized the class. Some groups have found it helpful to designate a Facilitator for each of the remaining meetings during Meeting One. Others choose someone to facilitate the next meeting at the end of each meeting. It will be helpful if the Facilitator reads all the material (readings and curriculum) for "their" meeting thoroughly before the group meets to have a feel for timing, flow and content.

Setting and Timing: Ideally, this course would be held in group members' homes with enough time (about 1 1/2 to 2 hours) to experience and go through the material fully. Such an informal setting contributes to a more relaxed, community-building atmosphere.

The course can also be used in a Sunday School hour or adult education forum. Unlike other study guides which often specifically state how many minutes should be spent on each section, we chose to allow the group to make such decisions based upon the flow of the discussion and interest of the group. However, the Facilitator should have a general idea of how time might be spent during the meeting.

For those using the course in a 45-60 minute time slot, we suggest you start with the questions in bold text and address other questions as time allows. That said, feel free to modify meetings as you see fit. Some groups may choose to take two weeks to cover all the material in each meeting.

Group Size: Ideal group size is between six and eight participants. If your group is larger, we suggest breaking out into appropriate size groups for the discussion periods.

Book Sharing: Of course, it's best if everyone has a copy of *Simpler Living, Compassionate Life!* On the other hand, and in the spirit of this book, if sharing works out well, great. It is important for the person facilitating the next meeting to make sure they have a copy of the book the week prior to "their" meeting.

Journal: There is space within the study guide—though you may also wish to bring a journal or notebook—to take notes and jot down feelings, ideas and impressions while you are together and during the week. Your notes will become a valuable resource, charting how your thoughts and feelings may have changed over time.

A Note on the Readings: We see this study guide as an attempt to help you form a learning community. This community will hear from a variety of "voices." Some of those voices will be your own and those of your fellow group members. There are also readings. We feel it is important not to treat these readings as authoritative. Think of these as the stories and ideas of other group members not able to join your discussion in person. Not all of the perspectives will be meaningful or useful to everyone. Focus on what you do find meaningful. In a learning community different people find different things helpful. The object is not that everyone will emerge from this experience thinking, doing, and believing the same things. Rather, that in an open sharing of ideas and experiences, each individual's own exploration of the issues will be enhanced and supported.

Length of Readings: There are approximately 30-60 minutes of reading each week. If you think you may not have time, we suggest you read the brief introduction (found on the first page of every reading) to each essay and decide which one you would like to start with. (As much of the learning and discussion emanates from your perceptions and thoughts on these readings, we think your experience will be more full if you can complete the suggested articles. If not, perhaps you can get to them at a later date.)

Course Ethos and Guidelines:

This course seeks to value your own perspectives, life-experiences and wisdom. We encourage you to interact with each other and the materials honestly and to be open about your questions, misgivings and hopes. The Seattle guru of simplicity study circles, Cecile Andrews, has a number of helpful guidelines for creating a community-oriented group. Below find her suggestions:

- *No leaders. Be participatory.* This is a circle, not a pyramid, so no one can be a dictator, everyone is responsible.
- *Respond as equals.* In this course we act on the idea that we are all equal.
- *Be authentic.* We spend a lot of our lives trying to look successful. No one really gets to know us. In this group, try not to pretend. Describe what you really think or feel.
- *Focus on the heart.* Some conversations come just from the head. When you communicate from the heart you bring in the whole of yourself: emotions, imagination, spiritual insight and thoughts.
- *View conversations as barn-raising instead of battle.* Ways to do this include:
  —Listen and focus on understanding. As others speak, try to suppress the instinct to criticize or compare;
  —*No attacking, dismissing or denigrating.* The facilitator should be especially committed to responding to others with support, thus modeling a caring response;
  —*No persuading.* It is enough to state what you think—you do not have to convince people that you are right;
  —*No playing devil's advocate.* Although this is a common form of communication, it violates just about all of the above guidelines.
- *Question conventional wisdom and seek out alternative explanations and views.*
- *Discover wisdom through stories.* Throughout human history people have learned through story-telling. Everyone can tell their story and there's no right or wrong interpretation. Ultimately, stories connect people; in listening to someone else's story, we often hear strains of our own.

(These guidelines are taken from two sources: Cecile Andrews' *The Simplicity Circle: Learning Voluntary Simplicity Through a Learning For Life Study Circle*, 1994; and her more recent book *The Circle of Simplicity: Return to the Good Life* published by HarperCollins, 1997.)

Meeting Format

The meeting format is fairly self-explanatory. Each meeting has all or most of the following components:

The "Facilitator Overview" should be read by the facilitator prior to the meeting. Specific instructions for the meeting will be given in this section.

"Tools Everyone Needs" generally include this book and, if you wish, a pen and journal/notebook. If other supplies (such as a flip chart) are suggested, they will be indicated in this section.

Participants should be familiar with the "Purpose" and "Overview" sections before the meeting starts.

The "Opening Meditation and Prayer" provides a brief centering time, reminding us of the spiritual essence of simplicity and the foundation for this course. This time can be led by the facilitator or whoever feels comfortable doing so. Feel free to bring in prayers of your own or pray spontaneously as you are comfortable. This goes for the "Closing Prayer" as well.

The "Check-In" is a *brief* (one-minute) report back to the group about the "action step" you took during the week. If you are pressed for time, you may wish to skip this section. People should also feel free to pass.

A few of the meetings include a "Group Reading" which should be read aloud cooperatively by the group.

Each meeting's discussion emanates from that week's readings. There will be time for "Group Discussion" as well as "Small Group/Pair Discussions." The themes of these latter discussions will frequently be shared with the whole group.

Many meetings end by considering and sharing with the group an "Action Step" which would be both meaningful and "do-able" for members. Integrated into a number of the meetings' action steps is a powerful tool developed by The Center for a New American Dream. Called "Turn the Tide," this tool consists of nine simple actions you can take individually and as a faith community, which have a positive, measurable impact on the well being of God's Creation. What is especially exciting about Turn the Tide is that you get immediate feedback about that "measurable impact" via web-based technology. Using The Center's website, you can record your action and find out just how much water, or how many trees, you and your group have saved—or how much you have cut your emissions of climate-warming gasses. (Further information about Turn the Tide for faith communities is available at (301)891-3683 or at www.newdream.org/turnthetide/faith.) We hope this tool will help many put their faith into action!

Finally, the shaded column on each Meeting's opening page lists readings for the next meeting under "Read Before Next Gathering."

One Final Important Note

This is *your* course. Use it as a resource to engage your life with the ideas presented, not as a course to be "mastered." Your creative adaptation to your own needs is encouraged. You may find you don't have time to answer every question, or feel drawn to discuss only a few of the suggested questions, or have questions of your own. Perhaps you will want to spend two weeks on certain meeting topics. Please modify as needed.

Course Overview

Below find brief summaries of each meeting. Following the summaries are possible shorter and theme-based alternatives to the twelve week course. As you read through the meeting summaries, you may also find another theme or length that works well for your group. Be creative!

Meeting One sets the tone for the course by providing time for participants to share a piece of their own story. Our hope is that the group becomes a community of support for those interested in simplifying their lives. We also wish to value the perspectives of each participant as much as the perspectives represented in this curriculum and the readings. Beginning with personal stories and sharing of one's experiences is a good place to start.

We each inherit a certain worldview (way of perceiving reality) which colors our whole life, from our relationship with the natural world to our views on simplicity. **Meeting Two** takes a look at the Western view of reality and suggests characteristics of a worldview which can help us address our society's ecological and social ills.

Meeting Three reviews the rich history of simplicity within both American culture and the Christian tradition.

We feel that movement toward simplicity is intimately connected to caring for the earth and environmental justice. **Meetings Four and Five** include discussions of environmental theology, and how that theology challenges our culture's central value of economic growth. Meeting Five especially focuses on ways to express that theology in the daily practice of simplicity.

Meeting Six emphasizes our experience of time (how busy we are!) and contrasts time as a commodity to be spent with time as a sacred gift to be fully experienced and offered back in gratitude to God and our communities. Meeting Six sees simplicity as making room (time) in our lives for an awareness of God's presence.

Meeting Seven highlights our relationship with money, an issue which often serves to first draw people to simplicity.

Meeting Eight takes a revealing look at our economic system. It does so not in an esoteric or theoretical way but with the purpose of discussing some of that system's fundamental problems and how those problems impact daily life. It introduces the topic of overconsumption in Western nations and how today's global economy affects the poor and the land.

Meeting Nine continues the themes introduced in Meeting Eight. Within the context of present-day inequity and injustice, it asks the important and difficult question, "how much is enough?"

We have no more intimate connection to the land than the food we eat. **Meeting Ten** provides time to consider food, and how our eating habits affect land and people. This meeting ends by providing hopeful alternative food purchasing options based on supporting local food economies, one practical expression of a move toward simplicity and living more lightly on the earth.

Meeting Eleven focuses on the very important (but often neglected) reality that the simplicity movement needs a "politics of simplicity." Ways to create a society which encourage the values and practices associated with simple living are explored.

Meeting Twelve focuses on simplicity and community. There is an exercise to help participants reflect on how they may feel motivated (or called) to respond to this course. It concludes with a potluck and time for individual participants as well as the group to decide what next steps, if any, they may wish to take.

If You Have Four, Six Or Eight Weeks. . .

If your group has **eight weeks** in which to complete the study, we recommend the following:

    Meeting One—Storytelling: Listening to Our Lives
    Meeting Two—Worldviews: The Lens Through Which We See
    Meeting Three—Simplicity Is Nothing New: A Brief Historical Overview
    Meeting Five—Theology for the Practice of Simplicity
    Meeting Seven—Your Money or Your Life: The Place of Money in Modern Life
    Meeting Eight—The Big Economy, The Great Economy
    Meeting Ten—Broader Impacts of Our Everyday Food Choices
    Meeting Twelve—Widening Our Circle of Community: Journey to
                       Abundant Life

We recommend the following if your group has **four weeks** in which to complete the study:

    Meeting One—Storytelling: Listening to Our Lives
    Meeting Five—Theology for the Practice of Simplicity
    Meeting Seven—Your Money or Your Life: The Place of Money in Modern Life
    Meeting Ten—Broader Impacts of Our Everyday Food Choices

If your group would like to concentrate on a theme, we have identified the following six week thematic options:

Theme: Money, Economics and Justice

    Meeting One—Storytelling: Listening to Our Lives
    Meeting Four—Theology in Support of Simplicity and Eco-Justice
    Meeting Seven—Your Money or Your Life: The Place of Money in Modern Life
    Meeting Eight—The Big Economy, The Great Economy
    Meeting Nine—How Much is Enough? Lifestyles, Global Economics and Justice
    Meeting Ten—Broader Impacts of Our Everyday Food Choices
    (If you have time for a seventh meeting, conclude with Meeting Twelve.)

Theme: Community—Extending Our Circle of Compassion
  Meeting One—Storytelling: Listening to Our Lives
  Meeting Four—Theology in Support of Simplicity and Eco-Justice
  Meeting Eight—The Big Economy, The Great Economy
  Meeting Ten—Broader Impacts of Our Everyday Food Choices
  Meeting Eleven—The Politics of Simplicity
  Meeting Twelve—Widening Our Circle of Community: Journey to
        Abundant Life

Theme: Simplicity in Personal, Everyday Life
  Meeting One—Storytelling: Listening to Our Lives
  Meeting Five—Theology for the Practice of Simplicity
  Meeting Six—Time as Commodity, Time as Sacred
  Meeting Seven—Your Money or Your Life: The Place of Money in Modern Life
  Meeting Ten—Broader Impacts of Our Everyday Food Choices
  Meeting Twelve—Widening Our Circle of Community: Journey to
        Abundant Life

Theme: History and Theology Applied to Everyday Life
  Meeting One—Storytelling: Listening to Our Lives
  Meeting Three—Simplicity Is Nothing New: A Brief Historical Overview
  Meeting Four—Theology in Support of Simplicity and Eco-Justice
  Meeting Five—Theology for the Practice of Simplicity
  Meeting Eleven—The Politics of Simplicity
  Meeting Twelve—Widening Our Circle of Community: Journey to
        Abundant Life

Or, design your own course tailored to fit your group's needs!

Meeting One:

Storytelling:
Listening to Our Lives

Tools Everyone Needs:
Simpler Living,
   Compassionate Life
pen or pencil
Optional:
journal or notebook

Purpose:
To briefly introduce
the course as a whole
and clarify/discuss
course guidelines;

To begin to create a
comfortable setting
and sense of commu-
nity within the group
by telling life-stories;

To share expectations
and hopes for this
course.

**Read Before Next
Gathering:**
"Worldview as Inheri-
tance"   —p. 191

"Traditional Western
View of Reality"
            —p. 194

"Healing Ourselves
and the Earth"
            —p. 196

If time allows:
"Sacred Cosmology
and the Ecological
Crisis"   —p. 200

Read Before Meeting One

"Overview"   —p. 11
Introduction to "The Sacred Journey"   —p. 19
The Good Life and The Abundant Life"   —p. 23

Facilitator Overview

This is an important meeting as it sets the tone for
the rest of this course. As today's group facilitator,
please:

1. Welcome everyone and make sure everyone has
   access to a copy of this book;
2. After introductions, follow the flow of the
   readings and associated questions;
3. Lead (or ask someone to lead) the opening
   meditation and prayer;
4. Read aloud the group reading (we suggest
   members take turns reading);
5. Keep track of time, ensuring that all have
   adequate time to tell their own stories;
6. Determine how the group wants to choose each
   meeting's Facilitator and designate one for the
   next meeting.

Important Note: If you are not going through the
curriculum in order, the articles listed in the shaded
box to the left are not your readings for next week!
If, for example, your next session is Meeting Four,
refer to Meeting Three for the appropriate readings.

Overview

This first meeting is dedicated to hearing a portion of each person's story and a little about why they feel drawn to a course combining faith and simplicity. The entire course emphasizes and values individuals' experiences and wisdom. Themes: *Simplicity as enjoyment of each other. Simplicity and our own stories: an element of our calling.*

Introductions

Briefly introduce yourself. (Soon you will get a chance to say more!)

Opening Meditation

Read aloud to the group:

The call to simplicity and freedom for Christians is the call to move from achievement-oriented spirituality to a life centered on a shared vision of relatedness to people and things, a relatedness of gentleness, of compassion, of belonging to one another.

—*Richard Bower*, Living Simply

Prayer

Creator, Sustainer, Redeemer, thank you for the gift of another day and for the chance to be together. We remember that you have promised your presence where "two or three are gathered." May we grow in compassion as you are compassion. May we learn from our own lives, from each other and from your presence in our world. *Amen.*

Ask:

In one sentence, what does the title of this book, "Simpler Living, Compassionate Life," suggest to you? (Feel free to use the space below to jot down your ideas.)

Group Reading (We suggest members take turns reading.)

An introductory reading by Michael Schut.

So, here you are! Beginning a course on simplicity. Perhaps you are excited, expectant; perhaps wary, nervous, unsure of what this is all about; perhaps wondering if you can hang out with these assembled folks!

No matter how you are feeling, we hope this first meeting is fun and relaxed. All you have to do is listen to stories and tell one of your own. So settle in and enjoy the undivided attention of the group and the opportunity to talk about yourself.

This entire course can be seen as a sharing of stories—your own as well as those represented in the readings. In other words, this course begins with you, where you are, who you are, and what brings you here. You will also see that there is great emphasis placed on sharing your own life-experiences within a supportive environment. Doing so is, in itself, participating in one of life's simpler joys: learning more about other people and developing a sense of community.

Hopefully, you have had a chance to read today's articles. "How to Use This Material" provides a brief overview to the course and also suggests guidelines for group interaction. Those guidelines are important and can help create an open and caring community as you meet together. The introduction also briefly discusses logistics. Everyone should be clear about how this course is organized, the role of the Facilitator, course guidelines and so on. Take ten minutes or so to answer the following questions, or other ones group members may have, about these guidelines and logistics.

Group Discussion

- **Are there any questions about course format, organization or leadership?**
- **Any questions or comments on the Facilitator's role?**
- **Any comments or questions about the group process (see "Course Ethos and Guidelines") hoped for?**

Group Reading—*continued*

As you begin today, remember Cecile Andrews' guidelines for interaction: Listen carefully and non-judgmentally to one another. Speak from your hearts, from the depth of your own experience. We all long for connection and to be known on more than a superficial level. This requires a certain amount of openness and trust, and Cecile's ideas can help in this process.

Buechner and Storytelling

Frederick Buechner (pronounced *Beekner*), author and minister, is someone who has listened deeply to his own life and shared it in such a way as to bring light and hope to many others. Buechner believes that all good theology is autobiography. He thus begins his celebrated autobiographical trilogy with the following:

> What I propose to do now is to try listening to my life as a whole for whatever of meaning, of holiness, of God there may be in it to hear. My assumption is that the story of any one of us is in some measure the story of us all.

He listens to his life as a whole for whatever "of meaning, of holiness, of God there may be in it to hear." This course asks you to do the same. Listen to the joy, for therein lies the kernel of God's call and passion in your life. Listen to the laughter, for laughter is immeasurable. Listen to that which society often tells us to muffle—the pain and alienation—for therein lie clues to that which needs healing and hope.

I would like to tell you about a time when I "listened to my life as a whole" and heard a good deal of pain. It is a story of how over time, with the help of friends and community, that listening led to greater freedom and joy.

I went to a Christian college that preached the gospel of grace, freely given to all. But the stronger, implicit message (at least for me) told me I had to be a *certain kind of Christian* to receive such grace. This silent instruction communicated a gospel of its own—a gospel of duty and guilt. That dualistic message and the "do's and don'ts" I thought I had to follow became life- and spirit-draining for me. What mattered was "following God's will," something I wanted to do. But as I felt the gospel of duty and guilt more and more strongly, I began to believe that if I were doing God's will, I would be miserable. That, however, was inconsequential because my own feelings of gladness and joy were not to be considered.

After college I moved to Washington, D.C., where I worked with Church of the Savior's Samaritan Inns, a program providing a home for homeless men. While there, I realized that what I really wanted in my life was to ultimately *share love*, and yet I felt I had little experience of God's love—in spite of all my efforts. Most all that effort had been motivated by duty and obligation. I had to start over. Within the context of a caring community I began to feel the pain of living a prescribed Christianity and the exhaustive effort of trying to please everyone else.

I began to listen to my joys and passions. I began to accept that, perhaps, such joys were hints of God's call in my life. I began pursuing an earlier love, being in the out-of-doors, and gradually gained enough skill to become a wilderness backpacking and rock-climbing guide. This whole process began by facing loss: the many years of trying to please a seemingly overly demanding God, of not valuing many of my own joys, and the sense of burden and "heaviness" I felt as a result.

Facing the pain associated with that loss has made a wonderful difference in my life. Pain (whether emotional, mental or physical) is often a sign of a broken relationship and of that which needs healing and restoration. In this case, it actually seems God used that loss to help heal my relationship with God. God no longer seems so much the never-to-be-pleased, demanding divinity, motivating through duty and guilt, but rather more of a relational being, wooing us with love and deeply interested in healing our relationships with self, God, each other and all of creation.

In our day, one relationship in need of restoration is the relationship between humanity and the rest of the natural world. As David Orr, a leading environmental thinker and educator, states, "Our alienation from the natural world is unprecedented. Healing this division is a large part of the difference between survival and extinction." So while this course emphasizes listening to *your* story (particularly as it relates to simplicity), it is set in the larger context of recognizing all of our relationships, not only those with people, but also with the larger community of life. It is also set in the larger context of the effects of our lifestyles on those relationships.

I believe that if we listen, the larger community (of all creation) has a story to tell as well. Surely part of this story is heard in the environmental crises facing our earth-home as the creation groans under the weight of our consumer society. Moving toward simplicity and reducing consumption is one important step toward healing the division to which Orr refers.

Finally, the psychologist Rollo May suggests that "only the truth that is experienced at all levels of being has the power to change the human being." Education capable of bringing about change, then, will educate not only the mind but the heart and soul as well. This course will focus on such an educational process, where reflection on experiences, feelings, and thoughts (your own, those of other group members, and those of the authors we will read) might lead to healing alienation in our own lives and our communities.

It is my hope that this course will engender a simplicity of compassion. That, as possible connections are seen between simplicity and the Christian faith, between simplicity and consumption, between simplicity and contemplation, we might move toward compassionate responses.

Storytelling

The rest of this meeting is dedicated to introducing yourselves more fully. Take your time; say more, and in more depth, than your name and your job. Try to let people see *you*. Below are some suggested questions. Each person should have equal time to speak. (Reminder: for those going through the course in a 45-60 minute time slot, we suggest you start with the questions in the bold text.)

1. **Briefly, what are your historical and geographical roots? (Where are you from, your family background, what sort of work have you done, etc.)**

2. "The Good Life and The Abundant Life" discussed just that. When have you experienced the abundant life? Besides those things mentioned in the essay, what else is good about the good life?

3. How does listening to one another foster your understanding of simplicity as compassion?

4. How did you come to be interested in this course?

5. In your own life, do you perceive connections between your faith and simplicity? What might they be?

After everyone has spoken, take a moment to consider your answer to the following:
6. What are your hopes and/or expectations for this course? *In one phrase or sentence* share those with the group.

Action Step

As this course on simplicity has started with an emphasis on listening, with an ear toward healing relationships (with human and non-human members of our communities), is there some relationship in your life which could use a little more time and attention? Can you think of some *small step* you might take in that direction this coming week? Although thinking of the step is all that is asked for now, you might choose to actually try taking it and notice what happens. If you are comfortable doing so, take a moment to share this with the group.

Closing Prayer *(Read in unison.)*
Creator God, you have made us and our world; you have made us as deeply relational beings; you have put in us a hunger for love and joy. Help us to listen attentively to our lives; help us to discern the leaning of our hearts; help us to hear your calling to us out of the dailiness of our own experiences. In your name we pray, *Amen.*

A Reminder

Select next week's Facilitator! You may also want to look ahead and choose facilitators for each of your gatherings. (If some do not feel comfortable, they should not feel pressure to facilitate; someone else could do two meetings if necessary.)

Meeting Two: Worldviews: The Lens through Which We See

Tools Everyone Needs:
Simpler Living, Compassionate Life
pen or pencil
Optional:
journal or notebook

Purpose:
To share our personal views about simplicity;

To discuss how our worldviews shape our lives, relationships, and views about simplicity.

Read Before Next Gathering:
"Introduction to *The Politics of Simplicity*" —p. 141

"Epilogue from *The Simple Life*" —p. 144

"Simplicity Among the Saints" —p. 149

Facilitator Overview
As facilitator today:
1. Serve as timekeeper;
2. Facilitate discussions, making sure everyone who wants to has the opportunity to speak;
3. Lead (or ask someone to lead) the opening meditation and prayer;
4. Designate next meeting's Facilitator.

Overview
This meeting encourages reflection on the effects our worldviews have on our lives and includes discussion of our individual feelings and thoughts about simplicity. Theme: *Simplicity: how do we experience it?*

Opening Meditation
You may wish to begin with a few moments of centering silence and then read aloud:

"Therefore I tell you, do not worry about your life, what you will eat or drink; or about your body, what you will wear. Is not life more important than food, and the body more important than clothes? Look at the birds of the air; they do not sow or reap or store away in barns, and yet your heavenly Father feeds them. Are you not much more valuable than they? Who of you by worrying can add a single hour to his life?"

"And why do you worry about clothes? See how the lilies of the field grow. They do not labor or spin. Yet I tell you that not even Solomon in all his splendor was dressed like one of these. If that is how God clothes the grass of the field, which is here today and tomorrow is thrown into the fire, will he not much more clothe you, O you of little faith? So do not worry, saying, 'What shall we eat?' or 'What shall we drink?' or 'What shall we wear?' For the pagans run after all these things, and your heavenly Father knows that you need them. But seek first God's kingdom and God's righteousness, and all these things will be given to you as well. Therefore, do not worry about tomorrow, for tomorrow will worry about itself. Each day has enough trouble of its own."

—Matthew 6:25-34

In this well-known passage, what particularly speaks to you?

Check-In

Share thoughts about the Action Step from the last meeting. Did anyone think about, or take, a step toward healing a relationship? *Briefly* share about your thoughts and experiences.

Opening Prayer

God, it is difficult to not worry, to trust in you, to seek your kingdom first. We ask for your help in discerning what often seems a murky path. Grant us courage. *Amen.*

Small Group Discussion

Break up into groups of two or three members, and use the following questions as a guideline for your conversation. Add questions of your own.

1. **Reflect on your childhood: How did the church and those significant in your life help to define your sense of self?**

In the point of rest at the center of our being, we encounter a world where all things are at rest in the same way. Then a tree becomes a mystery, a cloud a revelation, each man a cosmos of whose riches we can only catch glimpses. The life of simplicity is simple, but it opens to us a book in which we never get beyond the first syllable.

—Dag Hammarskjold, Swedish (1905-1961)

2. As you grew up, did you receive a worldview and language that included care for and connection with the natural world? Share your thoughts.

3. How is your worldview similar to or different from Elgin's description?

Group Discussion

Gather together as one group again and discuss:

1. In what ways does the western worldview nurture, or fail to nurture, compassion (empathy and justice) toward others, both human and non-human?

2. Share your thoughts about Bhagat's essay. Are there other "beliefs that need rethinking" within Western Christianity? What are they?

3. What two words would you use to describe *your feeling,* on a gut level, when you hear the word "simplicity?"

4. What two words or phrases would you use to capture the essence of *your ideas* about simplicity? Share your thoughts with the group.

Closing Prayer *(Read in unison.)*

Loving God, you have created a vast, rich and beautiful world, of which we are a part. In our search for you, help us not to assume our picture of you or your world to be *the* truth. Grant us an honest humility in all these undertakings. *Amen.*

Action Step

What more could you do to stay centered and focused on your deepest values and heartfelt aspirations? (Keep a journal? Meditate? Pray? Take time in nature? Slow down? Work less?) Choose one, share it with the group, and work on that this week.

 *Meeting Three:*

Simplicity Is Nothing New:
A Brief Historical Overview

Facilitator Overview

As facilitator today:

1. Serve as timekeeper;
2. Facilitate discussions, making sure everyone who wants to has the opportunity to speak;
3. Lead the opening meditation and prayer;
4. Designate next meeting's Facilitator.

Overview

This week provides a historical overview of simplicity, in American culture generally and Christianity specifically.

Opening Meditation/Prayer

Begin with a few moments of silence to prepare to hear the following quotes which represent a few Christian historical perspectives on simplicity:

(Job, speaking to his "counselors" about his life, recognized the wisdom of the natural world):

> But ask the animals, and they
>   will teach you;
> the birds of the air, and they
>   will tell you;
> ask the plants of the earth, and
>   they will teach you;
> and the fish of the sea will declare
>   to you.
>
> —*Job 12:7-8*

Tools Everyone Needs:
Simpler Living, Compassionate Life
pen or pencil
Optional:
journal or notebook

Purpose:
To consider historical Christian traditions of simplicity as background and support for a contemporary expression of simple living.

Read Before Next Gathering:
"Some Notes from Belshaz'zar's Feast"
—p. 161

Prayer

Thank you, Creator God, for the gift of breath. Be here with us. In humility, we ask for the grace to seek first your kingdom and to trust ever more fully, resting in you. *Amen.*

There was not a needy person among them, for as many as owned lands or houses sold them and brought the proceeds of what was sold. They laid it at the apostles' feet, and it was distributed to each as any had need.

—*Acts 4:34-35*

(**Note:** Remember to feel free to pick and choose questions as interest and time permit. Also, please remember that the authors you read are not meant to be "authorities," but voices of other group members not able to join the discussion in person.)

Pairs

Members pair up to discuss the following questions on David Shi's "Epilogue":
1. **What draws *you* to simplicity?**

2. **Do you agree with Shi's assessment that the movement toward simplicity will remain a minority concern? How might it become a "majority concern?"**

3. How do Shi's views fit with your own experience?

4. Shi quotes Mumford, "If our new philosophy is well grounded we shall carry into the future many elements of quality that this culture actually embraces." What "elements of quality" would you carry into the future while still expressing your sense of living simply?

Group Discussion

A member from each pair should summarize and share their impressions to the group (briefly, with no group discussion). Then discuss together:
1. **Did any common themes emerge in the pair discussions?**

Regarding Foster's "Simplicity Among the Saints," and/or Segal's introduction to "The Politics of Simplicity":

2. **Did any of the described traditions intrigue or attract you? Were you wary of or "turned off" by any? Why?**

> **Jesus as a concrete historical personality remains a stranger to our time, but His spirit, which lies hidden in His words, is known in simplicity, and its influence is direct.**
>
> —*Albert Schweitzer*

3. **How do these traditions relate to your own experience?**

Action Step

(Facilitator: please read the action step aloud, provide enough time for people to reflect and "answer" the suggested action, and then begin the closing prayer.)

Here's an idea to help you simplify one thing in your life. Take out a piece of paper. On one side jot down three or four things that you own, from which "you derive inner help and comfort" (Gandhi). On the other side jot down three or four things that do not offer that inner help and comfort. These have to be things that you currently own. Over the next week, you might try to give away one of the items in your unnecessary column to someone who may find it necessary. Next week, you'll have the chance to report back on your experience.

> **Dependence on God is the only independence, for God has no heaviness; only the earthly and especially the earthly treasure has that.**
>
> —*Vernard Eller,*
> The Simple Life

Closing Prayer

Creator God, thank you for the depth and richness of our own tradition. It is good to know that in our interest in, and expressions of, simplicity we stand in a long line of "witnesses and supporters," from our Jewish roots, through Jesus, the early church, and throughout the history of Christianity. May we go from this place in peace and joy. *Amen.*

Meeting Four: Theology in Support of Simplicity and Eco-Justice

Tools Everyone Needs:
Simpler Living, Compassionate Life
pen or pencil
Optional:
journal or notebook

Purpose:
To consider one example of a theologian's call to reform theology to include the natural world and to a life of greater simplicity and justice.

Read Before Next Gathering:
"Creation's Care and Keeping"
—p. 175

"The Discipline of Simplicity"
—p. 180

Facilitator Overview
As facilitator today:
1. Remind group members to bring something from home to the next meeting for the meditation (see below);
2. Serve as timekeeper;
3. Facilitate discussions, making sure everyone who wants to speak has the opportunity;
4. Lead (or ask someone to lead) the opening meditation and prayer;
5. Designate next meeting's Facilitator.

Overview
This meeting (and next) connects simplicity to a theology of care for the earth and all her creatures. Theme: *Simplicity: connection to all creation.*

Opening Meditation

Begin with a few moments of silence and then read aloud:

> Love all God's creation, the whole of it and every grain of sand. Love every leaf, every ray of God's light! Love the animals, love the plants, love everything. If you love everything, you will perceive the divine mystery in things. And once you have perceived it, you will begin to comprehend it ceaselessly, more and more every day. And you will at last come to love the whole world with an abiding, universal love.
>
> —*Fyodor Mikhail Dostoevsky*

> He [Jesus] is the image of the invisible God, the first-born over all creation. For by him all things were created: things in heaven and on earth... all things were created by him and for him. He is before all things, and in him all things hold together.
>
> —*Colossians 1:15-17*

Share any comments or reflections on the above passages.

Check-In

For those who feel so inspired, *briefly* share your experience of working through last meeting's action step.

Group Discussion

Note: "Some Notes from Belshaz'zar's Feast" can be a disturbing essay. It's hard to know what would happen to our economy, and our well-being, if the religion of growthism was seriously challenged. In this context, keep two things in mind. One, as Weiskel recognizes in his closing paragraph, the global economic system does not currently serve the well-being of "the mass of humanity," or the rest of the natural world. Second, if growthism is challenged there will need to be something better in its place. Certain characteristics of that "something" will be found in future meetings. For example, meetings 8, 9 and 10 address characteristics of a more sane and fair economic system.

Prayer

God, thank you for our time together, for the gift of life, for your ongoing work of creation in our world, and for your presence in each of our lives. Be with us now and when we leave this place. In your name, *Amen*.

Discuss:

1. **Did anything especially "grab you" in this essay? Share with the group your reactions to Weiskel's thoughts.**

2. **Weiskel states "our theology determines the character of our engagement with [the world]." How do you see this as true in your own life?**

3. Weiskel identifies "growthism"—more is better, growth is good—as our culture's most pervasive religiously held belief. Do you agree? What are some of the ramifications of this belief?

Pairs

Weiskel says "a sense of moral compulsion cannot be imposed effectively from above... moral and ethical imperatives emerge spontaneously from a shared sense of community—a feeling that what 'I' do or what 'we' do matters to others within a community of which I wish to be a part. Our past record as a species is not encouraging in this regard. Historically, those considered to be outside the moral community have simply been ignored or—worse yet—persecuted....Clearly, our notion of what is outside and what is inside must change if we are to survive much longer as a human species in a wider biological community."

Form pairs to discuss the following questions:

1. **Do you agree with Weiskel, that our notion of community must expand? Can you think of, and share with your partner, a time when your sense of community expanded? How did that happen and what was the experience like?**

2. To quote Weiskel again: "what we need... is a thoroughgoing reformation of our public theology of growthism." Drawing on your life experiences and the readings and discussions in this course so far, what might some of the characteristics of that reformation (and resulting theology) be?

Pair Share
Each pair summarizes their answers to the whole group.

Discuss the common themes that emerged.

Action Step
Today's action step has two parts. First, for the next meeting's opening meditation, please bring something natural—rocks, plants, bark, dirt, etc.—that has some special significance for you. (This can be an object or a picture.) Plan to briefly describe the story or significance behind the object you choose.

Second, this meeting has suggested various connections between justice, theology and caring for creation. One way to express those connections is to modify certain everyday actions. For example, global warming is already impacting island nations as sea levels rise. To decrease your contributions to global warming, you could try a couple of Turn the Tide's action steps: install four compact flourescent lights and move your thermostat 3 degrees.

Closing Prayer *(Read in unison.)*
Loving God, thank you for this time together. Spark our thinking, enliven our hopes, enter our worlds in ever-surprising and life-giving ways. Help us to listen to better understand your ways; help us to know "enough is enough and balance is best." In Jesus' name, *Amen.*

See www.newdream.org/turnthetide. For an introduction to Turn the Tide, see page 230.

Meeting Five:

Theology for the Practice of Simplicity

Tools Everyone Needs:
Simpler Living, Compassionate Life
pen or pencil
Optional:
journal or notebook

Purpose:
To consider biblical principles and the Bible as an "ecological handbook";

To specifically explore a perspective on biblical teachings as they relate to simplicity.

Read Before Next Gathering:
"Excerpt from *The Overworked American*" —p. 33

"The Spirituality of Everyday Life" —p. 37

"Entering the Emptiness" —p. 41

Facilitator Overview
As facilitator today:
1. Serve as timekeeper;
2. Facilitate discussions, making sure everyone who wants to speak has the opportunity;
3. Lead (or ask someone to lead) the opening meditation and prayer;
4. Designate next meeting's Facilitator.

Overview
Both DeWitt and Foster come from Evangelical backgrounds which they effectively apply to the many practical questions raised by everyday choices. Among other things, today's meeting shows that one's theology and beliefs have very practical ramifications in daily life.

Opening Meditation
Begin with a few moments of silence and then read aloud:

> For since the creation of the world God's invisible qualities—God's eternal power and divine nature—have been clearly seen, being understood from what has been made...
> —Romans 1:20

Take turns placing your natural object (or picture) in the center of your circle, either on the floor or a table. Briefly describe why it has special significance to you. For those who forgot, describe what you would have brought.

Small Group Discussion

In groups of three, discuss any of the following questions on Calvin DeWitt's "Creation's Care and Keeping: A Biblical Perspective."

1. **Which of the principles (earthkeeping, discipleship, Sabbath, fruitfulness, contentment, and practical application) most surprised you? Which did you find most helpful?**

Prayer

i thank You God for most this amazing
day: for the leaping greenly spirits of trees
and a blue true dream of sky; and for
   everything
which is natural which is infinite which is
   yes

—*e.e. cummings*

2. **Do you see connections between DeWitt's principles and the pursuit of simplicity? Between his principles and a simplicity of compassion?**

3. What did you think of this reading?

4. How does it relate to your experience (of God's creation, of how the Bible is taught, of being in the outdoors...)?

Small Group Reports

Anyone have a "hot topic" that came up in your small group which you would like to discuss with everyone?

Group Discussion

Discuss as a group any of the following questions on Foster's "The Discipline of Simplicity":

• **Foster refers to ten "controlling principles" for outward simplicity. Which is the most helpful to you? Do others seem unreasonable or unrealistic?**

• **How do inner and outer simplicity relate to each other? Do you need one to have the other?**

• **How did you like this reading? Did you find it useful in some way?**

• What would the concept of the Year of Jubilee (Leviticus 25:8-12) look like in a modern society?

Closing Prayer

The Lord is my shepherd, I shall not want. He makes me lie down in green pastures, he leads me beside the still waters, he restores my soul. He guides me in paths of righteousness for his name's sake. Even though I walk through the valley of the shadow of death I will fear no evil, for you are with me; your rod and your staff, they comfort me. You prepare a table before me in the presence of my enemies. You anoint my head with oil; my cup overflows. Surely goodness and love will follow me all the days of my life, and I will dwell in the house of the Lord forever. *Amen.*

—*Psalm 23*

Action Step

Calvin DeWitt's article discusses the notion of "Sabbath Rest." Are there ways you personally might try to give yourself such a respite in your week? List them below. Try out some of these ideas in the coming week.

Meeting Six: Time as Commodity, Time as Sacred

Facilitator Overview

As facilitator today:

1. Serve as timekeeper;
2. Facilitate discussions, making sure everyone who wants to has the opportunity to speak;
3. Lead (or ask someone to lead) the opening meditation and prayer (which includes part of the Group Reading and a time of silence);
4. Designate next meeting's Facilitator.

Overview

Many of us feel "too busy" and "don't have enough time." As a result we often feel disconnected from God and others. Meeting Six discusses our perceptions of time, silence, and contemplation. It focuses on slowing down our hectic pace—using silence and contemplation to be more in touch with ourselves and more aware of God's presence. Theme: *Simplicity: opening space in our lives for a greater awareness of God.*

Opening Meditation

Scripture readings:

- Psalm 46:10 "Be still and know that I am God ...."
- Matthew 14:22-23 (These verses follow the story of the feeding of the five thousand.) "Immediately Jesus made the disciples get into the boat and go

Tools Everyone Needs:
Simpler Living, Compassionate Life
pen or pencil
Optional:
journal or notebook

Purpose:
To explore how we experience and understand time;

To learn how silence and contemplation can enrich our lives and deepen our relationships with God.

Read Before Next Gathering:
"Spending Money as if Life Really Mattered"   —p. 59

"Money"   —p. 67

on ahead of him to the other side, while he dismissed the crowd. After he had
dismissed them, he went up into the hills by himself to pray."

Group Reading (The prayer follows this reading.)

An introductory reading by Jim Mulligan:
This session focuses on three related dimensions
of our experience of life: how we experience time,
silence as a way of experiencing time differently,
and contemplation as a particular use of silence.

> **There is nothing so
> much like God in all the
> universe as silence.**
>
> —*Meister Eckhart*
> (c. 1260-1327)

In our culture the familiar "time is money" equation
has been taken on with a singular obsessional devo-
tion. Cecile Andrews speaks about our culture's tendency to pressure pack as much
frenetic activity into our days as we possibly can. For many people having time to
enjoy life, or even just to experience it more sanely, is becoming a significant reason to get out of the rat race. Beyond release from the pressure, many seek a less
hurried pace of life, and through that, to experience life in greater fullness.

The desire to experience life more fully, more deeply, has long historical roots in
many religious traditions. In this search for depth, silence can help. Purposeful
times of silence are a feature of various traditions, including our Christian heritage.
Silence allows us to escape the press of time, to collect our thoughts, to relax our
tensed bodies, to have a break from constant "doing," and to be more reflective.
This space for reflection can help us to put life into perspective, to gain clarity, and
to experience our inner world more fully.

Contemplation is a particular way of experiencing silence, using it as a vehicle for
greater openness to God. Here we try not to think, nor to reflect about what we are
experiencing. Contempla-
tion seeks solely to *experience fully the present moment*
as meaningful in itself, not
needing to be understood,
or analyzed, just experi-
enced. Contemplation is
seen as a form of prayer:
not prayer in which we are
"speaking to God," but
rather one in which we are open to God, listening, receptive, and resting in God.
Contemplation can provide space in which God may speak to us (be present to us)
through all that is, all that God has created. It treats life as a gift of God, and
encourages us to experience God directly through this radical receptiveness to
God's presence in all things.

> **The call to simplicity and freedom is a reminder that
> our worth comes not from the amount of our involve-
> ments, achievements, or possessions, but from the
> depth and care which we bring to each moment, place,
> and person in our lives.**
>
> —*Richard A. Bower*

Unfortunately, in our day, contemplation is little understood. Seen as an esoteric and antiquated way of life, it has been largely relegated to the monastic life or at least to those who have either the leisure or dedication for it. This attitude reflects our society's entrenched view of God as removed from life, the earth, and the ordinary. It reflects our fixation on productivity, on the Christian life as solely doing good works. God's immediate presence to us seems alien, or merely a romantic ideal. However, it is God's presence to us all, in the daily ordinariness of living, that contemplation offers.

Moving towards voluntary simplicity can be a movement away from drivenness, a reclamation of time—life at an appropriate pace. It can provide for periods of silence, reflection, and contemplation. Such a life is often characterized as richer, fuller, more meaningful, more peaceful, more compassionate, more loving, more joyful. Today we will try to think about this use of the gift of time, and to experience it directly. (See prayer at right.)

Prayer

For our prayer today we will begin with 10-15 minutes of silence. Do whatever you need to do to make yourself fully comfortable. Some of you might wish to close your eyes. Let your muscles relax, letting go of the tensions of the day. Envision yourself in another pleasing setting: in the mountains, by the ocean, in the forest, somewhere where you are alone, peaceful, calm. Or, instead, be fully present to being here in this room with these people. Give yourself permission to do whatever you need to do to create a space of quietness. We will keep the silence for 10 to 15 minutes.

After the silence…
Creator God, you come to us in the stillness of this hour. Speak to us the word our lives need to hear. Grant us stillness, turn us from frantic striving, calm our drivenness. Help us to discern your presence through all of life and in all that you have made. Give us ears to hear, eyes to see, and hearts to know your grace. *Amen.*

Check-In

Last meeting's action step—exploring how you might want to incorporate "Sabbath Rest" into your life—fits in well with today's theme. Do any of you have something you would like to briefly share related to that?

Group Reading—*continued*

Below find a number of perspectives related to contemplation and silence. (Various people can read the quotes.)

Where shall the word be found, where will the word Resound? Not here, there is not enough silence.

—*T.S. Eliot*

Contemplation is...spiritual wonder. It is spontaneous awe at the sacredness of life, of being. It is gratitude for life... it is a vivid realization of the fact that life and being in us proceed from an invisible, transcendent and infinitely abundant Source. Contemplation is, above all, awareness of the reality of that Source. It *knows* the Source, obscurely, inexplicably, but with a certitude that goes both beyond reason and beyond simple faith.

—*Thomas Merton,*
New Seeds of Contemplation

Contemplative prayer "... is then not just a formula of words, or a series of desires springing up in the heart—it is the orientation of our whole body, mind and spirit to God in silence, attention and adoration... *a conversion of our entire self to God.*"

—*John J. Higgins,*
Thomas Merton On Prayer

Group Discussion

Discuss the following questions:

1. What most struck you about this week's readings by Cecile Andrews and Juliet Schor?

2. What struck you most about the readings we just read in this session?

3. What most characterizes the experience of time in your own life?

4. Gerald May says, "A... probing of spiritual growth shows that as people deepen in their love for God and others, they become ever more open: not only more appreciative of the beauty and joys of life, but also more vulnerable to its pain and brokenness." Do you see connections between this process of spiritual growth and developing a simplicity of compassion?

5. Can you recall a contemplative experience of your own? Would you share it with the group?

6. If you could shape your life in some new way (with respect to time, silence, and contemplation), what would that be?

Closing Prayer

Share a brief time of silence. Perhaps someone would also like to pray out loud to close the meeting.

Action Step

Between now and our next meeting, try one small step to put into practice your response to question 6 above. You may want to share your thoughts on this experience with the group next time.

Meeting Seven: Your Money or Your Life: The Place of Money in Modern Life

Tools Everyone Needs:
Simpler Living, Compassionate Life
pen or pencil
Optional:
journal or notebook

Purpose:
To consider our relationships with money;

To consider how our use of money reflects our core values.

Read Before Next Gathering:
"The Big Economy, The Great Economy" —p. 73

"Christian Faith and the Degradation of Creation" —p. 80

Facilitator Overview
As facilitator today:
1. Serve as timekeeper;
2. Facilitate discussions, making sure everyone who wants to has the opportunity to speak;
3. Lead the opening meditation and prayer;
4. Designate next meeting's Facilitator.
5. See the "Important Note" at the end of this meeting and make sure someone is responsible for getting the video.

Overview
The pursuit of wealth is an extremely powerful idol in our culture as is the growth of the economic system which supplies that wealth. This cultural idol is probably most obviously expressed in our personal lives in the ways we relate to money.

Opening Meditation/Prayer
You may want to begin with a time of centering silence and then pray together:

> Two things I ask of you, O Lord;
> do not refuse me before I die:
> Keep falsehood and lies far from me;
> give me neither poverty nor riches,
> but give me only my daily bread.
> Otherwise, I may have too much and disown you
> and say "Who is the Lord?"
> Or I may become poor and steal,
> and so dishonor the name of my God.
> Amen.
>
> —*Proverbs 30:7-9*

Check-In

At the end of Meeting Six, you were asked to try one small step to shape your life differently with respect to time and silence. *Briefly* go around the group, giving everyone the opportunity to share what they tried.

Group Reading

An introductory reading by Michael Schut:

Ah, money. What a sensitive topic! In Meeting Six we discussed how even the gift of time is so often thought about in terms of a monetary transaction. Both of today's readings, as well as my introductory essay "The Good Life and The Abundant Life," recognize money as a most conspicuous idol in our culture. It's an idol we rarely talk about openly and so are most often left alone to deal with the place money has in our lives. There is little room for a community of people to support the individual in their desire to have, use and give away money so as to reflect their sense of values.

After college I participated in the community life of the Church of the Savior in Washington, D.C. I remember a particularly helpful exercise in a class I took there. We were asked to write our "money autobiography." We were given the chance to write openly on, and then talk with others about, the story of our lives as it related to our relationship with money. For me that was a very liberating experience. Today's meeting will hopefully be liberating in providing a setting and place to begin to uncover this fairly taboo subject. Think of it, like Evy McDonald does, as listening to a certain part of your life's story.

> **In truth, all human beings are called to be saints, but that just means called to be fully human... The saints are simply those men and women who relish the event of life as a gift and realize that the only way to honor such a gift is to give it away.**
>
> —*William Stringfellow*

Group Discussion

1. **"Freedom from idolatry of money, for a Christian, means that money becomes useful only as a sacrament—as a sign of the restoration of life wrought in this world by Christ." (Stringfellow) What do you think of this idea of money as sacrament? Tell about an experience or time in your life when money was a sacrament to you.**

2. Do you know people or families whose use of money you respect? Tell about them.

3. McDonald wrote about her "inherited and learned notions about money and consuming," which revealed to her a pattern of purchasing things when she felt sad or insecure or had had a bad week. What are your inherited and learned notions about money?

4. *Your Money or Your Life,* written by Vicki Robin and Joe Dominguez, is a very useful book for examining your relationship with money. They define money as something "for which you trade your life energy—your time." Is that helpful to you? How have you tended to define money?

5. How much is enough? It's a difficult question, but necessary in a world where "human beings live at each other's expense, and the affluence of the few is proximately related to, and supported by, the poverty of the many." (Stringfellow) What are some of the ways you have found helpful in defining how much is enough?

Action Step

Evy McDonald had been told she would die soon. Often it is only in such times that we ask ourselves important questions. In this case, McDonald asked herself, "who do I want to be when I die?" Take a little time to consider your own answer to that question. Then you could ask what parts of your current life are, or are not, helping form you into that person.

Closing Prayer

Dear God, life itself is such a beautiful gift. We pause again to thank you. May we be filled with wisdom and grace because it is not easy to trust you more than the security we place in money. Help us down the road of "sainthood" where we might more and more resemble those who honor all your gifts of life both in their receiving and in their giving. In your name, *Amen*.

Another "action step" idea you might want to consider is writing your "money autobiography." Doing so can be a fun, thought-provoking and revealing exercise. If you do, it's helpful to share your story with someone else who has also written theirs. If your whole group would like to do so, you might add a session to this course using the next time you gather to talk about your money autobiographies.

Important Note: Meeting Nine involves watching a video. In addition to ensuring a TV and VCR are available, contact one of the resource centers listed below and ask for the "Chee Yoke Ling" video. There may be a nominal charge for postage. Each resource center can give you information on their policies regarding the loan of videos.

Attn: Tovi Harris
Diocesan House
P. O. Box 12126
1551—10th Avenue East
Seattle, WA 98102
(206) 325-4200

Attn: Jackie Fielding
Education Coordinator
Diocese of California
1055 Taylor
San Francisco, CA 94108
(415) 673-5015

Attn: Linda Scott
Resource Center, Atlanta Diocese
27444 Peachtree Road NW
Atlanta, GA 30363
(800) 537-6743
email: lscott@mindspring.com

 *Meeting Eight:*

The Big Economy, The Great Economy

Tools Everyone Needs:
Simpler Living, Compassionate Life
pen or pencil
Optional:
journal or notebook

Purpose:
To consider certain characteristics of our economic system in light of the Christian faith and its call to compassion and justice.

Read Before Next Gathering:
"How Much Is Enough?" —p. 90

"Word and Flesh"
  —p. 99

Facilitator Overview
As facilitator today:
1. Serve as timekeeper;
2. Facilitate discussions, making sure everyone who wants to has the opportunity to speak;
3. Lead the opening meditation and prayer;
4. Designate next meeting's Facilitator;
5. Make sure someone is responsible for the VCR/TV and video for next meeting; see "Important Note" below.

Overview
This meeting's readings attempt to uncover some of our economic system's fundamental problems. These problems have daily, practical ramifications in all of our lives.

Opening Meditation
Gather with a moment of silence.

Frederick Buechner defines compassion as "that sometimes fatal capacity for feeling what it is like to live inside another's skin, knowing that there can never really be peace and joy for any until there is peace and joy finally for all."

Pause for silent reflection.

> Compassion seems to be the greatest power.
> —*The Dalai Lama*

Pause for silent reflection.

> Love your neighbor as yourself.
> —*Mark 12:31*

Check-In

Last week you were asked to first consider who you want to be when you die and then which parts of your life are forming you to be that person and which are not. If you wish, briefly share with the group *one* thing that stuck out to you as you considered that question.

Pair Discussion

"The Great Economy, The Big Economy," began with a story. It's a story of how being in relationship with others makes it possible to grow in compassion for them. Those with whom we previously had no perceived relationship become our neighbor.

Break up into pairs and briefly share about a time or experience in your life when you feel your own "circle of compassion" expanded. A time when you realized your connectedness to this newly discovered neighbor—a person or a place or an animal. Or you could talk about a time when you were in need and received neighborly compassion from someone else.

Suggested In-Class Activity

If there is interest and time, consider the following activity:

The line of the big (human) economy and the circle of the great (nature's) economy (as discussed in Schut's article) can provide a helpful framework for understanding how our choices impact human and non-human communities. Actually *seeing* that framework can be even more helpful. Consider the diagram to the right (or use it for future reference). Does it make sense? Any questions about it? Discuss as you see fit.

Group Discussion

1. What most struck you about today's readings?

2. With what do you disagree or agree?

3. John Cobb lists three "positives" the current global economic system has brought us (such as bringing wealth to a high percentage of people in the "First World"). Do you agree with these? Can you think of other positives?

4. Discuss ways our economic system could change to express greater compassion. Does it seem that those changes would also reflect the view of human nature as "persons-in-community" rather than "individuals-in-a-market", (as John Cobb describes them)?

Closing Prayer

Loving God, our economic system is so vast and "making a difference" seems nearly impossible. Help us to see and act on the ways we might respond to your call in our lives. We place our hope in you. *Amen.*

Action Step

"The Big Economy, The Great Economy" discussed externalities (such as toxic waste, soil erosion, species extinction). Take a moment to consider your daily or weekly routine. Either individually or as a group find one externality to which you contribute. We encourage you to consider one of Turn the Tide's (www.newdream.org/turnthetide) action steps. For example, as a group you might all choose to take one less car trip this next week, or install efficient showerheads and faucet aerators. Using Turn the Tide's web-based calculator you could then actually quantify how much less you contributed to a certain externality (such as carbon dioxide emissions when driving a car).

Important Note: Next meeting involves watching a video. In addition to ensuring a TV and VCR are available, contact one of the resource centers noted on p. 261 to obtain a copy of the "Chee Yoke Ling" video.

 *Meeting Nine:*

How Much Is Enough?: Lifestyles, Global Economics and Justice

Facilitator Overview

As facilitator today:

1. Serve as timekeeper;
2. Facilitate discussions, making sure everyone who wants to speak has the opportunity;
3. Lead the opening meditation and prayer;
4. Read aloud the group reading;
5. Set up VCR/TV;
6. Designate next meeting's Facilitator;
7. Arrange to return video.

Overview

Today's global economy has far-reaching and often negative effects on people (particularly the poor) and our earth-home. Our lives most closely intersect with the global economy when we consume its products. This meeting presents a video of Chee Yoke Ling, a lawyer and formerly Director of Friends of the Earth, Malaysia, who passionately and articulately describes the effects of the global economy, and our overconsumption, on "developing" countries. Theme: *Simplicity: justice and compassion.*

Opening Meditation

What does the Lord require of you? To act justly and to love mercy and to walk humbly with your God.

—Micah 6:8

In one sentence, what does this verse bring to mind for you?

Tools Everyone Needs:

Simpler Living, Compassionate Life
pen or pencil
VCR and TV monitor
Chee Yoke Ling video
Optional:
journal or notebook

Purpose:

To consider our consumption habits as they relate to the effects of the global economy on people and the environment.

Read Before Next Gathering:

"The Pleasures of Eating"   —p. 105

"The Great Hunter-Gatherer Continuum"   —p. 110

Check-In

Briefly give those who would like to the opportunity to report on their experience of reducing "their" externality since the last gathering.

Group Reading

An introductory reading by Michael Schut:
Today's session (and this course) is not meant to induce guilt or to hold up one "form" of simplicity as better than another. However, it *is* meant to look openly at certain realities of our world today. Doing so, particularly when considering something as pervasive as the global economy, is overwhelming. Feeling rather powerless to effect any sort of positive change is a common and understandable response. Today's meeting, however, sets the stage for Meeting Ten, which offers hopeful, practical ideas for possible responses (related specifically to food and agriculture). Our hope is that we all might look openly at particular realities of today's world, and at the same time find small, practical steps that allow us to respond in positive ways.

Prayer

Loving God, thank you again for this chance to be together. We trust you are here with us. Open our eyes that we might see, open our ears that we might hear; open our minds and loosen that which binds us to injustice that we might act justly; open our hearts that we might love mercy; and set our feet free from paths of idolatry, that we might walk humbly with you. In your name, *Amen.*

As we have learned from ecology, all things are interconnected, and in today's global economy, the same is true of our consumer choices. They have wide ranging, often global implications. To remind ourselves of these implications, read the following statistics slowly.

In the last two hundred years the United States has lost:
- 50% of its wetlands,
- 90% of its Northwestern old growth forests, and
- 99% of its tall grass prairie.

Average time spent shopping per week: 6 hours;
Average time spent playing with children per week: 40 minutes.

The amount of energy used by one American is equivalent to that used by 3 Japanese, 14 Chinese, or 168 Bangladeshi people.

(Statistics taken from *All Consuming Passion: Waking Up From the American Dream,* New Road Map Foundation, Seattle, Washington, 1993.)

Group Discussion: Chee Yoke Ling Video
View the video together (about 35 minutes).

Yoke Ling is a passionate and articulate voice bringing a perspective from another country. Discuss the following as a group:
1. What did you agree or disagree with?

2. How are her views on trade different from or similar to your own?

3. How might her perspective affect your own?

Group Reading—continued
John Cobb, an eminent theologian, has spent the last 25 years looking closely at our economic system through theologically trained eyes. In his recent book, *Sustaining the Common Good*, Cobb discusses free trade. He uses the analogy of our economic system (and society in general) as a train speeding out of control:

If one finds oneself on a train speeding down a hill toward a bridge that has been destroyed, what is the realistic thing to do? Let us suppose that most of the people on the train do not know that the bridge is out and that there are powerful interests committed to maintaining their ignorance. The passengers are eager to reach their destinations on the other side of the gorge that the bridge crosses. They favor moving on as rapidly as possible and resent any

When you organize the global society primarily for the purpose of increasing production and consumption, you systematically destroy community (human and nonhuman).

—*John Cobb*

suggestion that the train should be slowed, much less stopped. Many of those who have reason to suspect that the bridge is out prefer not to think about it. To stop the train and take the long detour to the destination would require actions that would jolt the passengers and be quite disruptive of their plans.

Perhaps realism dictates that one should be silent and do what one can to make the remainder of the time pass pleasantly. After all, the chances of stopping the train in time are quite small given the lack of interest of those on board. But realism may not make a lot of sense in this context. It may be better to try to stop the train before it reaches the gorge, however unlikely one is to succeed. If so, the first step will be to persuade the realists on board to share in the effort.

Simplicity of living, if deliberately chosen, implies a compassionate approach to life. It means that we are choosing to live our daily lives with some degree of conscious appreciation of the condition of the rest of the world...As our actions have reverberations of global dimension, the capacity for conscious action has become a social necessity.

—*Duane Elgin*

My analogy is, of course, an alarmist one, and it is not fashionable to be an alarmist. Even those who see that our movement toward a global economy causes some problems are likely to find my cataclysmic analogy misleading. And, indeed, it is. In the analogy there is a single catastrophe awaiting the train. In the real world a continuing, single-minded emphasis on increasing production will lead to many smaller catastrophes, most of which will be explained in terms of particular local circumstances rather than attributed to global policies. Most of the suffering will be borne by the invisible poor, whereas we who make public opinion and shape policy will be largely unscathed for some time to come. Where we, the rich, will obviously share in the suffering, as with the destruction of the ozone layer, actions will be taken to contain the damage. (See Cobb, "Against Free Trade," in *Sustaining the Common Good*, pp. 108-109.)

Cobb is essentially writing about waking up, about awareness, about a change in perception. When we read or hear of the many catastrophes (whether environmental, economic or political) happening throughout different parts of the world, how do we perceive them? Do we see connections between our daily choices, resulting government policy and various crises facing peoples and places throughout the world? For example, is there a connection between our consumption habits and choices and how our country pursues international trade agreements?

Cobb and Chee Yoke Ling do perceive connections between such seemingly disparate acts as our consumer choices and unemployment in Mexico or Cameroon.

They suggest that "a continuing single-minded emphasis on increasing production will lead to many smaller catastrophes." These will be attributed to local circumstances rather than global or national policies.

1. What do you think about this perspective?

2. What struck you personally about the Wendell Berry and Alan Durning articles?

3. What do you see as the larger effects of your own patterns of consumption?

Action Step

Is there a first step you might think of that would change your own consumption patterns in a helpful direction? What would help you take such a step? Share this with the group.

Another way to tackle the question "how much is enough?" is to expose yourself to less advertising by declaring your independence from junk mail! See Turn the Tide's (www.newdream.org) fourth action step to do so. (See page 230 for an introduction to Turn the Tide.)

Closing Prayer *(Read in unison.)*
Loving God, our many interconnections draw us close to others and to the whole created order; and thus we may both care for or unwittingly oppress our neighbors and our world. Help us to be mindful of these potentials; encourage our acts of compassion; grant us the grace of loving community. *Amen.*

Meeting Ten: Broader Impacts of Our Everyday Food Choices

Tools Everyone Needs:
Simpler Living, Compassionate Life
pen or pencil
Optional:
journal or notebook

Purpose:
To reflect on and remember the joys of good food;

To consider our food choices as they relate to personal and environmental health.

Read Before Next Gathering:
"Christian Existence in a World of Limits"   —p. 117

"Structural Changes"   —p. 123

Facilitator Overview
As facilitator today:
1. Serve as timekeeper;
2. Facilitate discussions, making sure everyone who wants to speak has the opportunity;
3. Lead (or ask someone to lead) the opening meditation;
4. Designate next meeting's Facilitator.

Overview
Agri-culture is increasingly agri-business. This change has many economic, cultural, and environmental implications. Today's meeting considers these implications and discusses hopeful alternatives based on local food economies. Theme: *Simplicity as expressing elemental connection to the Earth: eating food that is healthy for us, the land, and its people.*

Food for Thought
Food reveals our connection to the earth. Each bite contains the life of the sun and the earth. We can see and taste the whole universe in a piece of bread! Contemplating our food for a few seconds before eating, in mindfulness, can bring us much happiness. Mindful eating can cultivate seeds of compassion and understanding.

—*Thich Nhat Hanh*

Opening Meditation
Berry describes "industrial eaters" as essentially ignorant of the history of the food they consume. Think of your lives, your parents' lives, your grandparents' lives. How far back in your family's history do you need to go to find people who knew where most of their food came from? Tell some of these family stories.

Check-In

Tell each other, briefly, about your ideas for reducing consumption. For those who had the opportunity to actually try something, how did that go?

Group Reading

Modern agriculture, addicted to oil and to poisons, strips the landscape of farmers, wildlife, biotic integrity, community, moral value and spiritual vitality; all in an unsustainable effort to feed restless urban populations. To sustain the world we must rebuild rural communities, dense with complex systems of life—human and natural—and rich with culture, ethics, and spiritual significance. Urban communities and choices play an indispensable role in this re-building.

—*Dr. Richard Cartwright Austin*

Opening Prayer

Loving God, thank you for the gift of life; for the everyday miracle of sun, air, water and soil becoming green, living things; for your care and sustenance. For seed and soil, green stem and air, fruit on vine, fallen fruit rotting on moist ground, new seed again, we give you thanks. Be with us here, may our hearts be open to you and one another. May the seeds of your truth take root in our hearts. *Amen.*

The air we breathe, the food we eat and the water we drink are our most direct connections to the natural world. In today's global market, what we eat has wide political, economic, community, and environmental health implications.

Find the shortest, simplest way between the earth, the hands and the mouth.

—*Lanza del Vasto*

Few of us are aware that the act of eating can be a powerful statement of commitment to our own well being, and at the same time to the creation of a healthier habitat. Your health, happiness, and the future of life on earth are rarely so much in your own hands as when you sit down to eat.

—*John Robbins*

Group Discussion

Reflect on the following questions related to Berry's article and the food continuum: (we recommend starting with those questions in bold if you have limited time.)

1. Share your thoughts about the readings. How has the "joy of good food" been experienced in your life?

2. Are there features of agribusiness that you see as unjust to people, animals and the land?

Berry describes the industrial food economy as a trap. He suggests escape comes via "restoring one's consciousness of what is involved in eating; by reclaiming responsibility for one's part in the food economy."

3. What from your own experience speaks to "the responsibilities of eating"?

4. What did you think of Berry's seven suggestions for reclaiming this responsibility?

5. Which of the seven do you already participate in? Which do you find more difficult to participate in?

Reflect on the Food Gathering Continuum:

6. Where do you see yourself on this continuum?

7. Where would you like to eventually be?

Closing Prayer *(Read in unison.)*
> Loving God, you open your hand and satisfy the desire of every living thing, giving them their food in due season. We thank you for sustaining such a rich and bountiful earth. Encourage in us our assumption of appropriate responsibility. Grant us gratitude at the richness you provide. *Amen.*

Action Step
Can you think of a first, small step in moving along the food continuum toward your eventual goal? What movement can you make in that direction in the coming week? Share this with the group.

Or, try Turn the Tide's two food-related actions: "Eat one less beef meal each week," or "Shift your shrimp consumption." See www.newdream.org/turnthetide.

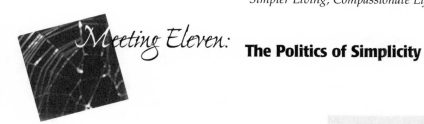

Meeting Eleven: The Politics of Simplicity

Facilitator Overview

As facilitator today:

1. Serve as timekeeper;
2. Facilitate discussions, making sure everyone who wants to speak has the opportunity;
3. Lead the opening meditation;
4. Designate next meeting's Facilitator;
5. If the group wishes to have a potluck or dessert-delight at the next meeting, discuss plans during this meeting.

(optional)
6. Arrange for a flip chart and markers for the next meeting.

Overview

Jerome Segal's quote nicely summarizes today's theme:

"If the simple living idea remains largely individualistic, it will not only be irrelevant to most Americans—in the end it will disappear under the influence of the dominant forces in American life. It is as a form of politics, a politics that is both personal and social, that simple living has enormous potential for deeply and lastingly transforming life in America." (*Tikkun*, volume 11, no. 4, page 20.)

Tools Everyone Needs:

Simpler Living, Compassionate Life
pen or pencil
Optional:
journal or notebook

Purpose:

To consider practical, political ideas that would help our society reflect and encourage simple living;

To remind ourselves that individual change and political action are both crucial elements to long-lasting, far-reaching societal change;

To consider Cobb's "appropriate Christian responses" to today's world.

Read Before Next Gathering:

"Building Community"   —p. 207

"Winter Solstice at the Moab Slough"   —p. 213

Opening Meditation

Begin with a brief silence and then read aloud, in unison:

> Oh Lord, how manifold are your works! In wisdom you have made them all; the
> earth is full of your creatures. Yonder is the great and wide sea with its living
> things too many to number, creatures both small and great. There move the
> ships, and there is that Leviathan which you have made for the sport of it. All of
> them look to you to give them their food in due season. You give it to them;
> they gather it: you open your hand, and they are filled with good things.
>
> —*Psalm 104:24-28*

Opening Prayer

Creator, Sustainer, Redeemer, we ask for your
presence here, and for your love and grace in
our lives. Thank you again for the gift of each
day. *Amen.*

Check-In

For those of you who had
a chance since your last
meeting, share briefly
about your experimenting
with movement along the
"food continuum."

Group Discussion

1. Any general comments or questions about today's readings?

2. John Cobb's essay presents five "images of appropriate Christian response":
   Christian Realism; The Eschatological Attitude; The Discernment of Christ;
   The Way of the Cross; Prophetic Vision. Do you feel drawn to any of them?
   How might church life be different if these areas of Christian response were
   incorporated?

3. Cecile Andrews says, "We need structural changes that allow people to behave in a caring way." What did you think of her concrete proposals (for example, limiting wealth accumulation, developing new standards of economic health, developing new kinds of taxation, and so on) for implementing such change?

4. Are there other structural changes—ones that would also encourage a simplicity of compassion—you could get excited about and support?

Small Group Discussion

Form groups of three members each to discuss the following:

1. Cecile Andrews briefly addresses regulating corporations. What are some of the better ways you know of to move corporations toward greater concern for people and the planet?

John Cobb says: "The rhetoric of identification with the poor and the oppressed has been around for some time. We have to ask what it means, and here diversity is legitimate. For some, it means functioning as advocates for the cause of the poor; for a few, joining revolutionary movements; for others, embracing poverty as a way of life. I believe this third meaning needs to be taken by Christians with increasing seriousness. The one who actually becomes poor will be a better advocate for the cause of the poor and freer to respond to other opportunities for identification."

2. What does this say to you?

Later in that same section (called "The Way of the Cross") Cobb says that these various ways of identifying need to be "supported by the churches." **Brainstorm together about ways the Church and/or other Christian communities could support such identification.** Be creative! Share examples you know exist and come up with your own! (Here's one example: a church has one or a number of couples who would like to purchase a home or create a co-housing project. They do not want to have a large mortgage and then both work full time for 30 years to pay it off. They would like to be able to volunteer their time in a variety of ways, providing service back to the community. A group of people from the church, or the church itself, could provide low-interest loans which the couples would pay back over time.)

Small Group Reports
Report back to the whole group some of the themes and hot ideas from your discussions.

Note: See Jerome Segal's new book *Graceful Simplicity: Towards a Philosophy and Politics of Simple Living,* published by Henry Holt, for further reflection on creating a society that encourages the richness of simple living.

Action Step
Perhaps, during your brainstorming, a specific action came to mind that some of you might want to actually implement!

Closing Prayer
Creator, Sustainer, Redeemer, thank you for this group of people; thank you for those communities which support us. Thank you especially for your great gift of grace and for laughter and joy in the midst of what is often a confusing and difficult world. May we be open to transformation through Christ's love and power. *Amen.*

...we are called to celebrate all life, including our own, not to repress it. But the celebration of life does not involve participation in the luxury and waste of a throwaway society that exists in the midst of world poverty.

—*John Cobb*

Meeting Twelve: Widening Our Circle of Community: Journey to Abundant Life

Facilitator Overview

As facilitator today:

1. Serve as timekeeper;
2. Facilitate discussions, making sure everyone who wants to has the opportunity to speak;
3. Lead the opening meditation and prayer;
4. Read the group reading together.

Overview

A time to celebrate and reflect on the course as a whole, generally, and on community specifically. Would the group like to continue meeting? How has the course affected lives and lifestyles? Have a potluck dinner or dessert-fest!

Opening Meditation

Begin with a moment of silence.

> If I choose not to become attached to nouns—a person, place or thing—then when I refuse an intimate's love or hoard my spirit, when a known landscape is bought, sold, and developed, chained or grazed to a stubble, or a hawk is shot and hung by its feet on a barbed-wire fence, my heart cannot be broken because I never risked giving it away.

Tools Everyone Needs:

Simpler Living, Compassionate Life
pen or pencil
flip chart and markers
Optional:
journal or notebook

Purpose:

To listen to our lives in order to hear "the voice of our own gladness";

To reflect on how this voice may connect to simplicity and to specific course content;

To express that voice creatively and share this with the group.

But what kind of impoverishment is this to withhold emotion, to restrain our passionate nature in the face of a generous life just to appease our fears? A man or woman whose mind reins in the heart when the body sings desperately for connection can only expect more isolation and greater ecological disease. Our lack of intimacy with each other is in direct proportion to our lack of intimacy with the land. We have taken our love inside and abandoned the wild.

—*Terry Tempest Williams*

Opening Prayer

Loving Creator, thank you for our time together, for the gift of life, for your on-going work of creation in our world, for your presence in each of our lives. Help us to hear your still, small voice. May your Spirit be here and with us when we leave. In your name, *Amen.*

Group Reading

An introductory reading by Michael Schut:

Over the last weeks/months you have gathered as a small community around the topic of simplicity. Much more could have been covered, but we hope that this course has provided some perspectives on how your faith specifically, and the Christian faith generally, might inform and possibly lead to greater simplicity.

Some or all of you may wish to continue meeting together as a way of supporting further exploration. Many of us need places in our lives where we can openly ask the kinds of questions raised in this course. We need to feel safe and supported when considering how the way we live our lives reflects our core values. For those interested, find listed on page 284 further resources ideal for small group use.

In this last meeting, we would like to discuss community. Cecile Andrews' essay acknowledges the loss of community many people feel today and identifies very practical ways to encourage the strengthening of communities. And Terry Tempest Williams' piece reminds us the circle of our community encompasses relationships with the rest of the natural world. We are impoverished, she says, when we think and act otherwise.

Why do we raise the place of community in our lives as the last topic in a course on simplicity? Because growth or inviting change into our lives rarely happens in isolation. Because M. Scott Peck may just be right when he writes, "in and through community lies the salvation of the world" (*The Different Drum*). And, because our hectic, individualistic culture contributes to the breakdown of community, living more simply may require us to re-discover, nourish and rely more and more on those around us.

In my own experience, community has often been the vehicle for ushering the love and grace of God into my life. Community, awareness of connection and relationship, has provided me with those moments where I sense sunshine breaking into my own darkness and where I relax into the love that I believe is at the center of the universe and holds it together.

So whether this recently formed community continues in a similar form or not, you hopefully have those places and people in your lives that offer support. Besides support, community can also help you to hear and respond to the stirrings of your own heart which, in today's noisy and wordy world, are hard enough to hear amongst all the voices clamoring for attention.

This course began with an emphasis on listening to your own voice, your own story, with an ear to hear "whatever of meaning, of holiness, of God there may be in it to hear" (Buechner). At its conclusion, once again do the same: listen to your lives to hear, as Buechner suggests, the voice of your own gladness:

> To Isaiah, the voice said, "Go," and for each of us there are many voices that say it, but the question is which one will we obey with our lives, which of the voices that call is to be the one that we answer. No one can say, of course, except each for himself, but I believe that it is possible to say at least this in general to all of us: we should go with our lives where we most need to go and where we are most needed.
>
> Where we most need to go. Maybe that means that the voice we should listen to most as we choose a vocation is the voice that we might think we should listen to least, and that is the voice of our own gladness. What can we do that makes us gladdest, what can we do that leaves us with the strongest sense of sailing true north and of peace, which is much of what gladness is? I believe that if it is a thing that makes us truly glad, then it is a good thing and it is our thing and it is the calling voice that we were made to answer with our lives.
>
> And also, where we are most needed. In a world where there is so much drudgery, so much grief, so much emptiness and fear and pain, our gladness in our work is as much needed as we ourselves need to be glad. If we keep our eyes and ears open, our hearts open, we will find the place surely.
>
> Jesus said, "Man shall not live by bread alone, but by every word that proceeds from the mouth of God," and in the end every word that proceeds from the mouth of God is the same word, and the word is Christ himself. And in the end that is the vocation, the calling of all of us, the calling to be Christs. To be Christs in whatever way we are able to be. To be Christs with whatever gladness we have in whatever place, among whatever brothers we are called to.

—*Frederick Buechner,* The Hungering Dark, *"The Calling of Voices," pp. 31-32*

Listen to the "voice of your own gladness." When was the last time someone encouraged you to do that? It's actually a very counter-cultural piece of advice, contrary to many of the voices beckoning us to the "good life." My sense is that the gladness Buechner refers to is closer to the joy that can come from the "abundant life" than the happiness promised by the good life. In this excerpt, Buechner discusses gladness in the context of discerning your call or your vocation. He does so primarily within the context of discovering one's "life-work." For today, though, we can set the word "vocation" in a broader context: from feeling called to a major life-change (including career) to simply one new direction or idea we may want to explore.

Group Discussion

With today's reading as a backdrop, explore the questions below:

1. **Are there points of intersection between the "voice of your own gladness" and things you've learned or been reminded of in this course?**

2. What has been the most meaningful part of this course for you personally?

3. **What actions/new directions might you take as a result of this time together?**

4. If this new direction/action is taken, what might be the outcome? How would your life be different? (Suggested Activity: Express these ideas or directions by writing a story, drawing an image, writing a song, or performing a skit for the rest of the group. Use a flip chart if helpful.)

In closing, consider your answer to question 4. As a way to reflect on this course as a whole, consider your answer in relationship to the following constellation of questions:

- How would this new direction be seen from the perspective of simplicity as compassion—compassion as empathy and justice?
- How does it achieve freedom from consumerism?
- How does it experience time, silence and contemplation?
- How does it experience the joys of food, community, and nature?
- How does it embody your theology of creation?
- What communities are you a part of and how might you express this action(s)/new direction(s) in those communities?

Celebration
Enjoy your potluck dinner or dessert-fest!

Future Action Step
If you are part of a faith community, a group of you could work with your congregation to gradually "green" your life together: from the music, worship and education, to lawn care and heating and lighting practices. *The Greening Congregations Handbook* is an excellent resource to guide that process. For information, call Earth Ministry at (206)632-2426, or visit www.earthministry.org.

Closing Prayer *(Read in unison.)*

Loving God, our hearts are restless until they find their rest in you. Help us as we search to combine our gladness with our compassion. Grant us a sense of perspective on our shortcomings, and open our lives to your encompassing joy.

We give you thanks for these times of sharing and learning; for your presence in our world and in our lives. Nourish our hearts that we may increasingly make room for love and thereby for your transformative presence. *Amen.*

Appendix A

About Earth Ministry

History

Earth Ministry was born out of a recognition of the underlying spiritual and moral roots of the environmental crisis, and the desire to help people of faith see more clearly the connections between their faith, their daily life and ecological concerns. Founded in March of 1992, we are a Christian, ecumenical, environmental, non-profit organization based in Seattle.

Earth Ministry's founders knew that Western Christendom has often been blamed for our environmental crisis. But they also knew that Christianity had much to offer in helping this culture live respectfully: in balance with all creation, grateful for its richness, nourished by its beauties, thankful for its life-sustaining bounty. They also knew the potency of its understanding of the convergence of social and environmental justice issues.

Out of these understandings and vision came our mission statement.

Mission

Earth Ministry's mission is to engage individuals and congregations in knowing God more fully through deepening relationships with all of God's creation. We believe that through this experience our personal lives and our culture will be transformed. These transformations include simplified living, environmental steward- ship, justice for all creation, and a worldview which sees creation as a revelation of God. Together these lead to a re-discovery of the vitality of the Christian faith.

Programs, Resources and Opportunities for Involvement

Consistent with Earth Ministry's mission, programs are designed both for individuals and church congregations. Primarily a grass-roots organization based in Seattle, Washington, much of Earth Ministry's work is targeted to local constituents; however, some of the programs and resources are equally applicable nationally.

National Resources:
• *Earth Letter*, a highly-acclaimed mini-journal of Christian environmental spirituality, is published five times a year. Each issue features engagingly well-written articles by respected voices in the fields of religion and/or the environment. In addition, it offers book reviews, highlights resources for congregations and gives updates on the work of Earth Ministry and local congregations.
• *Food, Faith and Sustainability* presents an anthology of essays and a five-session group curriculum. We all eat. What we eat directly effects how the earth is used

and how people's lives are affected. This book makes the connections between food choices, personal and environmental health, economics and the Christian faith. It concludes with a brief "Healthy Shoppers' Resource Guide."
- *Web Site Resources:* "www.earthministry.org" has numerous resources available either to down-load directly, or to order from us, by e-mail or by telephone.
- *Staff speaking, teaching and workshop/retreat leadership:* Earth Ministry's staff is available for these tasks both nationally and locally.

Local Resources:
- In addition to all of the above program resources, people who live within the Puget Sound region can take advantage of gatherings, lectures, field trips, a resource library, an annual Celebration of St. Francis and various action projects. Please visit Earth Ministry's web site or call for a current listing.

- For more information on these and other programs call or write:

Earth Ministry
6512 23rd Avenue, N.W., Suite 317
Seattle, WA 98117

(206) 632-2426
e-mail: emoffice@earthministry.org
website: www.earthministry.org

Appendix B

Resources For Further Study

Food, Faith, and Sustainability: Environmental, Spiritual, Community, and Social Justice Implications of the Gift of Daily Bread. An anthology and five-week curriculum published by Earth Ministry. Visit their website at www.earthministry.org or call 206-632-2426.

Cecile Andrews' book, *The Circle of Simplicity: Return to the Good Life* (published by HarperCollins, 1997), is not only very good but includes a wonderful curriculum as well. It's available at your local bookstore.

Your Money or Your Life: Transforming Your Relationship with Money and Achieving Financial Independence by Joe Dominguez and Vicki Robin is itself a very useful group study book. Contact your local bookstore or www.newroadmap.org.

Your Money or Your Life: A Group Study Guide for Contemporary Christians. This six-week study guide provides a rich framework for studying the book together. Contact the New Road Map Foundation, Department EM, P.O. Box 15981, Seattle, WA 98115; or visit their website at www.newroadmap.org for information.

Affluenza: The Cost of High Living. This lively, engaging and humorous video highlights environmental, social, community and spiritual costs of consumption. A portion of *Affluenza* focuses on a Christian response to over-consumerism. The video comes with a guide for group discussion. Check with your local library or public television station; to purchase a copy ($24.95) call (800) 937-5387. A follow-up video, *Escape from Affluenza*, has also been produced.

For very practical guides to exploring and implementing a lower-consumptive lifestyle in your own home or church see:

Household Eco-Team Workbook: A Six-Month Program to Bring Your Household into Environmental Balance. Contact: Global Action Plan for the Earth; (914) 679-9830

Eco-Church: An Action Manual. Contact: Resource Publications Inc.; (888) 273-7782; www.rpinet.com

The following organizations are a wealth of simple living related information:

The *Simple Living Network*. Check out their website at www.slnet.com where you can order most of these resources directly; call 1-800-318-5725; write P.O. Box 233, Trout Lake, WA 98650.

Alternatives for Simple Living produces an excellent catalog of resources. Contact them at 1-800-821-6153; 3617 Old Lakeport Road, Sioux City, IA 51106.

Endnotes:

1. "All-Consuming Passion," the New Road Map (NRM) Foundation, 1993, Seattle, Washington.

2. *Vital Signs 1998*, Worldwatch Institute. W. W. Norton, page 128.

3. Tom Athanasiou, *Divided Planet: The Ecology of Rich and Poor*, page 37.

4. Charles Lee, *Toxic Wastes and Race in the United States*, United Church of Christ Commission for Racial Justice, 1987, New York, NY.

5. Larry Rasmussen, "Returning to Our Senses," page 48 in *After Nature's Revolt*. Edited by Dieter Hessel.

6. For a critique of the idea of progress, see Juliet B. Schor, "Why I Am No Longer a Progressive," *Zeta*, April 1990.

7. Sahlins, *Stone Age Economics*, 2.

   For these estimates, see Leopold Pospisil, *Kapauku Papuan Economy* (New Haven, Conn.: Yale University Publication in Anthropology 67, 1963), 144-45 on Kapauku; Richard Lee, "What Hunters Do for a Living or How to Make Out on Scarce Resources," in Richard B. Lee and Irven DeVore, eds., *Man the Hunter* (Chicago: Aldine Publishing Company, 1968), 30-48 on Kung; C.S. Stewart on the Sandwich Islands (cited in Sahlins, *Stone Age Economics*, p. 56); Frederick D. McCarthy and Margaret McArthur, "The Food Quest and the Time Factor in Aboriginal Economic Life," reprinted from *Records of the American-Australian Scientific Expedition to Arnhem Land*, vol. 2 (Melbourne: Melbourne University Press, 1960), on Australia.

8. On stress, see Louis Harris, *Inside America* (New York: Vintage, 1987), 8-10. Fifty-nine percent have great stress at least once or twice a week, and 89 percent report experiencing high stress. These polls were taken in 1985–86.

   John P. Robinson, "The Time Squeeze," *American Demographics*, 12, 2 (February 1990): 30-33. The question asked was whether respondents "always," "sometimes," or "almost never" feel rushed to do the things they have to do.

   Robert Karasek and Tores Theorell, *Healthy Work: Stress, Productivity and the Reconstruction of Working Life* (New York: Basic Books, 1990), 166, on workers' compensation claims and "working to death."

   According to the 9 to 5 national stress survey, which was conducted in 1983, just over two-thirds of respondents reported that in the previous year there was an increase in the amount of work required or a speed-up. These women also reported increased levels of insomnia, pain, chest pain, tension, anger, depression, and exhaustion. See *The 9to5 National Survey on Women and Stress* (Cleveland, Ohio: 9to5, 1984), 35-38. See also Amanda Bennett, *The Death of the Organization Man* (New York: William Morrow, 1990), which chronicles speed-up in large corporations.

Karasek and Theorell, *Healthy Work*, on stressful workplaces.

9. Natalie Angier, "Cheating on Sleep: Modern Life Turns America Into the Land of the Drowsy," *New York Times*, 15 May 1990. Recent research by economist Daniel Hamermesh finds a relationship between employment and sleep in "Sleep and the Allocation of Time," *Journal of Political Economy*, 98, 5 (October 1990): 922-43.

10. MassMutual Family Values Study. (Washington, D.C.: Mellman & Lazarus, 1989), 3, on families and time.

Diane S. Burden and Bradley Googins, *Boston University Balancing Job and Homelife Study* (Boston University: mimeo, 1987), 26, on women and stress.

"When I'm at home," from Harris, *Inside America*, 95.

Paul Williams Kingston and Steven L. Nock, "Time Together Among Dual-Earner Couples," *American Sociological Review*, 52 (June 1987): 391-400. See also Arlie Hochschild, *The Second Shift: Working Parents and the Revolution at Home* (New York: Viking Penguin, 1989).

Harriet Presser, "Shift Work and Child Care Among Young Dual-Earner American Parents," *Journal of Marriage and the Family* 50, 1 (February 1988): 1330-48. This figure is for couples in which the wife works full time. Among part-timers, the proportion is over one-half.

Quote from Parents United for Child Care (PUCC) survey comments, mimeo, Boston, Massachusetts, 1989.

11. Hochschild, *Second Shift*, 212.

12. Sylvia A. Hewlett, *When the Bough Breaks: The Cost of Neglecting Our Children* (New York: Basic Books, 1991), 1.

John J. Sweeney and Karen Nussbaum, *Solutions for the New Work Force* (Washington, D.C.: Seven Locks Press, 1989), 209, n. 15, for 7 million figure.

Burden and Googins, *Balancing Job and Homelife*, 21, table 12, for the local study.

Preschoolers figure cited in Fern Schumer Chapman, "Executive Guilt: Who's Taking Care of the Children?" *Fortune*, 16 February 1987, p. 37.

Quote from PUCC, "Survey comments."

13. Ibid.

Victor Fuchs, *Women's Quest for Economic Equality* (Cambridge, Mass.: Harvard University Press, 1988), 111.

Hewlett, *When the Bough Breaks*.

Expert is Edward Zigler, Yale University, cited in Nancy Gibbs, "How America Has Run Out of Time," *Time*, 24 April 1989, pp. 61-64.

14. The definition of the YS root and its derivatives comes from John L. McKenzie, *Dictionary of the Bible* (New York: Macmillan, 1965), p. 760. The Hebrew name *Yeshua* (Jesus), common in New Testament times, literally means "God is saving us." The homemaking reference is from John 15:4, "Make your home in me as I make mine in you."

15. I use the term *soul* in the original Hebrew sense of *nephesh*, the essence of a person. See *Will and Spirit*, p. 32.

16. Tilden Edwards, *Sabbath Time* (New York: Seabury, 1982).

17. Manjusrimitra, *Primordial Experience*, p. 32.

18. Erica Jong, *Any Woman's Blues* (New York: HarperCollins, 1990), pp. 133-34.

19. Etty Hillesum, *An Interrupted Life* (New York: Washington Square Press, 1985), pp. 27, 30.

20. Frederick Douglass, "Narrative of the Life of Frederick Douglass, an American Slave," excerpted in Abraham Chapman, ed., *Black Voices* (New York: New American Library, 1968), pp. 241-55.

21. Rainer Maria Rilke, *Letters to a Young Poet*, trans. M. D. Herder Norton (New York: W. W. Norton, 1954), pp. 35, 38.

22. From chaps. 79, 82, and 86 of the long version of her "Shewings" (from Sloane Manuscript 2499), in Julian of Norwich, *Revelations of Divine Love*, trans. Clifton Wolters (New York: Penguin, 1982), pp. 203, 208, 212.

23. Adam Smith, *An Inquiry into the Nature and Causes of the Wealth of Nations* (1776; reprinted as *The Wealth of Nations* [New York: Knopf, 1991]). For a very popular history of economics featuring Adam Smith as the key initiator of the academic discipline, see Robert Heilbroner, *The Worldly Philosophers: The Lives and Times and Ideas of the Great Economic Thinkers*, 6th ed. (New York: Simon and Schuster, 1986).

24. The work of Hunter and Amory Lovins in the Rocky Mountain Institute is an especially important example. The ideas were first effectively articulated by

Amory B. Lovins in *Soft Energy Paths: Toward a Durable Peace* (San Francisco: Friends of the Earth, 1977).

25. See, e.g., Isaiah 1:17, Jer. 7:6, and Amos 2:6f.

26. Paul Tillich, *The Protestant Era*, trans. James Luther Adams (Chicago: University of Chicago Press, 1948), pp. 190f.

27. In the "sustainable society" production, distribution, consumption, and recycling will form a cyclical nexus, within which the material inputs to production will go through the cycle and start over. Recycling will be a major job-creating component of the economic process. It is possible now to identify many of the measures that would constitute a whole new orientation of society to conservation. Some of these if implemented immediately would have detrimental effects upon certain sectors of the economy because of the wastefulness presently inherent in much of our production and employment. We cannot foresee in detail the ramifications of stepping up the measures that consumers might take to oppose waste through their buying and conserving practices. These measures would, however, help to stimulate the coming into play of a host of adjustment mechanisms that would hasten the emergence of the cyclical patterns necessary for long-term sustainability.

28. John 10:10.

29. Luke 12:15.

30. See John V. Taylor, *Enough is Enough* (Naperville, Ill.: Allenson, Inc., 1975).

31. Richard B. Gregg, *The Value of Voluntary Simplicity* (Wallingford, Pa., 1936), 1.

32. *The Dialogues of Plato*, trans. B. Jowett, 2 vols. (New York, 1937), 1:636; Bradford Torrey, ed., *The Writings of Henry David Thoreau*, 20 vols. (Boston, 1906), 2:17.

33. Paul F. Boller, Jr., *American Transcendentalism, 1830–1860* (New York, 1974), 200; HDT, Writings, 4:362.

34. LM, *The Conduct of Life* (New York, 1951), 17-18.

35. Gregg, *Voluntary Simplicity*, 27; Aldo Leopold, *Sand County Almanac* (New York, 1949), vii.

36. Clara Barrus, *Life and Letters of John Burroughs*, 2 vols. (Boston, 1925), 2:156-57.

37. Quoted in D. Elton Trueblood, *The Best of Elton Trueblood: An Anthology*, ed. James R. Newby (Nashville: The Benson Co., 1979), p. 70.

38. John Woolman, *The Journal of John Woolman* (Secaucus: The Citadel Press, 1972), p. 41.

39. Quoted in Martin Hengel, *Property and Riches in the Early Church* (Philadelphia: Fortress Press, 1973), p. 45.

40. Tertullian, "The Apology of Tertullian" in Alexander Roberts and James Donaldson, eds. *The Ante-Nicene Fathers*, 8 vols. (Buffalo: The Christian Literature Publishing Co., 1887), 3:46.

41. "'The Teaching of the Twelve Apostles" in Roberts and Donaldson, *The Ante-Nicene Fathers*, 7:378.

42. Eusebius, *The Ecclesiastical History*, trans. Christian Frederick Cruse, reprint ed. (Grand Rapids: Baker Book House, 1958), Book IV, Chapter 23, p. 160.

43. "The First Epistle of Clement to the Corinthians" in Roberts and Donaldson, *The Ante-Nicene Fathers*, 1:15.

44. Quoted in *Quotations from Chairman Jesus*, ed. David Kirk (Springfield: Templegate Publishers, 1969), p. 175.

45. Ibid., pp. 42-43.

46. Quoted by Henri Nouwen in "The Desert Counsel to Flee the World," *Sojourners*, 9 (June 1980): 15.

47. Helen Waddell, trans., *The Desert Fathers* (Ann Arbor: The University of Michigan Press, 1957), p. 85.

48. Quoted by Henri Nouwen, "Silence, The Portable Cell," *Sojourners* 9 (July 1980):22.

49. Waddell, *The Desert Fathers*, p. 123

50. Ibid., p. 112.

51. Ibid., p. 114.

52. Ibid. p. 307.

53. Raphael Brown, trans., *The Little Flowers of St. Francis* (Garden City; Doubleday & Company, 1958), p. 68.

54. Ibid., pp. 58-60.

55. Theodore G. Tappert, ed., *Selected Writings of Martin Luther: 1520–1523* (Philadelphia: Fortress Press, 1967), p. 20.

56. Ibid., p. 43.

57. Ibid., p. 47.

58. John Calvin, *Commentaries on the Epistle of Paul the Apostle to the Romans* (Grand Rapids: Wm. B. Eerdmans Publishing Co., 1947), p. 481.

59. George Fox, *The Journal of George Fox* (London: Cambridge University Press, 1952), p. 11.

60. Quoted in Lewis Benson, *A Revolutionary Gospel* (Philadelphia: The Tract Association of Friends, 1974), p. 9.

61. William Penn, *No Cross, No Crown* (London: Richard Barrett, printer, 1957), p. 251.

62. George Fox, *Works of George Fox*, reprint ed. (Philadelphia: Marcus T. C. Gould, 1831), 4:194.

63. Taken from the bulletin of the First Centenary United Methodist Church, Chattanooga, Tennessee, June 29, 1980, p. 1.

64. John Wesley, *The Journal of John Wesley*, ed. Percy Livingstone Parker (Chicago: Moody Press, 1951), p. 409.

65. Kenneth Scott Latourette, *A History of Christianity* (New York: Harper & Brothers, 1953), p. 1186.

66. J. H. Worcester, *The Life of David Livingstone* (Chicago: Moody Press, n.d.), p. 75.

67. For more information see Dallas Lee, *The Cotton Patch Evidence* (New York: Harper & Row, 1971).

68. Ibid., p.100.

69. Quoted in Goldian VanderBroeck, ed., *Less Is More* (New York: Harper & Row, 1978), p. 223.

70. For a discussion of the millennial long waves in demographic history see Thomas M. Whitmore, B.L. Turner, Douglas L. Johnson, Robert W. Kates and Thomas R. Gottschang, "Long-Term Population Change", in B.L. Turner, ed., *The Earth as transformed by human action: global and regional changes in the biosphere over the past 300 years* (Cambridge; New York: Cambridge University Press with Clark University, 1990), pp. 26-39.

71. For the following citations from the demographer Paul Demeny see Paul Demeny, "Population," in B.L. Turner, ed., *The Earth as transformed by human action: global and regional changes in the biosphere over the past 300 years* (Cambridge; New York: Cambridge University Press with Clark University, 1990), pp. 42-54.

72. Paul Demeny, "Population," op. cit., p. 43.

73. For a description of the problems inherent in this rapid urbanization, particularly in Asia, see the United Nations Economic and Social Commission for Asia and the Pacific (ESCAP) study entitled, *The State of Urbanization in Asia and the Pacific, 1993* (Bangkok, ESCAP, 1993).

74. William James, The varieties of religious experience: a study in human nature; being the Gifford lectures on natural religion delivered in Edinburgh in 1901–1902 (London; New York: Longmans Green, 1904, 1902).

75. Richard E. Byrd, *Alone* (G.P. Putnam's Sons, Inc., 1938), p. 19.

76. Arthur G. Gish, *Beyond the Rat Race* (New Canaan, Connecticut: Keats Publishing, Inc., 1973), p. 21.

77. Kierkegaard, *op. cit.*, p. 322.

78. Wesley, *Journal*, Nov. 1767.

79. Ronald J. Sider, *Rich Christians in an Age of Hunger* (Downers Grove, Illinois: InterVarsity Press, 1977), p. 18.

80. Kierkegaard, *op. cit.*, p. 344.

81. Woolman, *Journal*, pp. 144-145.

82. *Ibid.*, p. 168.

83. George Fox, *Works* (Philadelphia, 1831, Vol. 8), p. 126 Epistle #131.

Bibliography

Adbusters: Journal of the Mental Environment, published by The Media Foundation, Vancouver, B.C.

Adler, Mortimer. *Desires Right & Wrong: The Ethics of Enough*. Macmillan Publishing Co., New York, 1991.

Andrews, Cecile. *The Circle of Simplicity: Return to the Good Life*. HarperCollins, New York, 1997.

Bender, Sue. *Plain and Simple*. Harper & Row, New York, 1989.

Berger, Peter, and Luckmann, Thomas. *The Social Construction of Reality*. Doubleday, New York, 1966.

Berry, Thomas. *The Dream of the Earth*. Sierra Club Books, San Francisco, 1988.

Berry, Wendell. *What are People For?* North Point Press, San Francisco, 1990.

———. *Sex, Economy, Freedom, and Community: Eight Essays*. Pantheon Books, New York, 1993.

———. *The Unsettling of America: Culture & Agriculture*. Sierra Club Books, San Francisco, 1977.

Birch, Bruce C. and Rasmussen, Larry L. *The Predicament of the Prosperous*. Westminster Press, Philadelphia, PA, 1978.

Bradley, Ian. *God is Green: Ecology For Christians*. Doubleday, 1992.

Brandt, Barbara. *Whole Life Economics: Revaluing Daily Life*. New Society Publishers, Philadelphia, 1995.

Brown, Lester, et al. *State of the World: A Worldwatch Institute Report on Progress Toward a Sustainable Society*. W.W. Norton, New York, NY, (annual publication).

Buechner, Frederick. *The Sacred Journey*. HarperCollins, New York, 1982.

———. *Now and Then*. HarperCollins, New York, 1983.

———. *Telling Secrets*. HarperCollins, New York, 1991.

Caldicott, Helen. *If You Love This Planet*. W.W. Norton, New York, 1992.

Carroll, John; Brockelman, Paul; and Westfall, Mary, editors. *The Greening of the Faith*. University Press of New England, Hanover, NH, 1997.

Christiansen, Drew, SJ, and Grazer, Walter, editors. "And God Saw That It Was Good." United States Catholic Conference, Washington, D.C., 1996.

Cobb, Clifford; Halsted, Ted; and Rowe, Jonathan. "If the GDP Is Up, Why Is America Down?" in *Atlantic Monthly*, October 1995.

Cobb, John B., Jr. *Sustainability: Economics, Ecology, and Justice*. Orbis Books, Maryknoll, New York, 1995.

————. *Sustaining the Common Good: A Christian Perspective on the Global Economy*. The Pilgrim Press, Cleveland, OH, 1994.

Crean, David & Ebbeson, Eric & Helen. *Living Simply: An Examination of Christian Lifestyles*. The Seabury Press, New York, 1981.

Daly, Herman and Cobb, John B., Jr. *For the Common Good: Redirecting the Economy Toward Community, the Environment, and a Sustainable Future*. Beacon Press, Boston, 1989.

DeGrote-Sorensen, Barbara. *Tis a Gift to be Simple: Embracing the Freedom of Living with Less*. Augsburg Fortress, Minneapolis, 1992.

de Mello, Anthony. *Wellsprings: A Book of Spiritual Exercises*. Image Books, Garden City, NY, 1986.

Dennis, Marie, et al. *St. Francis and the Foolishness of God*. Orbis, Maryknoll, NY, 1993.

Devall, Bill. *Rich in Means, Simple in Ends: Practicing Deep Ecology*. Gibbs Smith Publisher, Layton, UT, 1988.

Doig, Ivan. *This House of Sky*. Penguin Books, 1978.

DeWitt, Calvin. *Earthwise: A Biblical Response to Environmental Issues*. CRC Publications, Grand Rapids, 1994.

Dominguez, Joe and Robin, Vicki. *Your Money or Your Life*. Penguin Books USA Inc., New York, 1992.

Duchrow, Ulrich. *Alternatives To Global Capitalism*. International Books with Kairos Europa, Utrecht and Heidelberg, 1995.

Durning, Alan. *How Much is Enough? The Consumer Society and the Future of the Earth*. W.W. Norton, New York, 1992.

Easwaran, Eknath. *The Compassionate Universe*. Nilgiri Press, Tomales, CA, 1989.

Elgin, Duane. *Voluntary Simplicity: Toward a Way of Life That is Outwardly Simple, Inwardly Rich*. William Morrow, New York, 1981.

Eller, Vernard. *The Simple Life: A Christian Stance Towards Possessions*. Wm.B. Eerdmans Publishing Co., Grand Rapids, 1973.

Foster, Richard. *The Celebration of Discipline*. Harper & Row, New York, 1978.

————. *The Freedom of Simplicity*. Harper & Row, San Francisco, 1981.

Fox, Matthew. *A Spirituality Named Compassion*. Winston Press, Minneapolis, 1979.

Hall, Edward T. *Beyond Culture*. Anchor Books, New York, 1977.

Hallman, David, editor. *Ecotheology*. WCC Publications, World Council of Churches, Geneva, Switzerland, 1994.

Hawken, Paul. *The Ecology of Commerce: Doing Good Business.* HarperCollins Pub., New York, NY, 1993.

Hengel, Martin. *Property and Riches in the Early Church.* Fortress Press, Philadelphia, 1974.

Hessel, Dieter, editor. *After Nature's Revolt.* Augsburg Fortress Press, Minneapolis, MN, 1992.

Highwater, Jamake. *The Primal Mind.* Harper & Row, New York, 1981.

Janzen-Longacre, Doris. *Living More with Less.* Herald Press, Scottsdale, PA, 1980.

Kabat-Zin, Jon. *Wherever You Go, There You Are.* Hyperion, New York, 1994.

Kellermann, Bill Wylie, editor. *A Keeper of the Word—Selected Writings of William Stringfellow.* Wm. B. Eerdmans Publishing Co., Grand Rapids, 1994.

Kittredge, William. *Owning It All.* Grey Wolf Press, 1987.

Kung, Hans. *Global Responsibility: In Search of a New World Ethic.* Crossroad Publishing, New York, 1991.

Levering, Frank and Urbanska, Wanda. *Simple Living: One Couple's Search for a Better Life.* Viking, New York, 1992.

Macy, Joanna. *World as Lover, World as Self.* Parallax Press, Berkeley, CA, 1991.

Mander, Jerry. *In the Absence of the Sacred.* Sierra Club Books, San Francisco, 1991.

May, Gerald. *The Awakened Heart.* HarperCollins, New York, 1991.

McDaniel, Jay B. *Earth, Sky, Gods, and Mortals—Developing an Ecological Spirituality.* Twenty-Third Publications, Mystic, CT, 1990.

McDonagh, Sean. *Passion for the Earth: The Christian Vocation to Promote Justice, Peace, and the Integrity of Creation.* Orbis Books, Maryknoll, New York, 1994.

McFague, Sallie. *Models of God.* Fortress Press, 1987.

———. *Super, Natural Christians.* Augsburg Fortress Press, Minneapolis, 1997.

McKibben, Bill. *Hope, Human and Wild.* Little, Brown, Boston, 1995.

Meadows, Donella H. *Beyond the Limits: Confronting Global Collapse, Envisioning a Sustainable Future.* Chelsea Green Pub., Mills, VT, 1992.

Merchant, Carolyn. *Radical Ecology.* Routledge, New York, 1992.

Merck Family Fund. *Yearning For Balance.* July, 1995.

Merton, Thomas. *Contemplative Prayer.* Doubleday Books, New York, 1967.

———. *New Seeds of Contemplation.* New Directions, New York, 1961.

———. *Contemplation in a World of Action.* Doubleday Books, New York, 1973.

Naess, Arne. *Ecology, Community, and Lifestyle.* Cambridge University Press, Cambridge, MA, 1989.

Nash, James. *Loving Nature*. Abingdon Press, Nashville, TN, 1991.

Nearing, Helen. *Living the Good Life: How to Live Sanely and Simply in a Troubled World*. Schocken Books, New York, 1970.

———. *Simple Food for the Good Life*. Delacorte Press/Eleanor Friede, New York, 1980.

Nelson, Richard. *The Island Within*. Vintage Books, Random House, 1991.

New Road Map Foundation. *All-Consuming Passion*. Seattle, 1993.

Nhat Hanh, Thich. *Present Moment, Wonderful Moment*. Parallax Press, Berkeley, 1990.

Norwood, Ken and Smith, Kathleen. *Rebuilding Community in America: Housing for Ecological Living, Personal Empowerment, and the New Extended Family*. Shared Living Resource Center, 1995.

Nouwen, Henri J.M. *The Way of the Heart: Desert Spirituality and Contemporary Ministry*. Seabury, New York, NY, 1981.

O'Connor, Elizabeth. *Search For Silence*. Lura Media, 1986.

Orr, David. *Ecological Literacy*. SUNY Press, Syracuse, NY, 1992.

———. *Earth In Mind*. Island Press, Washington, D.C., 1994.

Quinn, Daniel. *Ishmael: A Novel*. Bantam/Turner Books, New York, NY, 1992.

Radford-Ruether, Rosemary. *Gaia and God: An Ecofeminist Theology of Earth Healing*. HarperSanFrancisco, San Francisco, 1992.

———. *Women Healing Earth: Third World Women on Ecology, Feminism and Religion*. Orbis, Mary Knoll, NY, 1996.

Robbins, John. *Diet for a New America*. Stillpoint Pub., Walpole, NH, 1987.

Roberts, Elizabeth and Amidon, Elias. *Earth Prayers From Around the World*. HarperCollins, New York, 1991.

Rohr, Richard. *Simplicity: The Art of Living*. Crossroad Publishing, New York, 1991.

Roszak, Theodore, editor. *Ecopsychology*. Sierra Club Books, San Francisco, 1995.

Ryan, John and Durning, Alan. *Stuff: The Secret Lives of Everyday Things*. Northwest Environment Watch, Seattle, 1997.

Saltzman, Amy. *Downshifting*. HarperCollins Publishers, New York, 1991.

Santmire, H. Paul. *The Travail of Nature: The Ambiguous Ecological Promise of Christian Theology*. Fortress Press, Philadelphia, 1985.

Schor, Juliet. *The Overworked American*. Basic Books/HarperCollins, New York, 1991.

Schumacher, E.F. *Small is Beautiful: Economics as if People Mattered*. Harper & Row, New York, 1973.

Shi, David. *The Simple Life*. Oxford University Press, New York, 1985.

———. *In Search of the Simple Life*. Gibbs M. Smith, Layton, UT, 1986.

Sherrard, Philip. *Human Image: World Image*. Golgonooza Press, Ipswich, England, 1992.

Thoreau, Henry David. *Walden/Civil Disobedience*. Houghton Mifflin/Riverside Editions, Boston, 1957.

Ueland, Brenda. *If You Want To Write*. The Schubert Club, St. Paul, MN, 1938, 1983.

Wachtel, Paul. *The Poverty of Affluence*. New Society Publishers, Philadelphia, 1989.

Wallis, Jim. *The Soul of Politics*. Orbis Books, The New Press, New York, 1994.

Williams, Terry Tempest. *An Unspoken Hunger*. Pantheon Books, New York, 1994.

———. *Refuge: An Unnatural History of Family and Place*. Pantheon Books, New York, 1991.

Periodicals and Resources

Northwest Environment Watch
1402 3rd Avenue, Suite 1127
Seattle, WA 98101-2118
(206) 447-1880

Plain Magazine
60805 Pigeon Point
Barnesville, OH 43713

Simple Living:
The Newsletter of Voluntary Simplicity
4509 Interlake Avenue North, Box 149
Seattle, WA 98103
(206) 464-4800

The Tightwad Gazette
(back issues/books for sale)
PO Box 201
Leeds, ME 04263-9710
(207) 524-7962

Yes! A Journal of Positive Futures
Box 10818
Bainbridge Island, WA 98110
1-800-937-4451

Worldwatch
1776 Massachusetts Avenue, NW
Washington, DC 20036
(202) 452-1999